The
Mercurian monarch

In memory of Noel Lees:
souls live on in perpetual echoes

The
Mercurian monarch

*Magical politics
from Spenser to Pope*

DOUGLAS BROOKS-DAVIES

Manchester University Press

First published by
Manchester University Press
Oxford Road, Manchester M13 9PL
51 Washington Street, Dover, N.H. 03820

British Library cataloguing in publication data
Brooks-Davies, Douglas
   The mercurian monarch.
   1. Alchemey in literature   2. English poetry—
Early modern, 1500–1700—History and criticism.
   3. English poetry—18th century—History and
criticism
   I. Title
   821'.309356   PR1195.A/

   ISBN.0–7190–0954–5

Library of Congress cataloging in publication data
Brooks-Davies, Douglas.
   The mercurian monarch.
   Bibliography: p.
   Includes index.
   1. English poetry—Early modern, 1500–1700—History
and criticism. 2. Kings and rulers in literature.
3. Magic in literature. 4. Hermetism in literature.
5. Mercury (Roman deity) in literature. 6. Politics
in literature. 7. Pope, Alexander, 1688–1744. Rape of
the lock. I. Title.
PR535.K56B76   1983   821'.3'093520621   83–12043
ISBN 0–7190–0954–5

Photoset in Plantin by
Northern Phototypesetting Co., Bolton
Printed and bound in Great Britain by
Biddles Ltd, Guildford and King's Lynn

Contents

Preface

This book is the product of two unfulfilled intentions, the first to write a detailed account of magic, and particularly Hermeticism, in seventeenth-century English literature, the second to write on Tudor and Stuart poetry and politics. The two eventually merged into the figure of the 'Mercurian monarch' whom, as a concept, I explain in the Introduction. He enables me to describe an alchemical and 'Egyptian' *Faerie Queene*, alchemical and Hermetic court masques, a Hermetic and deeply Arthurian early Milton, the Druidic interests of Drayton, Milton, Lovelace, and Marvell, and a Jacobite Alexander Pope who sees in Queen Anne the last of a line of magician monarchs.

I include a chapter on the court masque in a book which is otherwise about non-dramatic poetry because this was the medium through which the Mercurian monarch entered the seventeenth century. I have, though, had to reduce notice of pageants to a minimum and to ignore drama proper altogether because of lack of space, and this is the reason for the omission of other writers who might well have been considered here – for example, Robert Fludd, Henry and Thomas Vaughan, Drummond, William Browne, and Dryden.

The theme of the book is novel, but it will be apparent that I have been deeply influenced by the life-time's work of Frances Yates. Six months after her death it is difficult to believe that there will not be another book of hers, written with her unique humanity and fervour and filled with the kind of information that it was her gift only to discover and reveal.

Alastair Fowler has been a deeply formative influence. From exemplary tutorials with him twenty years ago dates my interest in mythography and many of the poems that I write about in the following pages. He knows perhaps more than I do how much I owe to him.

Pat Cummings shared my interest in alchemy and helped me during a difficult transitional phase in the history of the John Rylands University Library of Manchester. I am grateful to her, and to Penny Evans, who has produced an immaculate typescript from an impossible manuscript with care and cheerfulness, despite all the other term-time demands upon her. John Banks of M.U.P. has been kind and helpful over many years, and I should like to express my gratitude to him as well. Part of chapter IV appeared in somewhat different form as 'Marvell's Political Mysticism: Hermes and the Druids at *Appleton House*' in *Studies in Mystical Literature*, I (1980). I am grateful to the editor, Robert Eddy, for permission to reprint the substance of the article.

But this book would not have formed itself in my mind, nor would it have been written, without the knowledge, help, advice, and quiet understanding of Stevie Davies. She gave them, and time as well, at a period when no person could have been expected to give any, let alone all, of these.

Manchester   D.B.-D.
March 1982

Abbreviations, etc.

I have used the standard abbreviations for scholarly periodicals. In addition, I use the abbreviation O and S for Stephen Orgel and Roy Strong's *Inigo Jones: the Theatre of the Stuart Court*. I follow the old spelling of my copy texts, incidentally, except for modernising u/v, i/j, etc. References to the *Hermetica* are to Scott's English translation followed, where appropriate, by references to the more accurate text of Nock and Festugière.

Illustrations

Introduction

The concept of the magician king is a familiar one and an understandable corollary of the theory of divine right. Marc Bloch's study of the supposed healing power of kings, for example, takes as an epigraph Montesquieu's statement *Ce roi est un grand magicien*.[1] But Bloch's brilliant work is about magic and monarchy only in the very broadest sense and there has, so far as I know, been no other equivalent attempt to penetrate the mysteries that surround kings. The present book tries to understand a number of English poems which are linked, among other things, by certain attitudes to monarchy. As it was being drafted it turned out to be more and more concerned with the world of visionary politics of which the researches of Frances Yates have made us aware, and about the 'influence' (in the broadest sense) of Spenser and his faerie queene. The book starts with Spenser and Elizabeth; it ends with Pope and Anne, who regarded herself in many ways as a second Elizabeth. All the themes that I am concerned with, however, coalesce around the image of the planetary god Mercury who, identified with the monarch, then leads often (but not always) to consideration of the magical power of kings and queens.

The connection between monarchy and magic seems to begin in English poetry with Spenser under Elizabeth and to be intimately associated with – even if not dependent on – the identification of Elizabeth with Mercury. Spenser may have developed the idea from the traditional descent to epic heroes of Hermes–Mercury, the function of which was simply to warn: Mercury is a messenger.[2] But what Spenser recognised was that Mercury might be seen as bringing not just a message but divine benediction, or even divine power. As the intermediary between heaven and earth he is a channel of divine influence, pagan equivalent of the Judaeo-Christian angel who reveals the divine word and blesses at the same time. Spenser did not invent the equation of Mercury with angel.[3] His originality lay in deciding that angelic revelation was, by and large, reserved for his monarch and in using Mercury as a symbol for that revelation. As *The Faerie Queene* develops, moreover, Mercury stops being the agent of revelation and becomes a type of the sovereign herself.

There are several reasons why Spenser should have chosen Mercury as a symbol for his monarch rather than, say, Jupiter, the king of heaven. The first is that, as intermediary between heaven and earth, Mercury uniquely reflects the situation of the monarch with his 'two bodies' (the immortality and divinity of the office, the mortality, fallibility, and frailty of the individual holder of that office).[4] Another reason is that Mercury, as the originator of the lyre, represents the monarch as the principle of musically derived concord within the state. Yet another, and perhaps the most important, is that Mercury carries as his staff of office the white rod known as the caduceus. It symbolises wise, rational, government over himself and others, and since it is embraced by two serpents who, having been found fighting by the god, were pacified by him, it comes to be, in addition, an emblem of peace. In terms of the symbolism of monarchical regalia the caduceus is the sceptre of peace, self-control, and government. Mercury also leads the souls of the dead to and from the underworld with his caduceus, so that it develops a magical aura and can double for the magician's wand. In this way the Mercurian monarch becomes a magician king.[5]

This is one aspect of the political symbolism of *The Faerie Queene* that, unnoticed by modern readers, seems to have influenced a whole body of seventeenth-century poetry. Once we look for Mercury in this connection we find him in a surprisingly large number of places.

Mercury's significance as a symbol of sovereignty in Spenser and elsewhere is given special sanction, however, by the fact that he shares his name with the legendary Egyptian Hermes (or Mercurius) Trismegistus, Thrice-great Hermes, the Greek and Latin name for Thoth, supposed founder of all the arts and sciences (including all branches of magic), custodian of ancient mysteries, who was at once priest, magician, and king. Certain works believed to have been written by Hermes Trismegistus (who was alleged to have lived at the time of Moses), but now known to date roughly from the second to third centuries A.D., were received by the Renaissance in the Latin translation of the Florentine humanist Marsilio Ficino, whose translation was commissioned by Cosimo de Medici. (Cosimo was presented with the Greek manuscript, which became known as the *Corpus Hermeticum*, by one Leonardo da Pistoia somewhere around 1460.) These works were greatly revered for their supposed antiquity and their occasional similarities with Judaeo-Christian dogma. Hermes Trismegistus, it was believed, must have had truth revealed tò him by Moses or even Noah. He was, to use a phrase revived by D. P. Walker, an ancient theologian. He was also a magician – why else should he talk, in a long passage in the work known as the *Asclepius*, of the magical techniques used by the Egyptians to animate, by demonic power, their statues?[6]

The identification of Hermes Trismegistus as king and priest seems to have been particularly important to Spenser in his celebration of Elizabeth as temporal and spiritual leader, queen and supreme head of the reformed church. But Elizabeth was also interested in magic, and so she is Hermetic in that sense too. She consulted John Dee, who helped convince her that she was destined for an imperial role in Europe as restorer of a pure Christianity (the *Corpus Hermeticum* itself appears to have been influenced by ancient concepts of a world religion).[7] Elizabeth's dream was realised in *The Faerie Queene* rather than in Europe, where Gloriana–Elizabeth in her various guises revives for Protestantism the medieval notion of a world emperor who will restore the Golden Age and undo the ravages wrought by the Fall of man. Here magic is important because the unfallen Adam, it was believed, had possessed ultimate knowledge including magical (or, as the Renaissance termed it, 'occult') knowledge. Hence one way to undo the effects of the Fall was to master the liberal arts and then to proceed to the magical arts by becoming a magician or being advised by magicians.[8] And so Elizabeth consulted Dee as her 'ancestor' Arthur had been counselled by Merlin. As king, priest, and magician, the monarch is a Hermes Trismegistus.

The major piece of non-poetic evidence for the identification is John Dee's cabbalistic and alchemical treatise of 1564, the *Monas Hieroglyphica* (or *Hieroglyphic Monad*), the governing emblem of which is based on the alchemical and planetary sign for Mercury, ☿ , since Mercury signifies the beginning, middle, and end of the alchemical process. This symbol represents the complete magician–alchemist, a fact that takes on monarchical and political connotations when read in conjunction with Dee's fulsome letter of dedication to the Hapsburg king and emperor Maximilian. Indeed, the title page, addressed to 'Maximilian, by the grace of God the most wise King of the Romans, of

Bohemia and of Hungary', implicitly identifies Maximilian with Mercury since surrounding the Mercurian emblem, in an ornamental scroll, is the statement 'Mercury becomes the parent and King of all planets when perfected . . .'.[9] This seems to say that Maximilian will become the Mercurian monarch when he has mastered the mysteries offered within Dee's work. It is not surprising that Elizabeth, searching for the secret of stable monarchy and government, should not only champion the work but read it with Dee, telling him, if he would 'disclose [unto her] the secrets of that boke [she w]old *Et discere & Facere* [learn and do]';[10] for Dee's vision is in the end a religious vision, the twenty-four theorems of his tract reminding us, as Dee himself explains, of the twenty-four elders who worship God in Revelation.[11]

After Dee, in this Mercurian chronology, come the first three books of *The Faerie Queene* (1590). A few years later, in 1594, the 'prince' of the Christmas revels is advised in the *Gesta Grayorum* by one of his councillors to study philosophy (that is, magic):

> I . . . will wish unto your Highness the Exercise of the best and purest part of the Mind, and the most innocent and meriting Request, being the Conquest of the Works of Nature; making his Proportion, that you bend the Excellency of your Spirits to the searching out, inventing and discovering of all whatsoever is hid in secret in the World. . . . Antiquity, that presenteth unto us in dark Visions, the Wisdom of former Times, informeth us, that the Kingdoms have always had an Affinity with the Secrets and Mysteries of Learning. Amongst the *Persians*, the Kings were attended on by the *Magi*; the *Gymnasophists* [*sic*] had all the Government under the Princes of *Asia*; and generally, those Kingdoms were accounted most happy, that had Rulers most addicted to Philosophy.[12]

He then advises the 'prince' to collect a comprehensive library, lay out a microcosmic garden containing every species of animal and vegetable life, have a cabinet made in order to display curiosities and ingenious man-made devices, and then to have built

> Such a Still-house so furnished with Mills, Instruments, Furnaces and Vessels, as may be a Palace fit for a Philospher's Stone. Thus when your Excellency shall have added depth of Knowledge to the fineness of Spirits, and greatness of your Power, then indeed shall you lay a *Trismegistus*; and then, when all other Miracles and Wonders shall cease, by reason that you shall have discovered their natural Causes, your self shall be left the only Miracle and Wonder of the World.[13]

This is said in jest; but it was no joke to Elizabeth, Maximilian, Rudolf II, or the Danish Frederick III. Even James, despite his fear of 'demonology', could be praised as standing 'invested with that triplicitie which in great veneration was ascribed to the ancient *Hermes*, the power and fortune of a *King*, the knowledge and illumination of a Priest, and the learning and universalitie of a Philospher'.[14]

By 'philosphy' here is meant natural magic, the magic that, when practised by the virtuous adept, leads to a mastery of the secrets of nature, a revelation of the affinity between upper and lower worlds. It is largely (though not inevitably) astrological, often enabling the magus to control the lower world by mastering its astrological powers or virtues. As Henry Cornelius Agrippa remarks in his *Three Books of Occult Philosophy*:[15]

> Magick is a faculty of wonderfull vertue, full of most high mysteries, containing the most profound Contemplation of most secret things, together with the nature, power, quality, substance, and vertues thereof, as also the knowledge of whole nature, and it doth instruct us concerning the differing, and agreement of things amongst themselves, whence it produceth its wonderfull effects, by uniting the vertues of things through the application of them one to the other, and to their inferior sutable subjects, joyning and knitting them together throughly by the powers, and vertues of the superior Bodies. This is the most perfect, and chief Science, that sacred, and sublimer kind of Phylosophy, and lastly the most absolute perfection of all most excellent Philosophy.

The natural magician pursues his calling so that he may know God's creation. His magic is a branch of white magic. The other branch of white magic to which natural magic frequently leads among Renaissance practitioners is demonic magic (also known as angelic or ceremonial magic). This is the kind practised by Agrippa and Dee among many others. It was demonic magic that aroused the greatest fear amongst practitioners and observers because it could so easily appear to be a conjuring with evil (rather than good) spirits.

Demonic magic was heavily indebted to Jewish cabbalistic traditions, and particularly the assumption that by knowing the names of the angels you could, by observing certain rituals, summon up their powers. If natural magic enables you to 'know' the world and the planetary heavens, demonic magic enables you, like Moses or Ezekiel, to 'know' God. It is the goal of the magician who is always a theologian:

> ... the understanding of Divine things, purgeth the mind from errors, and rendreth it Divine, giveth infallible power to our works, and driveth far the deceits and obstacles of all evil spirits. . . . Yea it compels even good Angels and all the powers of the world unto our service *viz.* the

virtue of our works being drawn from the Archetype himself, To whom when we ascend, all creatures necessarily obey us, and all the quire of heaven do follow us.[16]

John Dee practised demonic magic. This was one of the reasons Elizabeth valued him; it was also the cause of his downfall. But the first three books of *The Faerie Queene* were written before his disgrace and so, as we shall see, contain elements of demonic (or angel) magic. These are excluded from the second part of the poem (Books IV to VI), which contains only natural magic.

And yet Ben Jonson can still allude to demonic magic as he celebrates James I, and demonic magic is in part the subject of Milton's *Il Penseroso*. The sylphs of Pope's *Rape of the Lock* come at the end of a long tradition of magician kings.

Another important figure in this book is the Italian heretic and visionary reformer Giordano Bruno (1548–1600), who lived in London in the early 1580s, became acquainted with leading Elizabethan courtiers, and dedicated his philosophical sonnet sequence *De gli heroici furori* (*The Heroic Frenzies*) and his strange reforming work *Lo Spaccio de la bestia trionfante* (*The Expulsion of the Triumphant Beast*) to Sir Philip Sidney. *The Expulsion* is a key text for the present study.[17] In it Bruno visualises the reform of the corrupt heavens by the expulsion of the vicious constellations (vicious because most of them remind Jupiter, the ageing king of heaven, of his younger and morally depraved self) and the replacement of the vicious constellations by their virtuous counterparts. Here, in the form of a long fable, Bruno preaches the individual moral reform which will lead to world reform, the instituting of a universal religion of love. I think it influences *The Faerie Queene* because its vision – not dissimilar to the almost inscrutable vision of Dee's *Hieroglyphic Monad*, perhaps – coincides with the vision underlying Elizabethan Protestant imperialism. The symbolism of the constellations, modified by Bruno from earlier traditions,[18] helps explain certain astronomical allusions in Spenser's epic. In particular, Bruno's interpretation of the constellation Ursa Major, often previously associated with Arthur, seems to be adopted by Spenser in *The Faerie Queene* and subsequently to influence the court masque, the early Milton, and finally *The Rape of the Lock*.

Bruno was in general, but especially in *The Expulsion*, dominated by the Hermetic writings. The most crucial passage for his purposes was the one in the third dialogue of the Hermetic *Asclepius* in which Hermes Trismegistus explains to Asclepius that Egypt is the image of heaven and home of the true religion. He also explains that Egyptians are so in communion with the gods that they can call down their spirits to animate their statues. But all this will change. Egypt will be overrun by barbarians and death, its religion lost. God will, however, sweep away the corruption through flood, fire, and war. The old Egypt will be restored.

This passage, known as the *Asclepian* lament, is quoted by Bruno at length in the second part of Dialogue III of *The Expulsion*.[19] Indeed, he is indebted to it for his overall apocalyptic vision. In this book I try to show how Bruno's interpretation of the lament (or sometimes perhaps the lament itself) lived through the seventeenth century to emerge, for example, in Marvell's *Upon Appleton House* as it agonises over the future of a war-torn England.

We have moved from Mercury to Hermes Trismegistus and thence to Bruno, who was influenced by Hermes Trismegistus. In the pages that follow I use the adjective 'Mercurian' whenever the imagery of the Graeco-Roman mythological deity is to the fore; I use 'Hermetic' to refer to the influence of the *Hermetica* or the possible presence of Hermes Trismegistus. Whenever I detect the influence of Bruno I try to indicate this by referring to him, though as the seventeenth century progresses distinctions become impossible and even undesirable – Robert Fludd, Thomas Vaughan, and many others begin to hover in the Hermetic twilight.

The book's main theme, then, is the literary consequences of the identification of monarchy and magic through the figures of Mercury and Hermes Trismegistus. It is an exploration of 'magic and politics' in so far as this identification always supposed that the magician monarch could achieve an ideal kingdom or empire (so that the myth of the Mercurian magician king fuses with Arthurian idealism). The fact that Hermes Trismegistus celebrated a divinely sanctioned Egypt led Spenser and others to see England as Egypt, an equation apparent in the celebration of Isis as, on the one hand, a domestic river and, on the other, as the Egyptian goddess and queen who has an important role in the *Hermetica* and in Bruno's Hermetic *Expulsion* (though not, it should be added, nearly so important as Mercury, the 'revealer' of the work).[20]

But there was a tradition of British magic, too, the magic of the Druids, supposed descendants of Noah, with whose son Cham knowledge of magic was sometimes thought to have originated.[21] As we shall see, the theme of the Mercurian magician king leads in the seventeenth century to a preoccupation with Druidism which was also an aspect of the search for the origins of ancient British liberty.

Apart from *The Faerie Queene*, the first part of *Poly-Olbion*, and a few court masques, the works considered here were produced after Isaac Casaubon, in 1614, dated the *Hermetica* as belonging to the early Christian era. The persistence of the Hermetic myth testifies to the persistence in the belief in 'magic' in general, of course. But my argument is that it lives as long as there was a historically effective belief in monarchical absolutism in Britain.

This is, however, not a book about the history of magic or specific magical sources used by writers. Consequently I have documented many statements solely from Agrippa because he was so popular. We know that he influenced Dee, for example; and his *Three Books* have the advantage of comprehensiveness as well as being, in many cases, repetitions of Renaissance magical commonplaces.

Notes

1 Marc Bloch, *The Royal Touch: Sacred Monarchy and Scrofula in England and France*, transln by J. E. Anderson of *Les Rois Thaumaturges* (London and Montreal: Routledge and Kegan Paul, McGill-Queen's U.P., 1973), p. 1 (Montesquieu's *Lettres Persanes*, 24).

2 This is the subject of Thomas Greene's *The Descent from Heaven: a Study in Epic Continuity* (New Haven, Conn. and London: Yale U.P., 1963).

3 See below, ch. I, sec. iv and n. 77.

4 E. H. Kantorowicz, *The King's Two Bodies: a Study in Mediaeval Political Theology* (Princeton, N.J.: Princeton U.P., 1957), ch. I and *passim*.

5 Evidence for the statements in this paragraph is offered in chapter I. Hermes was most anciently an earth god 'possessing magic forces': Edmund O. von Lippmann, 'Some Remarks on Hermes and Hermetica', *Ambix*, 2–3 (1938–1949), 21.

6 On the Hermetic traditions see A.-J. Festugière, *La Révélation d'Hermes Trismégiste*, 4 vols. (Paris: Gabalda, 1944–1954), Festugière's *Hermétisme et Mystique Païenne* (Paris: Aubier-Montaigne, 1967), and F. A. Yates, *Giordano Bruno and the Hermetic Tradition* (London and Chicago, Ill.: Routledge and Kegan Paul, University of Chicago Press, 1978 edn). There is a useful chapter on the subject in Wayne Shumaker, *The Occult Sciences in the Renaissance: a Study in Intellectual Patterns* (Berkeley and Los Angeles, Calif. and London: Univ. of California Press, 1972). For the general magical background to the period see Keith Thomas, *Religion and the Decline of Magic* (Harmondsworth: Penguin, 1978) and Brian Easlea, *Witch Hunting, Magic and the New Philosophy: an Introduction to Debates of the Scientific Revolution 1450–1750* (Brighton and Atlantic Highlands, N.J.: Harvester Press and Humanities

Press, 1980).

7   P. J. French, *John Dee: the World of an Elizabethan Magus* (London: Routledge and Kegan Paul, 1972); F. A. Yates, *Astraea: the Imperial Theme in the Sixteenth Century* (London and Boston, Mass.: Routledge and Kegan Paul, 1975).

8   For documentation see below, ch. I, n. 27 and (on revelation to a king), Festugière, *La Révélation*, I. ix, pp. 324 ff., 'Instruction d'un sage à un roi', based on Stobaeic Excerpt 24 on the origin of kings' souls as revealed by Isis: *Hermetica*, ed. Walter Scott, 4 vols. (Oxford: Clarendon Press, 1924–1936), I (1924), 495 ff.

9   John Dee, *Monas Hieroglyphica*, tr. C. H. Josten in *Ambix*, 12 (1964), 84–221. The points noted here can be found on pp. 103 and 113 respectively.

10 *Ibid.*, pp. 88–89.

11 *Ibid.*, pp. 216–19 (Theorem 24). The vision is religious but also mystical–political, since the twenty-four elders have 'on their heads crownes of gold' (representing 'Prophets and Apostles ... whom Christ hath made to be Priests and Kings') and subsequently prostrate themselves before God's throne and cast aside their crowns, showing that 'the godly, though made kings by Christ, doe willingly emptie themselves of all glory, mooved with a religious respect of the majesty of God': Revelation 4: 4, 10 with Geneva glosses (Geneva Bible (London, 1599?); all subsequent Biblical quotations are from the Geneva Bible and this edition, unless otherwise stated). Dee is probably more important than we so far realise to *The Apocalyptic Tradition in Reformation Britain 1530–1645* that has been traced by K. R. Firth (Oxford: O.U.P., 1979).

12 *Gesta Grayorum 1688*, ed. W. W. Greg; Malone Society Reprints (Oxford, 1914), p. 34. The councillors' speeches may have been written by Francis Bacon: *ibid.*, p. vi.

13 *Ibid.*, p. 35.

14 James Cleland, *Hero-paideia, or the Institution of a Young Noble Man* (Oxford, 1607), II. i, cit. Frank Kermode, *The Tempest*, New Arden Shakespeare (London: Methuen, 1961 edn), pp. xlix-l.

15 Translated by J. F. (London, 1651), I. ii, pp. 2–3. On Agrippa, see C. G. Nauert, *Agrippa and the Crisis of Renaissance Thought* (Illinois University Studies in the Social Sciences, 55 (1965)).

16 Agrippa, *Three Books*, dedicatory letter to Book III, p. 342. On demonic magic, see D. P. Walker, *Spiritual and Demonic Magic from Ficino to Campanella* (London: The Warburg Institute, 1958), and F. A. Yates, *The Occult Philosophy in the Elizabethan Age* (London, Boston, Mass. and Henley: Routledge and Kegan Paul, 1979).

17 For Bruno as a political visionary, see Yates's *Giordano Bruno*. I have used the text of *The Expulsion of the Triumphant Beast* ed. and tr. A. D. Imerti (New Brunswick, N.J.: Rutgers U.P., 1964).

18 E.g., Alan of Lille, *Anticlaudianus*, Book IX.

19 *Hermetica*, ed. Walter Scott, I. 339 ff.: *Expulsion*, ed. Imerti, pp. 241–242.

20   For Mercury, see the title page; for Isis, dialogue III, part ii.
21   Sir Walter Raleigh, *The History of the World*, I. xi.

[I]

The Mercurian monarch in 'The Faerie Queene'

Spenser had already begun *The Faerie Queene*, we gather from a letter he wrote to his friend Gabriel Harvey, by the spring of 1580. The first three books were published ten years later and dedicated to Queen Elizabeth. During those ten years Mary Queen of Scots had been tried and executed, the Armada had been defeated, and the question of the succession became more acute. Nobody has ever wished to deny that Spenser's poem meditates on these and related matters. His prefatory letter to Raleigh, after all, draws attention to the poem's political subject matter, and the choice of the Arthurian legend itself was a palpably political gesture. And yet these things are not as simple as they may appear, for to start from the assumption that *The Faerie Queene* is a political poem gives the reader a sense of critical direction while at the same time raising many interpretative problems. There is the problem of local detail, for example: while acknowledging that Book I is indeed in one sense about the political stability of the realm defined in terms of the oppposition between the Church of England and Roman Catholicism, how many readers even so find themselves bristling at the following description, by Frank Kermode, of cantos vii and viii?

> The subjection of Red Cross to Orgoglio is the popish captivity of England from Gregory VII to Wycliff (about 300 years, the three months of viii. 38). The *miles Christi*, disarmed, drinks of the enervating fountain of corrupt gospel and submits to Rome. He is rescued by Arthur, doing duty for Elizabeth as Emperor of the Last Days, saviour of the English Church.[1]

The answer, as we look at this apparently reductive account of a fairly sizeable episode, must be 'a large number', and this despite Kermode's own exploratory work on Spenserian allegory and the publication of more general works on the history, theory, and practice of allegory. Even the post-Nohrnberg reader of *The Faerie Queene* might be forgiven for still feeling bewildered about the poem's meanings while recognising that much of his bewilderment arose from the elementary difficulty that we have all lost the habit of reading and explicating a polysemous poem.[2] This means that we feel we are laboriously erecting damaging intellectual constructs upon what we intuitively regard as a fragilely beautiful work. Our instincts tell us that this is an unnatural action, that the poem as poem inevitably suffers. But the allegory *is* there: we should feel that we draw it out of the poem, not impose it thereon. Apparently bald statements like Kermode's are legitimate and admitted critical shorthand which we must accept and imaginatively integrate into our rereading.

There remains a more fundamental difficulty, however, and that is the knowledge, without which we cannot embark upon the process of imaginative integration. *The Faerie Queene* is an allegorical poem; its 'darke conceit' is to a greater or lesser extent political; but what are the political assumptions that underlie it? More than thirty years ago the question would hardly have seemed worth asking. It is the pioneering work of Frances Yates that has invited us to reassess the assumptions underlying Elizabethan politics and recognise the kind of poem that Spenser was writing. *The Faerie Queene*, she argues, celebrates Elizabeth in her imperial role as the monarch of Protestant empire, a role that developed from the medieval notion of the world emperor which itself had its origin in the unified Roman empire. Imperial significance must attach to the *Aeneid* echoes in Spenser's poem because, as she notes,

> The age of Augustus was the supreme example of a world united and at peace under the Roman Empire, and to that age had also belonged the supreme honour of witnessing the birth of Christ. By consenting to be born into a world ruled by Roman law under the greatest of the Caesars, Christ had consecrated the Roman world order and Roman justice.[3]

When she came to the throne and established herself as the supreme head and governor of the Church of England, Elizabeth also took to herself (or perhaps had thrust upon her) the concept of universal emperor. As the British queen descended from Aeneas via Brutus, the namer of Britain and founder of Troynovant on the banks of the Thames, she could claim the right to imperial rule, the governorship of the Roman empire. She could claim it, in addition, as a descendant of Constantine, the English-born Christian Roman emperor who had united under his one rule the previously divided eastern and western empires when he defeated Licinius, master of the eastern part of the empire, in 323 A.D. This, indeed, is the point of the opposition between Una, who is described in Book I as deriving from a 'Royal lynage . . . / Of ancient Kings and Queenes, that had of yore / Their scepters stretcht from East to Western shore' (i. 5), and Duessa, whose Roman father, ruling 'where *Tiberis* doth pas' (ii. 22), identifies her as the Catholic usurper of Una's rightful role as universal emperor.

What Yates's discoveries have achieved is a shift in our awareness: beyond practical politics lies a realm of mystical politics celebrated not so much, in the end, in theoretical treatises as in pageant, literature, and the visual arts. Even here, though, there is the problem of interpretation. When we look at the 'Rainbow' or 'Ermine' portraits of Elizabeth, what exactly are we seeing? When we look at engravings of the queen in imperial regalia with sceptre and orb, what should we really infer? Does the contemporary account of Elizabeth's coronation which describes 'the Queenes Maj^tie haveing the septer in the right hand and the world in the left hand'[4] imply the mystery of world rule or is it simply literalising an emblem? The evidence would seem, from our present historical perspective, to be in favour of the mystical interpretation. This, at any rate, is the assumption underlying the present study which, as I stated in the Introduction, is concerned with the myth of the Mercurian monarch. To the best of my knowledge it was Spenser who invented the myth from hints found in earlier monarchical panegyric, and the form in which it was embodied in *The Faerie Queene* seems to have defined the tradition of the Mercurian monarch as it is found in seventeenth-century English literature. I have indicated in the Introduction the implications of the myth, but it may be useful to recapitulate them here. The theory of the king's two bodies accepts, on the one hand, the divine and sacrosanct nature of the monarch's person but, on the other, the individual monarch's humanity (that is, his subjection to mortality). In effect it posits a tension between the office and the holder of the office, a tension between spirit and body, heaven and earth. Mercury is the intermediary between heaven and earth, uniquely appropriate as the symbol of this aspect of monarchy. Mercury's main attribute is the caduceus, emblem of wise government over self and others and emblem of peace. As the emblem of wise government it becomes identified with the monarchical sceptre; as the emblem of peace it represents the greatest achievement of any earthly monarch.[5] Mercury mediating between heaven and earth also suggests the monarch as magician, controlling the lower world by summoning down heavenly influences. The sceptre–caduceus becomes, on this reading, the magician's wand. At this point Spenser and those who follow him are able to draw on a happy coincidence: Mercury's Greek equivalent is Hermes and both were, among other things, gods of the liberal arts; the Greek name for the Egyptian priest–king Thoth, founder of all the arts and sciences (including magic, astrology, and alchemy), was Hermes Trismegistus. The Mercurian monarch, then, is potentially a Hermetic priest–king, master of the occult sciences. There remains one final point. Some at least of the Hermetic writings lived for the Renaissance through the Latin translations of Ficino, but for Spenser they were particularly alive through the work of Giordano Bruno. Bruno's great work embodying his own brand of Hermeticism and concerned with individual and universal reform, *The Expulsion of the Triumphant Beast*, was dedicated to Sidney. This work seems to have had considerable influence on *The Faerie Queene* and its concept of Elizabeth as reforming leader of Protestant imperialism. To the title of Hermetic Mercurian monarch, then, we should sometimes prefix the adjective 'Brunian'.[6]

[i] *Moses and the serpents*

We encounter Mercury's caduceus twice in *The Faerie Queene*, once in Book II and once in Book IV. In the former the Palmer's staff is described as follows:

> Of that same wood it fram'd was cunningly,
> Of which *Caduceus* whilome was made,
> *Caduceus* the rod of *Mercury*.... (xii. 41)[7]

In the latter Cambina possesses a Mercurian caduceus embraced by 'two Serpents ... / Entangled mutually in lovely lore' (IV. iii. 42). It is not immediately apparent that these two rods have monarchical implications, for Spenser unfolds his theme gradually and apparently indirectly. Mercury himself, indeed, does not appear until the *Mutability Cantos*. Again, his relevance to the poem's depiction of monarchy is not strikingly obvious. It depends, as do the references to the caduceus, on a subtly developing argument which is most readily grasped if we approach the poem book by book. The first Mercurian allusion occurs towards the end of Book II, but Book I is obviously concerned with magic. How does Spenser lead us to connect the two? The answer is, firstly through Book I's theological content, and secondly through its alchemical imagery.

The connection between magic and theology was, for the Renaissance, a commonplace. The white magician claimed that his ultimate aim was to know God, and that he practised his art within a Christian framework. Black magic, on the other hand, conjured with evil demons and was the devil's work. This contrast is simply expressed in the opposition of Una and Archimago, the former on her first appearance the whitest of whites (i. 4), the latter 'in long black weedes yclad' (i. 29). Archimago's name marks him out as a magician. On the level of theological allegory he represents Roman Catholicism, while Una represents Elizabeth as the queen of Protestant reform, the Act of Supremacy's one supreme head and governor of the Church. It was a Protestant commonplace that Catholicism was to be identified with the black arts. Spenser develops the logical corollary that the Protestant monarch–emperor should be endowed with the virtues of white magic.[8] In this again, however, he was merely applying to Protestantism a concept that had its place in pre-Reformation claims to imperial rule: the Emperor Frederick II had seen the role of the world emperor in terms of sin and redemption from sin. Adam before the Fall was the first just world emperor; the function of the postlapsarian world emperor is the Christ-like redemptive one of leading his people back to the earthly paradise.[9] And we should note the further point that it was a function of magic and alchemy to try to repair the ravages of the Fall as well. The successful magician gained, like Adam, sovereignty over nature. Adam himself had known the magical as well as other secrets of the universe.[10]

Archimago and Una battle for possession of Redcrosse. Their battleground is his consciousness or, more precisely, his imagination, since Renaissance magic in its natural and demonic forms was essentially a psychological affair in which the magician produced his effects through his own imaginative power (as the receiver and dispenser of astral or demonic influence), which he then projected on to the imagination of his subject. It is through the dream that he conjures up for Redcrosse at the end of canto i that Archimago is announced as a black magician, therefore, as well as through his Catholicism. For, as a Catholic black magician, he possesses Redcrosse through the power of evil demons, literally establishing false idols within his imagination:

> Unto their lodgings then his guestes he riddes:
> Where when all drownd in deadly sleepe he findes,
> He to his study goes, and there amiddes
> His Magick bookes and artes of sundry kindes,
> He seeks out mighty charmes, to trouble sleepy mindes. (i. 36)

Redcrosse's dream is brought to him by the falsest of the 'Legions of Sprights' which Archimago 'forth . . . cald out of deepe darknesse dred' (st. 38). These sprites are 'like little flyes', a simile which associates Archimago the Catholic black magician with Beelzebub, Lord of the flies and 'the chiefe of the devils' (Luke 11: 15). In other words *The Faerie Queene* begins with a false magician monarch 'possessing' England in the form of its patron saint, George (the sleeping Redcrosse). As late as 1651 Hobbes discusses '*the Principality of Beelzebub over Dæmons*, that is to say, over Phantasmes that appear in the Air', classifies his and Satan's followers as 'Children of Darknesse', directs our attention to I Timothy 4: 1–2 ('in the latter times some shall depart from the faith, and shall give heed unto spirits of errour, and doctrines of devils, Which speake lyes through hypocrisie'), and triumphantly concludes that the Catholic kingdom of darkness is the same as that of '*Beelzebub*, Prince of Dæmons'.[11] The simile may, then, be Spenser's way of warning us of Archimago's claims to monarchy, but it is noteworthy that as a magician he is not given the rod or wand of power. In effect this denies him his kingdom at the moment of his possession of it. If as a magician he has no wand, as a prince he can wield no sceptre. The Palmer in Book II, however, does possess a rod. Moreover, it is a Mercurian rod. When we encounter him at the beginning of the book 'clad in blacke attire, / Of ripest yeares, and haires all hoarie gray' (i. 7), almost identical in appearance to the black-clad and aged Archimago at I. i. 29, we begin to detect the subtlety of Spenser's unfolding of his Mercurian monarchical theme. For he possesses the kingdom that Archimago claimed. His rod (as we shall see) can be related to the sceptre of monarchical regalia symbolising princely control over the realm, and it can be interpreted in this way because it explicitly controls the demons of the imagination. The Palmer undoes Archimago's work as a black magician and prince of the kingdom of darkness and demonstrates that the monarch's temperate self-control which enables him to govern his people is an external manifestation of his benign magical control over the imagination of his subjects.

Archimago is also reminiscent of Simon Magus, who had power over demons and was the grand heresiarch to whom the Pope was, by sixteenth-century Protestants, regarded as successor. He was identified as one of those who, in the last days, will resist truth 'as Iannes and Iambres withstood Moses' (II Timothy 3: 8).[12] This is illuminating for the relationship between Archimago and Una, since it suggests the possiblity of connecting Una with Moses which is again relevant to the concept of the magician monarch. As Nohrnberg notes,[13] Una as Elizabeth in her role as head of the reformed church embodies faith, the true faith abandoned by Redcrosse through his Archimago-induced idolatry of the golden calf Duessa. Moses was the leader of his people who had also enjoyed divine revelation:

> At Mount *Sinai Moses* only went up to God; the people were forbidden to approach on paine of death; yet were they bound to obey all that *Moses* declared to them for Gods Law . . . in a Common-wealth, a subject that has no certain and assured Revelation particularly to himself concerning the Will of God, is to obey for such, the Command of the Common-wealth: for if men were at liberty, to take for God's Commandements, their own dreams, and fancies, or the dreames and fancies of private men; scarce two men would agree upon what is Gods Commandement; and yet in respect of them, every man would despise the Commandements of the Common-wealth.[14]

Moreover, Moses possessed a serpent-rod, which makes him potentially identifiable with caduceus-bearing Mercury. The relevant text is Exodus 4: 2ff.:

> And the Lord sayd unto him [Moses], What is that in thine hand? And he answered, A rod.
> Then said he, Cast it on the ground. So he cast it on the ground, and it was turned into a serpent: and Moses fled from it.
> Againe the Lord said unto Moses, Put forth thine hand, and take it by the taile. Then he put foorth his hand and caught it, and it was turned into a rod in his hand. Doe this that they may beleeve . . .
> . . . thou shalt take this rod in thine hand, wherewith thou shalt doe miracles.

A related text is Exodus 7: 10 ff.:

> Then went Moses and Aaron unto Pharaoh, and did even as the Lord had commanded, and Aaron cast forth his rod before Pharaoh and before his servants, & it was turned into a serpent. Then Pharaoh also called for the wise men and sorcerers: and those charmers also of Egypt did in like manner with their enchauntments.
> For they cast downe every man his rod, and they were turned into serpents: but Aarons rod devoured their rods.

The Geneva gloss on 'sorcerers' reads: 'It seemeth that these were Iannes and Iambres: reade 2 Tim. 3. 8 . . .'.[15]

What we have here is confirmation of Moses's divine status as a leader and of his divinely appointed status as a magician who performed miracles with his serpent-rod. Exodus 7 offered a particularly knotty problem to Renaissance magicians: were both lots of serpents real,

Aaron's created by divine intervention and the sorcerers' by natural magic? Or were Aaron's real and the sorcerers' illusory? Either way, this was a Biblical *locus classicus* for consideration of the essential difference between miracle and the limitations of magic, and especially black magic. In effect this established Moses as a magician king especially when regarded as a religious leader (the function of the serpent-rod in Exodus 4 was, after all, to act as a test of faith).[16] It pitted him against the sorcerers whom, via the Geneva gloss, we may identify with Iannes and Iambres and thence with Archimago in his guise as Simon Magus. The serpents that they are associated with are, as it were, waiting to be mystically absorbed by Spenser into the Palmer's Mercurian caduceus in Book II. In Book I, in accordance with his theological subject, holiness, he treats of Elizabeth as magician monarch in her Biblical persona of Moses, because of his rod the nearest theologically sanctioned equivalent to Mercury.

It was a commonplace to identify the monarch with Moses.[17] A convenient example from the period of the composition of Book I of *The Faerie Queene* is the mayor of Windsor's oration of 7 September 1586 in which Elizabeth is addressed as Moses leading her people from the Catholic tyrannies of Mary Tudor. Moses's rod becomes a sceptre here which, despite the Elizabethan settlement, is still being challenged by Catholic sorcerers. The mayor's text is evidently based on Exodus 7; it also anticipates the opposition of Una and Archimago in Spenser's poem. After the troubles under Mary:

> GOD in his great mercy, looked upon us as he did upon the Israelites in Egypt and their captivities, sending us in high tyme this his holy handmayden, as it were another Moses . . . to be our helper, and advanced her (and that by just title) to the scepter and dyadem of this (then a most wofull) realme . . .

But even now, as the mayor wishes to praise the country's welfare under Elizabeth:

> miserably, nay devilishly, nay dampnably, am I interrupted with the oppositions of traytors, the overthwartinges of rebells, the enchaunting of witches, the charmings of sorcerers, the presagings and foretellings of soothsayers, the seducings of jesuites and seminaries, the conspyrings of domesticall hypocrites and traitors, the bandings of Popish Foreyne Princes, and the curses of the Pope himselfe, that Antychrist most accursed.[18]

If Archimago is the Moses-defying sorcerer or black magician he is also, by his magical power, his own dragon-serpent: 'For by his mightie science he could take / As many formes and shapes in seeming wise, / As ever *Proteus* to himselfe could make: / ... Now like a foxe, now like a dragon fell' (I. ii. 10).[19] We have symbolically encountered him in the serpent-dragon Errour, therefore; we symbolically encounter him again in the dragon under Lucifera's feet (I. iv. 10), the dragon on which Duessa rides (vii. 18), and the dragon overcome by Redcrosse in canto xi. They are opposed by the dragon on Arthur's helmet (vii. 31) and Fidelia's serpent in canto x. It is the latter that directs us to Moses again, suggesting that the opposition of bad and good dragon-serpents in the book relates to the miracles and sorcery in Exodus 7.

Fidelia appears with a serpent at x. 13:

> She was araied all in lilly white,
>   And in her right hand bore a cup of gold,
>   With wine and water fild up to the hight,
>   In which a Serpent did himselfe enfold,
>   That horrour made to all, that did behold. ...

Primarily, as commentators recognise, the serpent in the cup alludes to the attempt to kill St John the Evangelist with poisoned wine. Because of the attempt a cup with a snake in it became the Evangelist's attribute. But there is also an allusion, as commentators again recognise, to Numbers 21: 6 ff., where God commands Moses to set up a brazen serpent 'upon a pole' as a cure for those who have been bitten by the plague of fiery serpents. This piece of homoeopathic magic was interpreted in John 3: 14–15 as signifying Christ's power to bestow eternal life. From our point of view the Numbers text and its gloss in John should be connected with the serpent-rod of Exodus, the former signifying salvation, the latter, faith.[20]

Fidelia confirms the identification of Una as Moses since she is iconographically similar to Una: both are associated with the brightness of the sun and both are dressed in white. Fidelia is therefore a manifestation of an aspect of Una (herself a symbol for Elizabeth) as the faith of the true church and she, too, like Una, has a symbolic relationship with Archimago the sorcerer; for he operates through sprites and 'Magick bookes' (i. 36) and she has 'in her other hand . . . / A booke, that was both signd and seald with blood, / Wherein darke things were writ, hard to be understood' (x. 13). Her book of faith (the Bible), in contrast to the books of magic, contains miracles (so that she is like Moses; see especially stanza 20), and its 'darke things', in contrast to the black works of Archimago, reveal light and truth.

Spenser's emphasis on faith is central not only to the theological meaning of Book I but also to its magical meaning. For the key to white magic, which was after all constantly affirmed by its practitioners to belong to the Christian scheme of things, was faith. As Paracelsus had written:

> ... we must not regard as sorcerers all those who are so called in the Holy Scriptures. If we did we should have to look upon the three Wise Men of the East as arch-sorcerers, for they were more versed in the arts and things supernatural than anyone before them or anyone living in their time. But Holy Writ speaks of them not as sorcerers but as magi; and how should we interpret this? Only to mean that they did not misuse their art and their great occult wisdom. For magic is an art which reveals its highest power and strength through faith.[21]

Agrippa, in the process of reconciling magic and religion, devotes a chapter to the 'three Guides which bring us even to the paths of truth and which rule all our Religion', and these are the three theological virtues which we meet in Spenser's canto x, 'Love, Hope and Fayth':

> But Faith the superior vertue of all not grounded on human fictions, but divine revelations wholly, peirceth all things through the whole world, for seeing it descends from above from the first light, and remains neerest it, is far more noble and excellent than the arts, sciences, and beliefs arising from inferior things: this being darted into an intellect by reflexion from the first light. To conclude, by faith man is made somewhat the same with the superior powers and enjoyeth the same power with them ... Faith is the root of all miracles by which alone (as the *Platonists* testifie) we approach to God, and obtain the Divine power and protection.[22]

Una's battle for Redcrosse is the battle for 'Faith . . . [and] miracles' against black magic's demonic delusions. Archimago's sprites are answered at the other end of the book when, at the betrothal of Una and Redcrosse, the voices of angels are heard:

> During the which there was an heavenly noise
> Heard sound through all the Pallace pleasantly,
> Like as it had bene many an Angels voice,
> Singing before th'eternall majesty,
> In their trinall triplicities on hye:
> Yett wist no creature, whence that hevenly sweet
> Proceeded, yet eachone felt secretly
> Himselfe thereby refte of his sences meet,
> And ravished with rare impression in his sprite. (xii. 39)

Una and Redcrosse, religion and country, have been united in an image of Protestant *imperium* that is essentially magical. The burden of magical text books as of Pico's *Oration on the Dignity of Man* is the power of the magus to summon angels or to become as angels. Here Una and Redcrosse literally call down angels, and the 'sprite' (cosmic spirit) of all those in the palace receives the 'rare impression'.[23] It is a specific magical symbolism that is intended, a point confirmed by its being consequent upon the liberation of Una's parents, the king and queen of Eden. For the king and queen are Adam and Eve, and what is restored by their liberation is that magical sovereignty over nature which was Adam's before the Fall and which we encountered earlier in connection with Frederick II's theories of world emperorhood.

These angels are only heard, however. Earlier, again in canto x, Redcrosse has, like Moses, ascended a mountain and seen angels. This is when he encounters Contemplation, the Saturnian melancholic who is the true hermit counterpart to the false hermit Archimago in canto i, the embodiment of contemplative wisdom in whom the Renaissance magus would have recognised his ideal self. Despite, or perhaps because of, its theological subject, Book I of *The Faerie Queene* asserts the necessity for compromise between the active and contemplative modes of life.[24] The magician–philosopher's life is essentially contemplative; the monarch, be he Moses or Elizabeth, has to find a middle way. If we may anticipate our Mercury theme: Mercury sees the king of heaven but communicates with mortals too. The monarch, similarly, partakes of both realms. For a moment, though, we, with Redcrosse, experience the ideal as, in an allusion to Jacob's ladder, that image so crucial to the Renaissance magician and humanist, the knight sees the Heavenly Jerusalem and 'The blessed Angels to and fro descend'. Agrippa can be our guide to the identification of the contemplative melancholic with the magician who, under the influence of a melancholic fury or frenzy, receives celestial power through his imagination and then, through mind, supercelestial revelation:

> ... this power is in every man ... but it is varied in diverse men in strength and weakness, and is encreased and diminished according to his exercise and use, by which it is drawn forth from power into act, which thing he that rightly knoweth, can ascend by his knowledge, even untill his imaginative faculty doth transcend and is joyned with the universall power ... and his imagination is made most strong, when that Etheriall and Celestiall power is poured out upon it, by whose brightness it is comforted, untill it apprehend the species, notions and knowledge of true things, so that that which he thought in his mind, cometh to passe even as he thought, and it obtaineth so great power, that it can plunge, joyn and insinuate it self into the minds of men, and make them certain of his thoughts, and of his will and desire, even thorow large and remote spaces,

as if they conceived a present object by their senses . . . yet these things are not granted to all, but to those whose imaginative and cogitative power is most strong and hath arrived to the end of speculation: and he is fitted to apprehend and manifest all things, by the splendour of the universall power, or intelligence and spirituall apprehension which is above him: and this is that necessary power, which everyone ought to follow and obey, who followeth the truth; if therefore now the power of the imagination is so great, that it can insinuate it self unto whom it pleaseth, being neither hindred nor let by any distance of time or place. . . . There is no doubt but that the power of the mind is greater, if at any time it shall obtain its proper nature, and being no way oppressed by the allurements of the senses, shall persevere both incorrupted and like it self; but now for example, that the souls abound with so plentiful Light of the Celestiall Stars, and hence, a very great abundance of light redoundeth into their bodies; so *Moses* face did shine, that the children of *Israel* could not behold him by reason of the brightness of his countenance. . . .

This is from chapter xliii of Book III of the *Occult Philosophy*. The manuscript version[25] is more precise when it tells of the mind learning 'the secrets of divine matters' including 'the angelic hierarchy' and possessing the power to foresee 'the emergence of a new religion', and this version, together with the passage quoted above, explains clearly what revelation Redcrosse receives from Contemplation. Chapter xliii is about the relationship between imagination, reason, and mind. Mind (which we share with God) is enlightened by God and his supercelestial demons; it in turn 'illuminates reason, reason floweth into the imagination'. Reason and imagination are, as we shall see, an important aspect of the magical subject matter of Book II; but the province of Book I, 'Of Holinesse', is mind. As Agrippa adds in that same chapter, if reason chooses, 'the soul by reason ascendeth into the mind, where it is replenished with divine light'. This is the state that Contemplation perpetually enjoys and that he shares for a moment with Redcrosse. It includes visions of angels (for this is an intense moment of ceremonial magic) and also, we are to infer from Redcrosse's connection of Cleopolis with the New Jerusalem combined with his discovery of his name and identity (x. 55 ff.), a revelation of the new religion established by his queen. Angel magic in the sixteenth century from Agrippa to Dee had frequently been the instrument of religious reform.

[ii] *The alchemical king and queen*

The good and evil dragon-serpents in Book I, indebted as they are to the serpents of Moses and the sorcerers in Exodus 7, also suggest the good and bad dragon—serpents of alchemy, where the good dragon symbolises regeneration and the bad dragon the putrefaction which inevitably precedes regeneration. Because of their interdependence the two dragons were often depicted as combined in a fashion reminiscent of the serpents round Mercury's caduceus (see plates 1 and 2).[26] Again we can detect Spenser preparing us for the explicit unfolding of his Mercury theme in Book II and elsewhere in the poem in a manner consonant with the theological subject of Book I; for the introduction of alchemy glorifies Elizabeth by connecting her with Adam and Moses, but this time seen as magicians possessing alchemical secrets.[27] Indeed, Mercurian associations come more to the fore when we attune ourselves to the alchemical suggestiveness of Book I: Hermes Trismegistus was the reputed founder of alchemy; 'Mercury' was often identified as the philosophers' stone itself, the alchemist's goal.[28]

The reader of alchemical texts is struck by certain obsessively recurring symbols. Among them are dragons, the lion, the eagle, and, above all, the white queen and red king who unite to produce a child, the philosophers' stone, which is white. The animals represent the stages of the alchemical quest;[29] the white queen and red king are usually identified as the lunar and solar principles respectively, for fundamental to the alchemist in his creation of the stone is the unveiling of

> The secrets both of *Sunne* and *Moone*,
> How they their kinde to multiplye,
> In one body togeder must wonne.

The 'one body' is a union in marriage:

> The Boke *Laudabile Sanctum* made by *Hermes*,
> Of the *Red Worke* speaketh in this wise:
> *Candida hunc rubeo jacet uxor nupta marito*,
> That is to saie, if ye take heede thereto,
> Then is the faire white Woman
> Married to the Ruddy Man.[30]

There are three alchemical 'plots' in Book I, all involving Una as the 'white' woman, royal because she is 'th'only daughter of a King and Queene' (vii. 43), and a queen because she represents Elizabeth. She is lunar by virtue of her virginity and her passing identification with Diana and Isis in canto vi.[31] The first and most remote plot is the union of Una's parents before the narrative begins to produce their daughter, herself the white stone. (Almost inevitably one links this with that commonplace of Elizabethan iconography, the union of the red and white roses of

1 Alchemical Mercury uniting solar and lunar principles

Lancaster and York to produce the one rose, Elizabeth.)[32] The second plot is Una's pursuit of Redcrosse, which culminates in their betrothal in canto xii. Redcrosse is red; he is also solar, as Alastair Fowler has argued at length.[33] His betrothal to Una announces the promise of a subsequent wedding after which they, too, will produce a child, and the inference is that this child will again be, symbolically, the white stone, the goal of monarchy. Whether the child would have been encountered by the end of Spenser's unfinished poem or whether he belongs to the eternal world must remain matter for conjecture. Conjectural, too, is the outcome of the third alchemical plot of Book I involving Arthur. Like Redcrosse, Arthur is solar. His armour shines 'Like glauncing light of *Phœbus* brightest ray'; he has a golden and 'glorious' helmet; his shield shines brighter than Phoebus (vii. 29 ff.). Tudor iconography had early on recognised a solar Arthur.[34] But Spenser renders his Arthur solar in a very particular way by giving him 'Athwart his brest a bauldrick brave . . . / That shynd, like twinkling stars, with stons most pretious rare' (st. 29). As Nohrnberg notes, 'baldrick' was commonly used in referring to the zodiac at this period; so that the mention of 'stars' must direct us to read Arthur here as solar lord of the zodiac.[35] It is at this point that Una joins with him to beg his aid in rescuing Redcrosse from Orgoglio's 'darkesome dungeon' (st. 51). The two come together only to part again, of course, for Una's solar companion is Redcrosse and Arthur's true lunar companion is the faerie queen, who has appeared to him, like Diana to Endymion, in the dream he recounts to Una at ix. 13–15. The faerie queen is traditionally Diana–Cynthia, the moon goddess.[36] Arthur's constant quest is for the faerie queen. Had Spenser finished his poem, and had Arthur found his queen, their coming-together, too, would have implied the alchemical conjoining of solar and lunar.

All this confirms the monarch's magical power. It even suggests a Mercurian Una if, as the child of the marriage of an alchemical king and queen, she is to be identified as 'our Mercury'. Now we could at this point leave the alchemical aspects of Book I, but to do so would be to ignore additional clues to its alchemical substance. The serpent-dragon Errour and the dragon vanquished by Redcrosse, for example, represent the dragon of putrefaction. Arthur's solar regeneration of Redcrosse is symbolised in part by the golden dragon on his helmet (the dragon of regeneration). In canto iii, having failed Una, Redcrosse is replaced by a lion; in canto x, undergoing repentance, Redcrosse himself roars out in pain like a lion (stanza 28; we note in passing the alchemical overtones of the 'corrosives' of stanza 25 and the 'firie' heat of stanza 26). Having

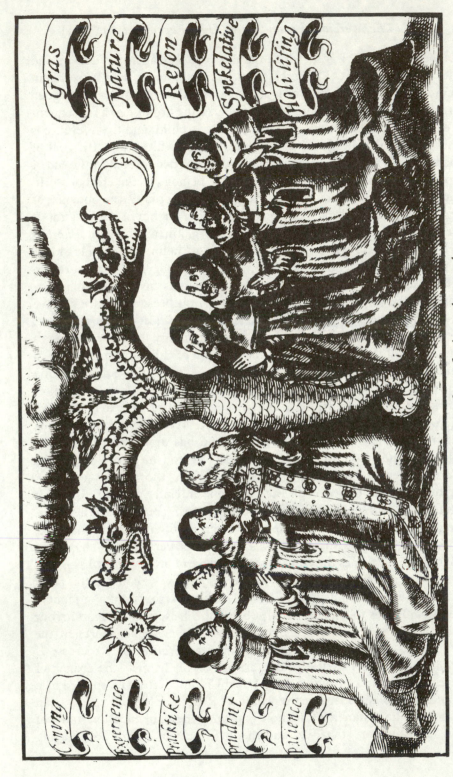

Gras · Nature · Reſon · Spekelatiſe · Holi lifing

Conyng · Experience · Practike · Prudent · Pacience

2   The alchemical dragons of putrefaction and renewal

been regenerated Redcrosse is one more scorched, this time by the dragon
of canto xi; encountering it he is compared to an eagle (st. 34). Alchemy
is a complicated affair, and rendered more so by the riddling texts in
which its mysteries are supposedly revealed. Nevertheless, it is based on a
continuing process of refinement which we can perhaps detect Spenser
alluding to in the process of Redcrosse's encounters which chart his
spiritual development. Spenser does not, it is true, present us with an
alchemical treatise. But when we discover that it is the function of the
alchemical lion to destroy the sun in order that the sun may emerge
reinvigorated and marry the moon, we gain added insight into the reason
for Redcrosse's displacement by a lion and the later leonine roarings he
emits as he is destroyed in order to emerge the fully-fledged solar knight
so that he may unite with Una. An extract from the relatively well-known
alchemical poem *The Hunting of the Green Lyon* will make the parallel
clearer: the lion can eclipse the sun

> And yet wythin he [the lion] hath such heate,
> That when he hath the *Sun* up eate,
> He bryngeth hym to more perfection,
> Than ever he had by Natures direccion.
> This *Lyon* maketh the *Sun* sith soone
> To be joyned to hys Sister the *Moone*:
> By way of wedding a wonderous thing,
> Thys *Lyon* should cause hem to begett a King.[37]

(The 'king' is the stone.) Similarly, Redcrosse's identification as an eagle
in the context of his dragon fight in canto xi suggests the conjunction of
eagle and dragon, in alchemical symbolism embodying the perennial
attempt to generate spiritual life from putrefaction, as in the following
stanza from Backhouse's 'The Magistery':[38]

> The *Eagle* which aloft doth fly
>   See that thou bring to *ground*;
> And give unto the *Snake* some *wings*,
>   Which in the *Earth* is found.

The alchemical images must be integrated by the reader into Spenser's
Christian framework (indeed, they were metaphors for spiritual
illumination), but they add a vital magical element to it. I should like to
end this section with a quotation from the medieval poem called by
Ashmole *Dastin's Dreame*. It includes king and queen, sun and moon,
the poisonous serpent-dragon, and the begetting of the infant 'stone',
and offers a gloss on the alchemical relationship between Redcrosse and
Una as I have tried to outline it. The quotation begins at stanza 40:

The King thus entred in his bed royall,
The Queene conceived under a Sun bright;
Under her feete a mount like Christall,
Which had devoured her husband anon right,
Dead of desire and in the Maidens sight;
Lost all the Collour of his fresh face . . .

The Serpent bold shed out his poyson,
The Queene and Maidens for feare tooke them to flight,
Seaven tymes assending up and downe
With in a vault, now darke, now cleere of light,
Their generation was so strong of might,
After death now passeth Purgatory;
To Resurreccion as any Sun bright,
Things that were lost to bring to his glory.

The Queene tooke her full possession,
The Soule reviving of the dead King,
But of old hatred the toxicate poyson,
Was by the Serpent cast in to their hindring;
The *Prince* was buried, but of his rising,
The Brethren were glad the truth was seene,
When they were washed by his naturall clensing;
And their old Leprie by Miracle was made cleane.

The full *Moone* halfe shaddowed the *Sun*,
To putt away the burning of his light;
Black shaddowed first the skyes were so dunn,
The Ravens bill began who looketh right,
Blacker then Jett or Bugle to sight;
But little and little by ordinary apparance,
The temperate fire with his cherishing might
Turned all to white, but with noe violence.

Tyme was the Queene approched of Childing,
The Child of Nature was ready to fly. . . .[39]

Alchemy's preoccupation with incest, inherited from mythological incest patterns, is evident enough from this extract and gives a useful insight into symbolic characterisation in Book I. In alchemy, incest affirms the ultimate identification of all matter and of the upper and lower worlds: as above, so below. Same copulates with same in order to produce the opposite, or refined version, of its corrupt self (king produces purer king; solar lion devours the sun to produce a refined sun, and so on). We find a similar phenomenon in Book I of *The Faerie Queene*, where it is not only the dragons that are different while being essentially the same but also many of the main characters: Redcrosse is solar; but so are Arthur and, in many respects, Una. As allegorical manifestations of each other they are, as it were, incestuously related, however dissimilar they may, in many ways, also be. The birth of the 'Child of Nature' from incestuous union of king and queen, sun and moon, in the end, then, offers a simple truth, and one that is at the root of Renaissance magical lore. Magical power is the product of the magus's own self-discipline: 'a firm and stout mind (saith *Hermes*) can we not otherwise obtain, than by integrity of life, by piety, and last of all, by Divine Religion'.[40] Another way of putting this is to say that we beget what is within, as Pico explains in his *Oration*.[41] Having communed with and purged ourselves, we then contemplate an incestuously produced purified version of ourselves. The political implications of this for Elizabeth and Book I are again simple: the queen's Protestant empire depends upon her fitness as emperor. Neither monarchs nor magicians can operate without theology and the moral virtues, and Elizabeth is both monarch and magician with her archetypes including Moses and the Hermetic alchemists. Her magical trappings represent a self-begotten wisdom engendered by her own virtues, while at the same time suggesting something specific about the external nature of the empire over which she rules. As a magician monarch she is, after all, in the line of Adam, Moses, and Solomon, and her empire is the material realisation of a God-given magical power.

[iii] *Hermes and the stars*

There is one further aspect to the unfolding of Spenser's Mercurian theme in Book I, and this is its stellar symbolism. It is through this that the notion of Brunian Hermetic reform enters the poem. Fowler has explicated the solar implications of the first book, and these have been confirmed by Yates, who observes that Spenser's solar scheme in effect calls down, like a magic talisman, the sun's astral influences to imbue the book with the powers of a unifying religion of charity and love.[42] Of equal interest is the other stellar symbol in the book, ignored by Yates and noticed only in passing by Fowler. We find it in the main *chronographia*, at ii. 1, by which Spenser times the dream that Archimago conjures up for Redcrosse:

> By this the Northerne wagoner had set
> His sevenfold teme behind the stedfast starre,
> That was in Ocean waves yet never wet,
> But firme is fixt, and sendeth light from farre
> To all, that in the wide deepe wandring arre. . . .

As well as establishing time in a manner as familiar from the Greeks as from Chaucer,[43] this passage symbolically relates to the larger narrative patterns of Book I. Specifically, it invites us to identify characters with stars. Thus, the 'Northerne wagoner' is the constellation Boötes, the Ploughman; the 'sevenfold teme' is the traditional seven stars of Ursa Major. Boötes suggests Redcrosse, discovered by, and brought up as, a ploughman, and hence named *Georgos* (I. x. 66; Greek *georgos* = husbandman, ploughman), while Una is 'the stedfast starre', or pole star. Popularly, but erroneously, Ursa Major was known as Arcturus, which led to the association of the constellation with King Arthur. It assumed particular prominence because of its mention in Job 9: 9 and 38: 32, verses influentially allegorised by Gregory the Great in his *Moralia in libros beati Job*. Here Arcturus (i.e. Ursa Major with its seven stars), set in the centre of heaven, signifies the Universal Church, with its constituent stars representing the Trinity together with the four cardinal virtues, and the seven gifts of the Holy Spirit. More generally, it signifies the qualities, and hence the life, of the virtuous Christian, and was used, as Sydney Anglo has shown, as a shorthand symbol for Prince Arthur in the 1501 London pageants.[44] The relevance of all this for Redcrosse as the knight of holiness is clear enough. Moreover, it confirms Redcrosse's relationship with Arthur, his symbolic counterpart, from whom he takes over (significantly) after his rescue by Arthur from Orgoglio and his subsequent stay in the House of Holiness in canto x. Holiness turns Redcrosse into Arcturus quite literally, for it is in this canto that he learns that his name is *Georgos*, and Arcturus as a star is actually in the Ploughman constellation Boötes.

The patristic interpretation is useful for directing us to the imperial Christian meanings of Ursa Major, hence of Arcturus, and hence of Spenser's Prince Arthur. But we might suspect a Brunian reading of the constellation to be operating here as well. It is the first constellation we encounter in *The Faerie Queene*; it is the constellation with which Bruno begins his *Expulsion of the Triumphant Beast* — that vision of external reform which must begin first with internal reform, and that was dedicated to Sidney — 'by virtue of the place's being the most eminent part of the heaven'.[45] In Bruno's work the old vicious constellations are banished and replaced by their virtuous equivalents. In the case of Ursa Major this means that the old bear of hypocrisy, imposture, and falsity (among other vices) is to have the bear of Truth substituted for it.[46] This, in brief, is what happens as Archimago's hypocrisies are expelled from Redcrosse and the influence of Una possesses him. The *chronographia* at the opening of canto ii, in other words, implies the possibility of a Brunian Hermetic interpretation of Spenser's vision of Protestant empire for Elizabeth, one that is entirely consonant with the alchemical monarch that we have already encountered.

The relevance of Ursa Major for Book I is reinforced by the presence of constellation symbolism in Book II, announced once more by a *chronographia* in the second canto, this time in stanza 46. Guyon has been telling Medina of his mission to investigate the Palmer's complaint about the 'mischiefes . . . wrought' by the witch Acrasia. Then:

> Night was far spent, and now in *Ocean* deepe
> > *Orion*, flying fast from hissing snake,
> > His flaming head did hasten for to steepe,
> > When of his pitteous tale he end did make. . . .

Orion is a stellified hunter, called by Ovid the companion of Boötes (*comesque Boötae*)[47] and linked with Arcturus in Job 9: 9: 'He maketh the starres Arcturus, Orion, and Pleiades . . .'. This would suggest that Guyon's 'like race' (II. i. 32) with Redcrosse should be interpreted in a slightly different way from that usually recognised. Guyon is not just the moon to Redcrosse's sun; he is, it would appear, Orion to his Boötes.

By the 'hissing snake' Spenser presumably means the scorpion sent by Diana that killed Orion. Like Orion it, too, was stellified. But since, as Scorpio, it rises in the east as Orion's sign sets in the west, the two were regarded as being kept forever apart, Orion perpetually avoiding in the heavens his vanquisher on earth. The scorpion is traditionally an emblem of treachery. But Spenser writes 'snake', not 'scorpion', and so the question must be, where is the snake that Guyon–Orion flees and vanquishes?[48] The answer lies initially in a pun in canto i when we encounter Mortdant's and Amavia's deaths, the consequence (in theological terms) of their human fallenness and hence their inheritance from the Satanic dragon-serpent of canto xi of Book I. The pun occurs when Guyon alludes to Amavia as 'this wretched woman overcome / Of *anguish*' (i. 58; my italics), and relies on our connecting *anguish* with Latin *anguis* (= snake, serpent). In ii. 45, the stanza preceding the chronographic one, Medina tells us that Guyon's tale of Acrasia instructs us 'from pleasures poyson to abstaine': in context, we suspect that the allusion is to snake poison. Similarly, in canto iv Guyon comes upon the squire Phedon who has been afflicted by Furor. The squire's tale begins with 'gnawing anguish' (st. 23) and concludes with Furor's 'mortall sting' (st. 33), while Furor's own 'great yron teeth' and 'burning eyen' (st. 15) are based on those of the dragon–serpent of I. xi.[49] Guyon, together with the Palmer, overcomes Acrasia and Furor. On both occasions he is Orion, but overgoes his stellified mythological counterpart by vanquishing the 'hissing snake' rather than merely avoiding it. Indeed, if we recall that in Agrippa's Hermetic astrology '*Orion* granteth victory',[50] it seems that Guyon cannot fail. Bruno is even more instructive. When, says Bruno, the vicious Orion is banished, he will be replaced by the virtuous Orion embodying 'exalted Militia, zealous against iniquitous, visible, and invisible powers'. This, from the Explanatory Epistle addressed to Sidney, is expanded in the body of the text to identify Orion with 'Military Art, through which the peace and authority of the fatherland may be maintained, barbarians be fought, beaten, and converted to civilized life and human society, and inhuman, savage, and bestial cults . . . be annihilated'.[51]. Here, surely, we have what amounts to one of the most concise descriptions of Spenser's moral and implied political programme in Book II. The capturing of Acrasia is the expulsion of the false queen of love for the benefit of Gloriana, whose emblem Guyon wears (ii. 42). With her capture is achieved the expulsion of the beast in man. There is, however, one slight difference between Spenser's vision and Bruno's, for Spenser's vision of reform still allows for the presence of infected will. Bruno's Orion achieves the annihilation of 'porcine, savage, and bestial cults', whereas Spenser's Guyon–Orion leaves his book with one uncorrected 'porcine' barbarian remaining: 'Let *Grill* be *Grill*, and have his hoggish mind' (xii. 87).[52]

Guyon's function as, in part at least, an embodiment of monarchical temperance symbolised in terms of Brunian astrological Hermetics will be confirmed if we can assimilate him into the other more obviously monarchical figures in the book, Belphoebe and Arthur. Belphoebe is, as the prefatory letter to Raleigh tells us, Elizabeth as 'a most vertuous and beautifull Lady'; Arthur's princely pedigree is of course beyond dispute. Now Belphoebe appears just once in Book II, in canto iii, and as a huntress. Spenser directs us to identify her with Diana, but as a huntess subduing wild beasts and with her 'golden bauldricke, which forelay / Athwart her snowy brest' (ii. 29) she also, as an androgynous figure, calls to mind hunting Orion, mentioned in the chronographic stanza which ends the immediately preceding canto. It is not just the hunting which is the clue; rather, it is the baldric, for the constellation Orion contains seven such bright stars that 'Virgil girds him with gold, *armatusque auro circumspicit Orion*'.[53] The baldric links her in addition with Arthur, whom we must imagine as still wearing in Book II the 'bauldrick brave' that he was equipped with in Book I. Earlier we identified Arthur's belt as zodiacal. We now see that it encourages us to associate him with Orion, especially since Arthur, too, is a hunter. For if Guyon–Orion vanquishes snakes, so does Arthur when he overcomes Maleger, perhaps the deadliest snake that inhabits Book II. His skin is 'as cold and drery as a Snake' we are told at xi. 22; at stanza 47 we hear of his stinging 'cursed darts'. It is no accident that Maleger corresponds structurally, in canto xi, to the dragon-serpent of I. xi with his 'two stings . . . / Both deadly sharpe' (st. 11); nor is it an accident that Spenser characterises him as a barbarian by comparing him to a Tartar (st. 26). Deadly Maleger is not just the barbarian within who has to be expelled, the demonically possessed Legion of the gospels of Mark and Luke. He is the external barbarian who has, in Bruno's words, to be 'fought [and] beaten' if civilisation is to prevail. Guyon's association with Orion connects him, then, with Belphoebe and Arthur. As Boötes governed Book I, so Orion in his Hermetic significances governs the second book.

[iv] *The Mercurian Palmer: sceptre and caduceus*

Bruno's *Expulsion of the Triumphant Beast*, through its Hermeticism, introduces Hermes Trismegistus covertly into Books I and II of *The Faerie Queene*. Mercury himself, however, is mentioned by name in Book II in a stanza from which I have already in part quoted. There we are told that the Palmer's staff, with which he supports himself from the moment of his first appearance (i. 7), is:

> Of that same wood . . . fram'd . . . cunningly,
> Of which *Caduceus* whilome was made,
> *Caduceus* the rod of *Mercury*,
> With which he wonts the Stygian realmes invade,
> Through ghastly horrour, and eternall shade;
> Th'infernall feends with it he can asswage,
> And *Orcus* tame, whom nothing can perswade,
> And rule the *Furyes*, when they do rage:
> Such vertue in his staffe had eke this Palmer sage. (xii. 41)

The Palmer's staff has the power to defeat 'charmes' and subdue 'monsters' (st. 40), and although it is only of the same wood as the caduceus and not the caduceus itself, it is not going too far to suggest that mention of the caduceus carries with it inevitably the idea of serpents. If Book I is about good and evil dragon-serpents with magical and related connotations, then Book II is equally about serpents in the form of

Orion's 'hissing snake' and its manifestations. The Palmer's staff, which implicitly reminds us that the Mercurian caduceus was traditionally entwined by serpents, is the master symbol to which the serpents of Moses's rod and the other serpents in Book I, and the snakes in Book II, all relate.

We should at this point recall that one of the 'analogies' observed in *The Faerie Queene* by Nohrnberg and others is the thematic and structural kinship between Books II and V, expressing the dependence of Temperance (Book II's virtue) and Justice and Equity (the subjects of Book V's 'legend').[54] These concepts are interdependent since it is a commonplace that the governor cannot govern justly unless he first govern himself: 'it is not ynough to be a good King, by the scepter of good lawes well execute to governe . . . if he joyne not therewith his vertuous life in his owne person'.[55] Alexander Ross repeated an equally illuminating commonplace when he reported that the two serpents on Mercury's caduceus 'signified, that eloquence must be joyned with wisdom . . . and where wisdom and eloquence are conjoyned there the State is well governed, which is signified by the rod or Septer, the symbol of Government'.[56] If we consider the Palmer from the point of view of his possible political significance, his relevance to our theme of Mercury and monarchy becomes apparent. He represents the power of rational control without which individual and law cannot function. This includes the power to overcome hostility, both within and without, 'for all anger and hostility falls to the ground when that rod doth mediate . . .: therefore Princes Embassadors that are employed to mediate a peace, are called *Caduceatores*'.[57] The Palmer's caduceus-staff of temperance, in other words, becomes interchangeable with the monarchical sceptre.

This is subtly apparent from Spenser's narrative strategy in one of the more overtly political cantos of Book II, the second, where we encounter Medina and Guyon talks of his sovereign whom, in stanza 40, he describes as

> Great and most glorious virgin Queene alive,
> That with her soveraigne powre, and scepter shene
> All Faery lond does peaceably sustene.

We note the emphasis on 'peace' (repeated at the end of the stanza), a consequence of the good government symbolised by the 'scepter shene' which relates it to the peace-bringing caduceus of Mercury. The relationship is confirmed when we recall that Guyon describes the queen to Medina in the presence of the Palmer, who is undoubtedly supporting himself on his caduceus-like staff, and when we observe the 'hissing snake' of stanza 46. The shining sceptre brings peace by virtue of its caduceus-like qualities which are also transferred to and received from the Palmer's staff. Sceptre and staff cancel out the malevolent snake present in the *chronographia* and elsewhere in the book.

The sceptre passage should be linked with an equivalent passage in Book III when Merlin prophesies to Britomart of her descendant Elizabeth, the British prince who unites Welsh and English:

> Thenceforth eternall union shall be made
>   Betweene the nations different afore,
>   And sacred Peace shall lovingly perswade
>   The warlike minds, to learne her goodly lore,
>   And civill armes to exercise no more:
>   Then shall a royall virgin raine, which shall
>   Stretch her white rod over the *Belgicke* shore. . . . (iii. 49)

Peace and the sceptre again;[58] and this time we are given more information. The sceptre is a manifestation of the virgin's 'goodly lore', thus anticipating Cambina's specifically Mercurian 'rod of peace' in Book IV (again in canto iii) with its 'two Serpents . . . / Entrayled mutually in lovely lore' (st. 42). Lore/learning recalls the common interpretation of the rod or caduceus as the 'rod of teaching' (*doctrinae virga*) and suggests in Cambina's case a magical lore which we must retrospectively read into the lore of the 'royall virgin' of Book III.[59] We are also told that the sceptre, 'shining' in Book II, is white, the colour of Mercury's caduceus.[60] This would seem to clinch the identification of monarch with Mercury, and of sceptre with caduceus; while the phrases 'goodly lore' and 'lovely lore' allude in addition to the monarch's magical power, to establish in the poem the type of the Mercurian magician monarch.

The Palmer's staff; Gloriana's 'scepter shene'; the 'royall virgin['s] . . . white rod'; Cambina's 'rod of peace'; and, from Book I, Moses's serpent rod, must all be viewed, whatever their differences from each other, as aspects of an archetype which itself assimilates serpent rod and monarchical sceptre.[61] In the case of the 'white rod', this sceptre is easy to identify as 'The Ivorie Rod with ye Dove', one of the two rods or sceptres with which the monarch is presented during the coronation ritual. Elizabeth's coronation service was in Latin. In the translation used at Charles I's service the archbishop handed the monarch 'y^e Rod with y^e Dove' with the words: 'Receive the Rod of vertue and equity . . .'.[62] The qualities of this sceptre take us back, through the 'scepter

3 Mercury as peace-bringer, with Ceres holding corn and the infant
Pluto/Plutus

shene' of Book II, to the relationship between Books II and V, which suggests the 'analogy' between Temperance and Justice. Further confirmation for the 'analogy' comes from the significance of the 'Scepter with ye Crosse' which is handed to the monarch by the archbishop immediately before he is given the sceptre with the dove. The sceptre with the cross is 'ye signe of Kingly Power, ye Rod of the Kingdomes, the Rod of vertue, that thou mayst governe thy self aright ....'.[63] The two sceptres together symbolise self-government, monarchical rule, and equity. Spenser fuses them, and then identifies this composite with the Mercurian caduceus.

The Palmer's staff unfolds its meanings, like so many of Spenser's images, only slowly. And yet its relationship with Gloriana's 'scepter shene' is evident enough to give it political significance as the symbol of, among other things, monarchical temperance, or inner virtue. In moving on to Mercury, however, we have not escaped Orion, for he, too, is related to Mercury. Indeed, Orion numbered him among his parents, who also included Jupiter and Neptune. To quote Ross once more: '*Orion* may be the type of an excellent Governour, who for his Justice and Authority is begot by *Jupiter*; for his Eloquence of *Mercury*; for his skill in Horsemanship and Navigation, of *Neptune*'.[64] In addition to his Brunian meanings, Orion might represent governorship to Spenser, then, in which case he was unlikely to forget Mercury's place in his pedigree. Guyon–Orion is the monarch in his private capacity as temperate human being who is unfolded further into the Mercurian Palmer. But since in the monarch private always impinges on public, we must make public equations as well. For example, the identification of caduceus-staff with sceptre. Indeed, the meaning of Book II is not fully established until we read Book V and connect the Mercurian images of the former with the Mercurian images of the latter, focussing as they do on the public figure of the Mercurian Queen Mercilla and her anticipation, Cambina.

Book II, like Book I, has magic for one of its themes. Acrasia is, after all, an enchantress and a witch. As in Book I, the theme of magic involves the imagination. Book I, however, is concerned with the realm of mind, so that its consideration of magic involves the three-way relationship between mind, imagination, and reason, as we saw earlier when we explored Redcrosse's encounter with Contemplation. The province of Book II is the less elevated realm of the moral being and of reason. Even in the turret of Alma's castle (cantos ix and x), which structurally corresponds to Contemplation's mountain in I. x, we concentrate on the sensitive soul, and this despite the presence of the rational soul in the figure of Alma herself. And in ascending to the turret with Arthur and Guyon we confront, allegorically embodied in Phantastes, that most essential part of the sensitive soul for magicians, the imagination or fantasy. To cite once more the chapter from Agrippa quoted in connection with Contemplation, from the point of view of magical theory Book I relates to the ability of the mind to commune with supercelestial demons; Book II relates to the corruptible nature of the soul as 'it descendeth into sensitiveness and is affected by the influences of the heavenly bodies, and qualities of naturall things, and is distracted by the passions and the encountring of sensible objects'.[65] The 'passions' are embodied obviously enough in the book, and so are 'the influences of the heavenly bodies' in their malign aspects if we read passional characters like Acrasia, Phaedria, Furor, Pyrochles, and Cymochles, for example, as channels of astral influences (so that Acrasia is venerean; Pyrochles solar and martial, etc.).[66] Phantastes is so important because he demonstrates not how the soul is distracted by the passions, but how it can be distracted by 'the encountring of sensible objects'. Indeed, he, as the fantasy, represents a veritable storehouse of such objects and others too:

> His chamber was dispainted all within,
>> With sundry colours, in the which were writ
>> Infinite shapes of things dispersed thin;
>> Some such as in the world were never yit,
>> Ne can devized be of mortall wit;
>> Some daily seene, and knowen by their names,
>> Such as in idle fantasies doe flit:
>> Infernall Hags, *Centaurs*, feendes, *Hippodames*,
> Apes, Lions, Ægles, Owles, fooles, lovers, children, Dames. (ix. 50)

We meet these, or similar, monsters of the mind on the way to Acrasia's bower at the beginning of canto xii. At stanza 36 the 'ill-faste Owle' and other 'fatall birds' fly about Guyon's company. Before that 'an hideous hoast . . . / Of huge Sea monsters, such as living sence dismayd. . . . Most ugly shapes, and horrible aspects, / Such as Dame Nature selfe mote feare to see' have rushed at them and been dispelled by the Palmer, who, 'lifting up his vertuous staffe on hye, / . . . smote the sea, which calmed was with speed, / And all that dreadfull Armie fast gan flye / Into great *Tethys* bosome . . .' (st. 22 ff.). The pacifying power of the 'staffe' anticipates a main theme of Books III and IV, Elizabeth's sovereignty over the ocean, and is the corollary to it: the quelling of the sea monsters (monsters of the fantasy) must precede the orderly procession of the denizens of ocean, symbol of that sovereignty. Now the Palmer's rod is finally unveiled in its caducean aspect at stanzas 40–41, when it quells the wild beasts that inhabit Acrasia's Circe-like island. These, too, are the monsters of the mind that the caduceus, as an emblem of reason, vanquishes.[67] Spenser seems to be presenting us with a specific state of soul here that Agrippa again describes in the forty-third chapter of his Book III. As we recall, 'the soul by reason ascendeth into the mind, where it is replenished with divine light' (the subject of Spenser's Book I from our point of view); 'sometimes it descendeth into sensitiveness . . . and is distracted by the passions' (a matter considered in Spenser's Book II); but 'sometimes the soul revolveth it selfe wholly into reason', and this is the state considered here in canto xii with the banishing of the different beasts by the caduceus. To quote at greater length:

> it is possible that that part of the reason, which the *Peripateticks* call the possible Intellect, may be brought to this, that it may freely discourse and operate without conversion to his Phantasmes: for so great is the command of this reason, that as often as any thing incurreth either into the mind, or into the sensitiveness, or into nature, or into the body, it cannot passe into the soul, unless reason apply it self to it; by this means the soul perceiveth it self neither to see, nor hear, nor feel, not that it suffereth any things by the externall senses, until cogitative reason first apprehend it; but it apprehendeth it when it is at leasure, not when it earnestly gapeth after another thing. . . . Know therefore that neither the superiour influences, nor naturall affections, nor sensations, nor passions either of the mind or body, nor any sensible thing whatsoever, can work or penetrate into the soul unless by the Judgement of reason it self.

This, then, is what the Mercurian Palmer represents: that reason through which the magician receives 'superior influences' which enable him to banish evil spirits, both as objectively real creatures and as mental phantoms.[68]

Without reason as embodied in the Palmer you can descend into a self-made hell. As the occult philosophers pointed out, there were indeed evil as well as good spirits, and each individual has his good and evil spirit or genius:

> . . . amongst the good spirits there is a proper keeper or protector deputed to every one, corroborating the spirit of the man to good; so of evil spirits there is sent forth an enemy ruling over the flesh, and desire thereof; and the good spirit fights for us as a preserver against the enemie, and flesh; Now man betwixt these contenders is the middle, and left in the hand of his own Counsell, to whom he will give victory. . . .[69]

It is of your 'own accord' that you 'decline ... from the right path, adhering to the spirits of errours, giving victory to the Devill', thrusting yourself 'down ... unto the lowest degree of misery',[70] and this, whatever its other meanings, is one meaning of Guyon's descent into Mammon's underworld where again he encounters 'Owles and Night-ravens' (vii. 23) and where he is pursued by a 'feend' or evil spirit (st. 26–27). He descends with Mammon because he is without the Palmer (vii. 1–2); and in view of the allusive context that I have been outlining, we must suspect that the Mammon who seduces Guyon is not just the lord of wealth but the Mammon who, in his magically sanctioned function, is the prince of the individual's evil genius as well. Agrippa alludes to 'Tempters and Ensnarers ..., one of which is present with every man, which we therefore call the evill *Genius*, and their Prince is *Mammon*, which is interpreted covetousness'.[71] The pursuing 'feend' is, presumably, Guyon's evil genius. But there is another genius presiding over the individual, the 'threefold good Demon ... the one whereof is holy, another of the nativity, and the other of profession'.[72] We do not meet Guyon's demon (or genius) of the nativity or of his profession, but we do meet his holy demon. For is not this what the angelic figure, whom the Palmer is summoned by a mysterious voice to view sitting by Guyon's head, signifies? On one level the angel reminds us of the inflowing of God's love for man, and the redemption of the realm of nature through grace. But he is placed 'beside' Guyon's head, presiding over him, having charge 'Of his deare safetie' (viii. 8), so that his function sounds remarkably like that of

> the holy Demon ... assigned ... from a supernaturall cause, from God himself, the president of Demons. ... This doth direct the life of the soul, & doth alwaies put good thoughts into the minde, being alwaies active in illuminating of us ...; when we are purified, and live peaceably, then it is perceived by us. ... Also by the ayd of this Demon we may avoid the malignity of a Fate, which being religiously worshipped by us in honesty, and sanctity ... we may be much helped by it, as by dreams, and signs, by diverting evill things, and carefully procuring good things.[73]

It is as a dream that the angel-genius appears to Guyon, which is one reason he sits 'beside his head' (compare the 'ydle dream' at I. i. 47). Spenser imples something else too. When in stanza 1 of the eighth canto he tells us that this is one of the angels that God 'sends to and fro, / To serve to wicked man, to serve his wicked foe', he says 'angels' and means it.[74] The image here is based on Jacob's ladder, which we have already encountered on Contemplation's mountain. These angels come 'like

flying Pursuivant, / Against foule feends to aide us millitant' (st. 2).
Guyon's angel, then, is a manifestation of divine love; it is his holy
demon or genius; it is, in addition, an embodiment of the quasi-divine
state of the magician as expressed earlier in Redcrosse's meeting with
Contemplation. Book II's good magician, however, is the Palmer, and so
it is no surprise that the Palmer, too, sees the angel and receives from him
the role of Guyon's guardian: 'The charge, which God doth unto me
arret, / Of his deare safetie, I to thee commend' (viii. 8). This is a strange
moment in the book of Temperance, and it says as much about the
Palmer as about Guyon. For while Guyon is 'dreaming' his holy demon
the Palmer is being granted a vision that is the consequence of his role as
magician and especially of his role as adumbrator of the power of the
monarch magician. He receives angelic power.[75] It is also a consequence
of his specifically Mercurian function, since Mercury as a planetary deity
endows one with 'a piercing faith and belief, clear reasoning, the vigour
of interpreting and pronouncing, gravity of speech': a complete enough
summary of the Palmer's character and role as it is revealed in Book II.[76]

We can go even further. Iconographical tradition connects and even
identifies Mercury with the Judaeo-Christian angel, so that the angel
seen by the Palmer is his exact celestial counterpart.[77] Moreover, if
Mercury gives you 'faith and belief . . . [and] the vigour of interpreting',
then this is almost exactly the virtue bestowed on the magician by angels.
Because of their role, as messengers, in the heavenly hierarchy they
enable you to 'be a messenger of the divine will and an interpreter of the
mind of God'.[78] We now understand why, in describing the Palmer's
staff as a caduceus, Spenser directed attention to the caduceus's power to
'invade' the 'Stygian realmes' (xii. 41). This part of stanza 41 recalls
Virgil's account of Mercury's descent to Aeneas:[79]

> Then [Mercury] took his wand; the wand with which he calls the pale
> souls forth from the Nether World and sends others down to grim
> Tartarus, gives sleep, and takes sleep away. . . .

Spenser alludes to it to remind us that Book II no less than Book I is a
book of dreams, 'guilefull semblaunts' (xii. 48), and visions. In Book I the
serpent–rod of Moses defeated the snakes of the sorcerers and overcame
the images induced by Archimago; in Book II we see how Mercury's
snake-entwined wand can guide us from the hell of self- and magically
imposed delusion to the heaven of the mind, symbolised in the angel as
messenger of God. Mercury as leader of the soul (psychopompos), for
which role his caduceus was frequently interpreted as the emblem,

parallels that of Moses, the leader of God's chosen people, the emblem of whose authority, too, is a serpent-rod. In Book II, however, we approach nearer than in the previous book to our theme of the Mercurian monarch, for caduceus and 'scepter shene' are one and the same. Both achieve internal as well as external peace by banishing 'infernall feendes' (xii. 41) and bestowing visions of angels.[80]

[v] *Mercury and Merlin*

The Palmer in Acrasia's spring-like Bower of Bliss suggests another Mercurian tradition, that of *Mercurius Ver*, or Mercury as spring god, which we are perhaps most familiar with nowadays from Botticelli's *Primavera*.[81] This becomes a dominant *motif* in Book III, and we are introduced to it in the first canto when the Palmer hands over his Mercurian mission to Britomart, who has an 'enchaunted' spear, the 'secret vertue' of which the Palmer detects through 'his mightie Science' (i. 7, 10). Britomart is a Minervan figure, and her spear is the emblem of wisdom; but it is also the symbolic double of the caduceus. It continues for Book III the role that the Palmer's staff had in the previous book, and it reminds us, too, that Mercury (Hermes) and Minerva (or Athena) were often associated or even united into the composite Hermathena (see plate 4).[82] Britomart is indeed Minervan, and in being Minervan, and so exemplifying the warrior as well as virginal aspects of Queen Elizabeth, she is Mercurian as well. This must be one of the primary meanings of Britomart's disguise in the armour of the Saxon virgin Queen Angela (iii. 56 ff.), about whom little is said by the chroniclers. Angela is the angel-messenger, and her armour makes Britomart the inheritor of the quest of the Mercurian Palmer, who has himself seen an angel.

Britomart becomes *Mercurius Ver* when we notice that her approach to Malecasta's castle at III. i. 20 over 'a spatious plaine, / Mantled with greene' echoes the earlier approach to Acrasia's bower made by the Palmer and Guyon: 'they behold around / A large and spacious plaine, . . . / Mantled with greene, and goodly beautifide / With all the ornaments of *Floraes* pride' (II. xii. 50).[83] Both are false springs confronted by a true Mercury. Over the span of Books III and IV spring will be restored through the release of Florimell, whose story has so much in common with seasonal myth. She is the true Flora, goddess of flowers. Flora's lover was Favonius/Zephyrus, the west wind of spring who was frequently identified with Mercury as spring god.[84] The larger movement of these two central books, then, is Mercurian, for Florimell is

4   Mercury and Minerva (Hermathena)

not released until the last canto of Book IV. But into this larger movement smaller Mercurian patterns are assimilated. As a spring god, for example, Mercury was leader of the three Graces, and the Graces, as Nohrnberg has noticed,[85] appear in Book III as the three subsidiary heroines Florimell, Amoret, and Belphoebe. Each of them has moral qualities that are infolded in Britomart and hence the queen. As *Mercurius Ver*, Britomart–Elizabeth is their leader.

Britomart, however, can become Mercury by acquiring Angela's spear and armour only after she has encountered Merlin in canto iii. In canto ii we learn how she has seen her lover Artegall in Merlin's magic globe (a present to her father, King Ryence). In the succeeding canto, to quote the argument stanza, he reveals '*the famous Progeny / which from them springen shall*'. In essence this is a confrontation with her Cambro-British (Tudor) roots which, Spenser implies, are knowable through Merlin alone. The implication is that the monarch is dependent upon the magician, that she becomes Mercurian by consulting a magician adviser.

At this point we might pause over Merlin's globe, variously described as 'A looking glasse' and 'glassie globe' (ii. 18 ff.). Stanza 19 tells us that 'it round and hollow shaped was, / Like to the world it selfe, and seem'd a world of glas'. It was given to King Ryence by Merlin:

> It was a famous Present for a Prince,
> And worthy worke of infinite reward,
> That treasons could bewray, and foes convince. . . . (st. 21)

Its particular 'vertue' is 'to shew in perfect sight, / Whatever thing was in the world contaynd, / Betwixt the lowest earth and heavens hight' (st. 19). As a gift to a king symbolising the world, it would seem to answer the sceptre of Book II; in terms of coronation liturgy it can only be the orb, emblem of the monarch's Christian *imperium*. It is complemented by the 'white rod' of the 'royall virgin' at ii. 49. It is, though, a magic glass. Contemporaries might have associated it with John Dee's smoky polished 'Glass which had occasioned much conversation, and given rise to a report that he was a Magician'.[86] Elizabeth's relationship with Dee had been – even if it was not to be in the last years of her reign – an intellectually close and sympathetic one, and Dee was in many ways a key historical testament to the phenomenon of the magician-monarch. It should be no surprise that he appears, however fleetingly, in this first part of *The Faerie Queene* to confirm the magical power of the queen.[87]

The phrase 'magical power' is too vague, though, for this globe bestows upon the fit viewer 'What ever thing was in the world contaynd'.

Spenser is being precise, and his precision enables us to identify it with the third in the hierarchy of four philosophers' stones, the 'Magicall or Prospective Stone', by which

> it is possible to discover any Person in what part of the World soever, although never so secretly concealed or hid; in Chambers, Closets, or Caverns of the Earth. . . . In a Word, it fairely presents to your view even the whole World, wherein to behold, heare, or see your Desire. . . . [and] To convey a Spirit into an Image, which by observing the Influence of Heavenly Bodies, shall become a true Oracle.[88]

Merlin bestows upon Ryence, and by implication upon Britomart, one of the ultimate goals of the alchemist's quest. This is one of the places in the poem where the alchemical promise of Book I is fulfilled.[89]

But in a sense much of this is peripheral to Britomart's experience in Book III, for she goes to Merlin suffering from love melacholy. Because of the strange and ambiguous power of love it had, at least since Plato, been regarded as a demon to which we succumb either for good or bad.[90] It acts, inevitably, upon the imagination (hence Britomart's melancholic fantasies). From one point of view Britomart is a public figure; but in this most private of books we see her battle with love the demon and with his black magician, Busirane, as they attempt to manipulate her fantasy. As Mercury, or a Mercury–Minerva, she can win the battle, but only after she has encountered and learned from Merlin.

Merlin's cave is inhabited by 'cruell Feends', which he controls but which might 'devowre' the unwary intruder (iii. 8). This makes it Book III's equivalent to Mammon's cave with its pursuing demon, and the 'feends' in Merlin's cave are to be interpreted in part as love demons which Merlin knows how to control because he, too, having succumbed to the Lady of the Lake, has suffered from love and has learned from his suffering. We now understand why, when Britomart first sees Merlin and he is 'writing strange characters in the ground, / With whiche the stubborn feends he to his service bound' (iii. 14), the wording echoes John 8: 6.[91] Christ's reaction to the scribes and Pharisees as they remind him that the woman taken in adultery should, according to Mosaic law, be stoned, is to stoop down 'and with his finger [write] on ye ground'. His reply to their persistence is, 'Let him that is among you without sinne, cast the first stone at her'. In other words, anyone (including the white magician) can become love's victim, and the problem is to learn how to control the demon and harness his energies for good. It is this that Merlin reveals to Britomart when he tells her that from this 'hard begin' will emerge a progeny of 'Renowmed kings, and sacred Emperours'. Public and private fuse as we realise that the 'civill jarre' that will, under their rule, be turned to 'universall peace' alludes to Britomart's psychology as well as to the realm (iii. 22–23). The answer to the control of love's demon lies in a realisation of one's Mercurian self, the bringing forth not just into history but from one's own moral being of the 'royall virgin' with her Mercurian 'white rod' (iii. 49). As Merlin shows Britomart, she is engendered from strife (as, we might add, the caduceus itself was born from the strife of serpents).[92]

Books III and IV, then, deal with the magical education of the monarch with respect to love. Mercurian Britomart's mastery of love's black magician Busirane, ultimately through the power bestowed on her by Merlin (a victory over her own fantasies), releases Amoret into the following Book IV, which then relates love in its private aspect to love in its cosmic function, the binding-together of the elements and its moral corollary, concord, one of the main virtues of Mercury. We meet Dame Concord at the Temple of Venus in canto x. 'According' Cambina with her Mercurian caduceus appears early on, in canto iii. In effect the movement from Book III to Book IV is an extended allegory of the development of the Mercurian monarch from childhood to adulthood, an exploration of the way in which the vulnerable and dangerous inner impulses can be channelled outwards to embrace another individual – lover or friend – and beyond that to magical mastery over the elements. When you achieve the latter stage, however, the private self is not superseded or necessarily transcended. Book IV might in many ways be more 'public' than its predecessor, but these 'public' aspects are complemented by the private allegory of Scudamour's quest for Amoret.

It is Mercury, in fact, who is the symbolic meeting point of public and private. For, if at one end of the spectrum he becomes the Mercurian monarch, at the other end he fuses with Minerva–Athene to produce the wise, but inexperienced, virginal Britomart, or with Aphrodite to produce the Hermaphrodite, the emblem of sexual union with which Book III originally ended, and which Spenser then transferred to the tenth canto of Book IV to express the inner identification of Scudamour and Amoret. The point seems inescapable: the teleology of Book III (1590) and of Books III and IV (1596) is towards Mercury and the release of love and peace.[93]

But, although Book III is Mercury's, it belongs almost as much to Merlin. As a white magician he commanded fiends to build a 'brasen wall . . . / About *Cairmardin*' (iii. 10). Ultimately this is the power bestowed by him upon Britomart and through Britomart to Elizabeth, the 'royall virgin' who will command 'sacred Peace' with her Mercurian staff. And yet such a wall can be a prison as much as a fortification. Merlin's magic wall, created for good, is echoed for bad in Malbecco's castle at ix. 7, where we are told of Malbecco's attempt to imprison Hellenore that it is good will and 'gentle curtesyes' that will control a woman and 'not yron bandes, nor hundred eyes, / Nor brasen walls'. We notice it later in Danaë's 'strong brasen towre' (xi. 31), and finally at xii. 30, slightly metamorphosed, where the captive Amoret's 'small wast [is] girt round with yron bands, / Unto a brasen pillour'. Merlin's power to command is a benevolent one that can be parodied by the weak and evil Malbecco, Danaë's father, Acrisius, and Busirane. The point is that each of the latter is defeated: Hellenore escapes with Paridell; Jupiter enters Danaë's tower in 'a golden showre'; Amoret's bonds are released by Britomart. Furthermore, each instance suggests a political reading, the vanquishing of the tyrant Malbecco in the first instance so that the Trojan myth and its consequence, the building of New Troy, can be recapitulated; the defeat of the tyrannical father-king Acrisius in the second instance by the superior monarch Jove (with his magical power of metamorphosis); the defeat of the tyrannical Busirane, finally, through the greater power of Britomart.

It is this last confrontation that is crucial to our understanding of the relationship between monarchy and magic in Book III. Britomart is the book's embodiment of Elizabeth as the Mercurian monarch, and her power to defeat Busirane derives from Merlin. It is significant, then, that Busirane should parody Merlin as closely as he does. For example, Merlin's cave with its fiends (iii. 8–9) is imitated by Busirane at xi.16:

> For he the tyrant, which her hath in ward
> By strong enchauntments and black Magick leare,
> Hath in a dungeon deepe her close embard,
> And many dreadfull feends hath pointed her to gard;

while at xii. 31, when Britomart finds 'the vile Enchaunter . . . / Figuring straunge characters of his art', we catch the echo of Merlin 'writing strange characters' at iii. 14. Busirane parodies Merlin because of Merlin's connection with the monarch magus, for he himself is based on Busiris, the Egyptian tyrant who killed strangers and 'defiled his temples with [their] blood', and who was identified with the Pharaoh of Exodus.[94] In other words, when Mercurian Britomart compels Egyptian Busirane to reverse his charms so that Amoret can be released (xii. 36 ff.), we are witnessing monarchy overthrowing tyranny, a political statement expressed through a magical metaphor. The Exodus context, moreover, recalls Book I, the battle between Una and Archimago described in terms of the contest between Moses and Aaron with their magic rod and the Pharaoh's Egyptian sorcerers.

Does Busirane's political significance end there, though? I think not, since his connection with Busiris and the spilling of strangers' blood recalls, in this book of Merlin, a tale told by Geoffrey concerning Merlin and King Vortigern in which the young Merlin almost became a sacrificial victim of Vortigern's, who had been advised by his magicians to sprinkle a tower that was being built for him with the blood of a youth in order to prevent it from collapsing. Merlin proved that their remedy would not work by revealing, through his greater magic, the cause of the collapse.[95] The story parallels that of the Pharaoh and his sorcerers, and it would appear that Spenser conflated them to give us the oppositions Britomart–Merlin–Moses on the one hand and Busirane–Vortigern–Busiris on the other. Now Vortigern appears in Spenser's chronicle of British history at II. x. 64 as the usurping king who, according to Gildas, Nennius, and others (including Geoffrey), was the tyrant who invited the Saxons to Britain, thus becoming the betrayer of his land. Anti-Vortigern material is common at this period when the Cambro-British myth was so strong, and there is little doubt that Spenser's contemporaries would have made the connection between Vortigern and Busirane. After all, the burden of Merlin's vision in canto iii is the enmity of Britons and Saxons.[96]

The relationship between magic and monarchy as I have outlined it so far in Book III has, however, been oversimplified by the omission of Proteus, the third magician of the book. Indeed, he stands literally midway between Merlin and Busirane, appearing as he does in cantos iv and viii. As the god of metamorphosis, sophistry, and magic he, like Merlin, is an apt symbol for the double aspect of love and magic.[97] But this Proteus appears to tend towards black magic rather than white, particularly when he displaces Arthur as redeemer by rescuing Florimell in canto viii and then attempts to seduce her by transforming himself 'To dreadfull shapes . . . / Now like a Gyant, now like to a feend' (viii. 41). Like the Protean Archimago and Busirane he works by trying to posses her imagination, and in doing so bears a marked similarity to that lesser order of evil spirits who, according to Agrippa, 'do contrive rather to weary men, then to hurt them, some heightning themselves to the length of a Giants body, and again shrinking themselves up to the smalness of Pigmies, and changing themselves into divers forms, do disturb men with vain fear'.[98] This makes him considerably less harmful than Busirane, and it would seem that one of his main meanings from our point of view emerges directly from his relationship with Florimell. If Florimell is Flora, the spring goddess, then Proteus is winter, since at viii. 35 he kisses her with 'frory lips' and has 'cold ysickles [hanging] from his rough beard'. Subsequently he imprisons her. Critics have long recognised the seasonal mythology here, but they have not been attuned to Mercury's role in it; for Flora/Florimell's true partner, attained with her release and the simultaneous arrival of spring, must be Zephyrus, commonly identified with Mercury as spring god. In terms of Book IV's mythological and narrative structure this Mercurian figure is Neptune, who orders Florimell's release and, as we shall see, symbolises Elizabeth's maritime dominance. The fact that Proteus (a sea god) yields to Neptune, ruler of the sea, is a statement of his hierarchical inferiority. He must obey the true king. As a figure in a seasonal myth he can merely delay spring (so becoming an anti-Mercury) for its just annual period, not destroy it; as a creator of illusions he can only 'disturb . . . with vain fear'. This, in conjunction with his displacement of Arthur as rescuer from canto viii, suggests that he is yet another parody magician monarch, a view that is confirmed by the sea god Proteus's frequent confusion with the 'King of *Ægypt*' of the same name, 'a wise politick man, and a great Prophet, therefore he was said to change himself into all shapes; wisdom, policy, and fore-knowledge, are gifts very requisite in a Prince; and if he will govern his people well, he must change himself into many shapes . . . he that cannot dissemble, cannot govern'.[99] Spenser would have agreed with the 'wisdom, policy, and fore-knowledge', but the dissembling would have sounded a little too Machiavellian to be openly admitted in his idealising poem. This, presumably, is why Proteus in Books III and IV fails as a monarch magus. He is not a Busirane-like tyrant; neither is he a Neptune or a Britomart–Merlin.

He is, however, Egyptian, as Busirane is, and as the Mercurian monarch is through his connection with Hermes Trismegistus. The Egyptian preoccupation of Book III helps confirm the presence of Brunian Hermetics in Books I and II while at the same time drawing attention to a Brunian element in Book III itself. We recall that Bruno, following the *Asclepius*, writes of the corruption of Egypt and its religion and of its restoration to its pristine purity. This restoration is announced in *The Expulsion of the Triumphant Beast* by the reform of heaven, to be achieved by the banishing of the vicious constellations, many of which commemorate the king of heaven's lusts. Can it be an accident that we find these very stellified lusts in the castle of Busirane, the 'Egyptian' black magician, whose prototype was king over a sterile land? They are portrayed for us in canto xi, stanzas 30–35; so that in vanquishing Busirane Britomart actually effects the expulsion of the beast, acting not just as a Mercurian monarch but as a Brunian Hermetic magician as well. Closer inspection of these stanzas, moreover, reveals that they contain themes and motifs found elsewhere in the book. Thus, Jove's capacity for metamorphosis suggests Proteus; the ram and Helle (xi. 30) call to mind horned Malbecco and Hellenore; the bull in the same stanza appears earlier as the inhabitant of forests at i. 14, the sacrificial ox to which Marinell is compared (iv. 17), and the Minotaur of x. 40; Danaë was imprisoned in a 'brasen towre', as we have seen (st. 31); when Leda was seduced she was sleeping among 'daffadillies' (st. 32) as Cymoent was 'Gathering sweet daffadillyes' when she heard of her son Marinell's wound (iv. 29); Jove's 'thunderbolts and lightning fire' with which he killed Semele (st. 33) are borrowed by Busirane at xii. 2 in an attempt to frighten Britomart; 'the *Trojane* boy' of xi. 34 suggests Trojan Paridell, and so on. Jove's metamorphoses govern the book in this way because his unchaste history can be interpreted as a precedent for a connection between lust and kingship. But the Brunian meaning is there too, to remind us that Jove repented and purged himself and the heavens. It is with this reminder that the 1590 *Faerie Queene* ended, and in the reminder was embodied the supreme compliment that Britomart–Elizabeth had vanquished the corruptions of the old religion and established in its place the pristine religion and chaste virtues envisioned in the *Asclepius* and Bruno's *Expulsion*.

[vi] *Mercury, Venus, and Isis*

The key Mercurian figure in Book IV is Cambina, whose function it is to 'accord' the battle over Canacee. Cambina is 'learned ... in Magicke leare' (iii. 40) and

> In her right hand a rod of peace shee bore,
>> About the which two Serpents weren wound,
>> Entrayled mutually in lovely lore,
>> And by the tailes together firmely bound,
>> And both were with one olive garland crownd,
>> Like to the rod which *Maias* sonne doth wield,
>> Wherewith the hellish fiends he doth confound. . . . (st. 42)

She is Book IV's equivalent to Merlin and the Palmer, and so becomes its image of the Mercurian-magician-monarch as prince of peace. Later we will meet her serpents again in the figure of the hermaphroditic Venus encountered by Scudamour in canto x. For the moment it is important to notice that Cambina enters 'in a charet ... drawne ... Of two grim lyons' (st. 38–39), which recalls the chariot of Cybele, goddess of the created earth on whom civilisations and cities are raised (see plate 5).[100] Book IV, with its legend of friendship, is ultimately about the friendship which Plato, in the *Timaeus*, recognised as binding the four elements together to produce cosmos from chaos. Cybele takes us from cosmos to city and state. She is fused here with Mercury to complete the chain that, through the monarch, links base matter with the divine. Magic is, again, not a mere metaphor but essential to Spenser's definition of monarchy, for the monarch's power to sustain civilisation derives from a God-given revelation like that enjoyed by Moses. Cambina's 'rod of peace' is a sceptre, wand, and Moses's serpent-rod as well as Mercurian caduceus.

We meet Cybele once more at the end of Book IV, in the great procession for the wedding of Thames and Medway in which the bridegroom, Thames himself, wears a turreted coronet like Cybele's:

> Like as the mother of the Gods, they say,
>   In her great iron charet wonts to ride,
>   When to *Joves* pallace she doth take her way:
>   Old *Cybele*, arrayd with pompous pride,
>   Wearing a Diademe embattild wide
>   With hundred turrets, like a Turribant.
>   With such an one was Thamis beautifide;
>   That was to weet the famous Troynovant. . . . (xi. 28)

The bride is described some twenty stanzas later as being bedecked with flowers so that she heralds 'a new spring; and likewise on her hed / A Chapelet of sundry flowers she wore' (st. 46). Brides traditionally wore and carried flowers; but these flowers, in connection with the reference to 'spring', turn her into Flora. She is the spring queen who announces the release in the next canto, as a direct consequence of her wedding, of that other Flora, Florimell, from the dungeons of Proteus's palace. Her bridegroom is a Cybele-like Thames who, because of the earlier association of Cybele with Mercury, suggests that the marriage, on the practical political level signifying armed peace,[101] symbolises on the level of mystical politics the union of *Mercurius Ver* with his bride Flora–Venus in the figure of Elizabeth. Their union releases Florimell. In other words the Mercurian monarch has the power to release a

5 Cybele

springlike Golden Age.

But in fact it is Neptune who formally redeems Florimell. This is only fitting since, as one of the mythological founders of Troy, he can at once embody Elizabeth's Trojan ancestry and, as ruler of ocean, her maritime supremacy.[102] It is he who leads the procession to Proteus's house for 'the spousalls' of Thames and Medway, and significantly he is described 'with his threeforkt mace' of monarchical supremacy and wearing 'his Diademe imperiall' (xi. 11). He is the double – in a sense progenitor – of Thames, who himself recalls the peace-bringing Mercury–Cybele Cambina. Neptune's trident echoes Cambina's caduceus and, when he achieves Florimell's release from Proteus, it is seen to be more powerful than Proteus's 'staffe' (or wand), which we have been introduced to in the previous book (viii. 31). He is able to effect Florimell's release because, we are told, he is 'the seas sole Soveraine' and therefore she is his 'by high prerogative' (xii. 31–32).[103] He can thus compel the undoing of Proteus's magic and liberate Flora–Florimell and is therefore another manifestation of the monarch as Mercury, leader of spring, and his Mercurian role is confirmed when we notice the parallel between the end of Book III and the end of Book IV. For Neptune vanquishes Proteus to liberate Flora as the Hermathena Britomart vanquished Busirane to liberate Amoret. The final canto of Book III glosses the twelfth canto of Book IV to suggest that Neptune's power derives from his own Mercurian wisdom which is greater than, and so can penetrate the illusions generated by, Proteus's inferior magic.

Neptune's defeat of Proteus is, indeed, symbolically anticipated in the description of Thames's bride, Medway, thus again confirming the doubling between Neptune and Florimell and the bridal couple. She is 'Clad in vesture of unknowen geare' which

> seem'd like silver, sprinkled here and theare
> With glittering spangs, that did like starres appeare,
> And wav'd upon, like water Chamelot,
> To hide the metall, which yet every where
> Bewrayd it selfe, to let men plainely wot,
> It was no mortall worke, that seem'd and yet was not. (xi. 45)

As Hamilton perceptively notices,[104] this echoes Busirane's tapestry at III. xi. 28,

> Woven with gold and silke so close and nere,
> That the rich metall lurked privily,
> As faining to be hid from envious eye;

> Yet here, and there, and every where unwares
> It shewd it selfe, and shone unwillingly;
> Like a discoulourd Snake, whose hidden snares
> Through the greene gras his long bright burnisht backe declares.

Medway, as a Flora-like symbol of love, dissolves through the echo part of the apparatus of Busirane's demonic magic, just as her name, in its Spenserian form *Medua*, cancels out the witch Medea on whom Acrasia at the end of Book II was based. Similarly, the pun in Chamelot makes the fabric, camlet, into Arthur's Camelot to suggest that in this marriage all the main myths of the poem fuse. To them, however, one is added: Thames is the son of Tame and Isis. In the developing Egyptian context of the poem it is inevitable that Isis, described in xi. 24, should recall the Egyptian goddess Isis, herself the daughter of a river god and, it turns out, the symbolic centre of Book V.[105]

Medway's robe is similar to, but crucially different from, Busirane's tapestry in that it conceals no harmful snake. The spousal at the end of the book reminds us that the book began with a wedding feast — the feast celebrating the union of Scudamour and Amoret from which 'that same vile Enchauntour *Busyran*' abducted her (i. 3). Scudamour's search for her is the quest for the impulse to love within himself which he confronts in the Temple of Venus, in canto x, embodied in the mysterious figure of the hermaphroditic Venus.[106] One of the important points about this figure is that 'both her feete and legs together twyned / Were with a snake, whose head and tail were fast combynd' (x. 40). This bisexual Venus, combination of Hermes and Aphrodite, corresponds to Book III's Hermathena and symbolises marriage and the just union of mind and body. Its circular snake reconciles still further the entwined serpents of Cambina's caduceus to produce an image of the cosmic cycle,[107] which at the same time celebrates the supremely magical power of Elizabeth as receiver and diffuser of divine love. Whatever the psychological allegory, the political implications of the temple are clear. The reconciled serpents of the caduceus express the integrating power of the monarch whose power in this respect is in addition announced by the presence of Concord at the temple's entrance (Concord was invariably portrayed holding a caduceus).[108] It is this serpent of reconciliation that vanquishes Busirane's snake in the grass to enable us to proceed to the marriage of Thames and Medway, a further image of political stability assured by the monarchical ability to impose peace.

The book's images of monarchical magic have again been centred on Mercury and his caduceus. We can now see that its energies have been

6   Isis as Cybele

directed almost remarkably single-mindedly to undoing the political threat posed by strifeful Ate, herself the undoer of sovereigns. In her dwelling 'Hard by the gates of hell' are her equivalent to Busirane's tapestries and Medway's robe:

> And all within the riven walls were hung
> > With ragged monuments of times forepast,
> > All which the sad effects of discord sung:
> > There were rent robes, and broken scepters plast.... (i. 21)[109]

Book IV traces the means by which these 'broken scepters' can be replaced by the pacific wand of Mercury, the sceptre of the magician king.

[vii] *Mercury and Isis*

At the end of Book V Artegall, on his way to Gloriana's court, is beset by two hags, Envy and Detraction. Envy, subscribing to an iconographical commonplace, holds a venomous snake. Detraction's tongue, complementing it, 'Appear'd like Aspis sting, that closely kils' (xii. 30, 36). They command the Blatant Beast and, in order to sully Artegall's good name, 'These two now had themselves combynd in one, / And linckt together gainst Sir *Artegall*' (st. 37). This echoes the hermaphroditic Venus of IV. x. 41 who 'hath both kinds in one'; but through this allusion to Mercury we detect a further echo of Cambina's caduceus with its entwined serpents. Envy and Detraction, like Ate, are another manifestation of discord, the reverse of the Mercury archetype. If the monarch is a Mercurian magician, it is inevitable that they should erupt at the end of this fifth book in which political concerns have been supremely to the fore,[110] and in which the monarch has for the first time appeared in her own person complete with 'Scepter in her royall hand, / The sacred pledge of peace and clemencie' (V. ix. 30). Two stanzas earlier we are told:

> All over her a cloth of state was spred,
> > Not of rich tissew, nor of cloth of gold,
> > Nor of ought else, that may be richest red,
> > But like a cloud, as likest may be told,
> > That her brode spreading wings did wyde unfold;
> > Whose skirts were bordred with bright sunny beams,
> > Glistring like gold, amongst the plights enrold,
> > And here and there shooting forth silver streames,
> Mongst which crept little Angels through the glittering gleames.

The angels accompanying her are reminiscent of Cupids, turning the monarch into the queen of heavenly love and so dispelling, once and for all, the demons of Busirane. But it seems that 'these little Angels did uphold / The cloth of state', and the queen herself is 'Angel-like' (st. 29). Echoes of the angel on Jacob's ladder (which we have encountered earlier in our pursuit of the magician monarch) fuse with our memory of Britomart–Angela to give us a culminating statement of the queen's Mercurian mediating role with heaven defined in terms of her ability to call down angels. The cloud is a dark veil which she alone has the power to penetrate, and this is the power of Mercury, whose passage through the gloomy clouds at *Aeneid*, IV. 245–246 was interpreted by Boccaccio as proof of his ability to dispel, with his caduceus, the clouds of mental obfuscation and darkness.[111] What Wind has written so beautifully of Botticelli's Mercury in the *Primavera* could be applied to Spenser's Queen Mercilla and her clouds: 'To "reveal the mysteries" is to move the veils while preserving their dimness, so that the truth may penetrate but not glare. . . . The highest wisdom is to know that the divine light resides in clouds'.[112] Remembering, too, the gold and silver of Mercilla's skirts, and that Mercury is the god of knowledge, we recall Plutarch's 'the Deity is not blessed by reason of his possession of gold and silver, nor strong because of thunder and lightning, but through knowledge and intelligence'.[113] Mercilla's gold is not real gold, nor is her silver real silver. Neither are her clouds thunder clouds. She is the divine monarch who possesses the power of angels presented to us in the guise of Mercury. For it is Mercury, surely, as well as the quality of mercy, that Mercilla's name conveys.[114]

My Plutarch quotation was from the *De Iside et Osiride* in order to remind us that we approach Mercilla herself through the mystery of Isis's church which Britomart penetrates in canto vii. The moon goddess and queen, Isis, surrogate for the moon queen, Cynthia–Elizabeth, is the goddess above all of veiled mysteries. She is the daughter of Mercury and revealer of her 'divine mysteries to those who truly and justly' are initiates.[115] Her name signifies knowledge and understanding. Britomart's sojourn at the church is a crucial stage in her private quest for her lover Artegall, but it also confronts her with an image of her public monarchical self. For the Isis she encounters is both lover and queen, and as a queen she is a proleptic unfolding of Mercilla as Egyptian queen and as Mercury. This episode reminds us, too, as indeed Mercilla herself does with her angel-Cupids, how important the vanquishing of the tyrannical Egyptian black magician Busirane is to Spenser's

ISIDIS
Magnæ Deorum Matris
APVLEIANA DESCRIPTIO.

Nomina varia
Ifidis.

Ifis
Minerua
Venus
Iuno
Proferpina
Ceres
Diana
Rhea feu
  Tellus
Peffinuncia
Rhramnufia
Bellona
Hecate
Luna
Polymor-
  phus dæ-
  mon.

Ἴσις παρδεχής πο-
λύμορφ©- δαί-
μων.
Μυελώνυμ©-φύσις,
ύλη.

Explicationes fym-
bolorum Ifidis.

A Diuinitatem, mun-
  dum, orbes cœleſtes
BB Iter Lunæ flexuo-
  ſum, & vim fœcun-
  dariuam notat.
CC Tutulus, vim Lu-
  næ in herbas, &
  plantas.
D Cereris fymbolum,
  Ifis enim ſpicas in-
  uenit.
E Byſſina veſtis mul-
  ticolor, multifor-
  mem Lunæ faciem.
F Inuentio frumenti.
G Dominium in om-
  nia vegetabilia.
H Radios lunares.
I Genius Nili malo-
  rum auerruncus.
K Incrementa & de-
  crementa Lunæ.
L Humectat. vis Lunę.
M Lunæ vis victrix, &
  vis diuinandi.
N Dominium in hu-
  mores & mare.
O Terræ fymbolũ, &
  Medicinæ inuentrix.
P Fœcunditas, quæ ſe-
  quitur terram irri-
  gatam.
Q Aſtrorum Domina.
R Omnium nutrix.
S ⎫ Terræ mariſque
M ⎭ Domina.

Ἀκρα Θεῶν Μήτηρ ταύτη πολιώμ©- ΙΣΙΣ

7 Isis

argument. For if Britomart is to be understood as wandering Isis searching for her husband Osiris—Artegall, whose union, foretold by Merlin, is reiterated here (st. 22), then we must recall first that Osiris was a just ruler whose wisdom and justice were sustained by Isis after his death, and second the report that 'while many tombs of Osiris are spoken of in Egypt, his body lies buried in Busiris'.[116] He is buried there because he was born there. In storming Busirane's castle in Book III and binding its tyrannical inhabitant Britomart—Mercury was in a way banishing the power of death (Mercury, after all, leads souls from as well as into the underworld with his caduceus). In Book V she encounters her beloved reborn: Mercurian Isis, as it were, resurrects the just king, and the result of their union will be Mercurian Mercilla.

This is evident enough from the iconographical relationship between the image of Isis in the church and Mercilla herself, enthroned with her sceptre (vii. 6–7):

> Uppon her head she [Isis] wore a Crowne of gold,
> To shew that she had powre in things divine;
> And at her feete a Crocodile was rold,
> That with her wreathed taile her middle did enfold.

> One foote was set upon the Crocodile,
> And on the ground the other fast did stand,
> So meaning to suppresse both forged guile,
> And open force: and in her other hand
> She stretched forth a long white sclender wand.

This wand becomes Mercilla's sceptre, the ivory rod of the coronation liturgy.[117] When we recall that the crocodile was emblematically interchangeable with the dragon-serpent, we see that this tableau defines Mercilla not only by connecting her with Isis, but also by harking back to the hermaphroditic Venus with her ouroboros.[118] Moreover, crocodile-serpent in conjunction with white wand indicates that Mercilla's sceptre is, once more, a caduceus, Mercury's white wand with its entwined serpents. And yet we do Spenser's inconographical subtlety an injustice if we treat the crocodile merely as a serpent, for the crocodile itself is, according to Plutarch, the only living creature without a tongue, so that it is 'a living representation of God . . . for the Divine Word has no need of a voice'. Mercilla's angels have confirmed her quasi-divine magical power. The crocodile suggests, through her affinity with Isis, that in her divinity she can transcend eloquent Mercury himself to enter, even if only momentarily, the world beyond words.[119]

The idol moves her wand in sign of favour to Britomart, reminding us that the Isis we encounter here is an animated statue (a point to which I shall return in a moment). After this, as the day is 'overcast', Britomart succumbs to sleep, during which she has her 'wondrous vision' in which Isis's wand checks the crocodile when it starts to swell with pride and in which Britomart herself becomes Isis. Since the crocodile emerges after being woken by 'An hideous tempest . . . from below' (st. 14), our identification of the wand with the caduceus would appear to be confirmed: it vanquishes the crocodile-serpent in its evil (underworld) aspect because Mercury has power over Hades. But the vision is too much for Britomart, who wakens 'full of fearefull fright' and 'With thousand thoughts feeding her fantasie' (st. 16, 17). When she wakens it is still night and she is still in the dark, physically and mentally the victim of the cloud which persuaded her to fall asleep in the first place. Mercurian Mercilla can comprehend and even rule her own clouds; but that tableau, as I have said, is dependent on this anterior tableau at Isis's church. Britomart has become Isis only in a dream; Mercilla is not yet Mercilla. Britomart needs an interpreter, and she finds one in a priest of Isis who acts literally as a hermeneut, interpreting under the influence of Hermes–Mercury, the god of all priests.[120] He explains and so dispels her delusions, as Merlin dispelled them in Book III and as the Mercurian Palmer vanquished the fantastic monsters of Book II. The message of both Merlin and the priest is the same: Britomart will marry Artegall; Isis will once again be reunited with Osiris. Mercilla will be the ultimate offspring of their union, the Mercurian monarch who is Mercurian in all the senses we have so far encountered it in this book: intermediary between heaven and earth; vanquisher of death; dispeller of illusions; pacific. More than that she will be, in the mystical sense, bisexual, reconciling within herself the parental opposites Osiris and Isis.[121] The clue here is the combination of 'sunny beams' and 'silver streames' on her robe at ix. 28, which takes us back to the alchemical theme of Book I and makes Mercilla into the bisexual *Mercurius noster* of the adepts, offspring of, and in herself uniting, gold and silver, sun and moon (see plate 1). This is one of the reasons why Spenser tells us so explicitly that '*Isis* doth the Moone portend; / Like as *Osyris* signifies the Sunne' (vii. 4). In canto vii, at Isis's church, we are present at an alchemical wedding, the issue from which will be Mercurian Mercilla, and the crocodile-serpent-dragon of double aspect is the alchemical dragon of putrefaction and renewal. It is no surprise that Spenser should return to alchemy as a theme in this book; for alchemy is one of the great Hermetic arts and a supreme affirmation of the monarch's magical power, and Book V, like no other book in the poem since Book I, is about Elizabeth's Protestant empire and the mystical vision that underlay it.[122]

The crocodile–dragon of renewal finds its corrupt opposite in the monster beneath the altar in Catholic Geryoneo's church, which emerges 'from under th'Altars smooke, / A dreadfull feend ... Borne of the brooding of *Echidna* base' (xi. 22, 23; Echidna is the snake woman who provides the archetype for the dragon Errour in Book I).[123] Elizabeth–Mercilla's Protestant empire, in other words, rises alchemically from the putrefied matter of Catholic imperialism. But, in fact, in physical appearance the monster is not a dragon (though it does have 'A Dragons taile'), but a sphinx, emblem of ignorance appropriate to Spenser's anti-Catholic bias. And yet the sphinx is far from being only evil. Its appearance here directs us back to Isis and Mercilla and so to the mystical vision that underlies the book's practical politics. For 'the Ægyptians placed the Image of *Sphynx* in the Porch of *Isis* Temple ... to shew, that the mysteries of Religion were not to be divulged among the Vulgar but Enigmatically';[124] and the well-known pavement at Siena cathedral portraying Hermes Trismegistus as the contemporary of Moses shows him holding in his left hand a table placed on two sphinxes which bears an inscription conflating a fragment from the *Asclepius* with one from the *Pimander*. This inscription strengthens the Christian implications of the Hermetic texts to remind us that 'God, the Creator of all things, made the second visible god, and made him first and alone, in whom He delighted and loved most exceedingly as His own son, who is called holy word'.[125]

So the spinx is connected with Thrice-great Hermes himself as revealer of divine mysteries. It would seem that with Book V Spenser's theme of the Mercurian monarch becomes specifically that of the Hermetic monarch, elaborating as it does on the Egyptian themes of earlier books. Moreover, Geryoneo's sphinx tells us that Catholic imperialism is to be understood as a perversion of the true religion of Isis and Hermes Trismegistus, whose mysteries it conceals. Therefore Elizabeth's Protestantism is a return to the old Egyptian religion. This is a typical gesture of Renaissance syncretism for which Spenser, if we are to take note of the clues laid earlier in the poem, is probably indebted to Bruno's *Expulsion of the Triumphant Beast*. In the second part of the third dialogue Bruno refers to, and quotes from, the *Asclepian* lament in a passage worth citing at length:

... the wisdom of the Egyptians, which is lost, worshiped not only the earth, the moon, the sun, and other stars of the heaven but also crocodiles. . . . This magic and divine rite (through which Divinity so easily imparted herself to men) is mourned by Trismegistus, who said when reasoning with Asclepius: 'Do you see, oh Asclepius, these animated statues full of feeling and spirit that are the cause of such and so many worthy works, these statues, I say, prognosticators of future things that bring infirmities, cures, joys, and sadnesses, according to the merits of human affects and bodies? Do you not know, oh Asclepius, that Egypt is the image of heaven or, better said, the colony of all things that are governed and practiced in heaven? To speak the truth, our land is the temple of the world. But woe is me! The time will come when Egypt will appear to have been in vain the religious cultivator of divinity, because divinity, remigrating to heaven, will leave Egypt deserted. And this seat of divinity will remain widowed of every religion, having been deprived of the presence of the gods, for which reason there will succeed in that land strange and barbarous people without any religion, piety, law, and cult.

'Oh Egypt, oh Egypt! Of your religion there will remain only the fables, still incredible to future generations, to whom there will be nothing else that may narrate your pious deeds save the letters sculptured on stones, which will narrate, not to gods and men (because the latter will be dead and deity will have transmigrated into heaven), but to Scythians and Indians, or other people of a similarly savage nature. Shadows will be placed before light. . . . The religous man will be considered insane . . . the most wicked man, good. And believe me, capital punishment will still be prescribed for him who will apply himself to the religion of the mind, because new justices will be found, new laws. Nothing holy will be found, nothing religious; nothing worthy of heaven or the celestials will be heard. Only pernicious angels will remain, who, mingling with men, will force upon the wretched ones every audacious evil as if it were justice. . . . And this will be the old age and the disorder and the irreligion of the world. But do not doubt, Asclepius, for after these things have occurred, the lord and father God, governor of the world . . . will doubtlessly put an end to such a blot, recalling the world to its ancient countenance.'[126]

It is Hermetic Elizabeth as Mercilla who restores justice in this book by banishing the false sphinx and pernicious angels of Catholic dominion so that the old religion may be revealed and the world be recalled 'to its ancient countenance'. This is what is anticipated by the animated statue of Isis, whose very appearance in this book is a sign that the true religion has returned.

[viii] *Mercury and Colin*

In Book VI Spenser most openly questions the values of the court. Accordingly, the monarch disappears from view except for one mention in canto ii when we are told that the young Tristram, 'a Briton borne / Sonne of a King', has been deprived of his birthright by his uncle, 'that did the kingly Scepter beare' (st. 27, 29). Tristram has been sent from Lyonesse to the land of faerie by his mother in accordance with the 'counsell of a wise man' (st. 30). He becomes Sir Calidore's squire and so parallels the noble foundling 'salvage' of cànto iv who later accompanies Arthur as – even if he does not technically become – his squire. The parallel asserts the book's pastoralism, Spenser's modulation from the courtly. And when we read in iv. 4 that the 'salvage' has been rendered invulnerable from birth 'by Magicke leare', we begin to suspect that the magical theme, too, has been modulated into the pastoral mode.

Confirmation comes at vii. 24 when this 'salvage' attacks the agents of the shameful Sir Turpine, who are themselves about to attack the sleeping Arthur, with

> an oaken plant, which lately hee
> Rent by the root; which he so sternely shooke,
> That like an hazell wand, it quivered and shooke.

'Wand' turns the traditional attribute of the wild man[127] into the symbol of magical power. The Mercurian monarch's chief emblem has been transferred, in this book in which the very bases of courtly culture are probed, explored, and exposed, to the monarch's apparent opposite, the good-natured wild man who has not even the Mercurian gift of language, 'But a soft murmure, and confused sound / Of senselesse words, which nature did him teach, / T'expresse his passions, which his reason did empeach' (iv. 11). The 'salvage' with his wand soon yields to another figure, however, that of the poet's *persona* Colin. For Colin does possess language, the Mercurian language of art and particularly the Mercurian language of music. As he plays his pipe (equivalent to wand and caduceus) he commands through its music the dance of 'An hundred naked maidens lilly white, / All raunged in a ring' (x. 11) as well as the three 'Graces, daughters of delight, / Handmaides of *Venus*' (st. 15) to become another *Mercurius Ver*, leader of the Graces.

This vision, equivalent to Redcrosse's glimpse of angels and the New Jerusalem in the corresponding canto of Book I, appears to Sir Calidore on the wood-enclosed mount Acidale, the scene, Spenser is careful to tell us, of Venus's non-sovereign exploits. Here she plays. It is on 'Cytheron . . . She used most to keepe her royall court' (st. 9). What we are seeing here is the private magic of the monarch off duty. And so the knightly Calidore has only to appear for the maidens to disappear and for Colin to break his pipe. In effect, he is silenced to become like the magic-learned wild man, and yet Colin enjoys the traditional position of sovereignty 'in the midst' of the 'troupe of Ladies' (st. 10).[128] What criticis have often, and rightly, seen in Book VI, a strangely questioning holiday from the world of courtly glory, applies to our Mercurian theme as well. In one way the obverse of the monarch, and yet in another way the monarch's equal, is the sovereign poet, whose imaginative power is equivalent to the monarch's power to call down angels.[129]

Moreover, if in earlier books Spenser has informed us of the Mercurian role of the monarch, in this pastoral book he reminds us that Mercury was originally a shepherd god[130] while at the same time, through the figure of Colin as musician, strengthening the links between Book VI and the monarchical Book V. For there is 'a legend that Hermes cut out the sinews of Typhon, and used them as strings for his lyre, thereby instructing us that Reason adjusts the Universe and creates concord out of discordant elements.'[131] It was chaos-bringing Typhon who killed Osiris, and from one point of view it is he who is embodied in the malevolent aspect of the crocodile that is controlled by the magical power of Isis's rod (V. vii. 15). Colin's musical pipe can be seen as a double of the Mercurian lyre which itself asserts the same control over chthonic forces as Isis's rod or wand.[132] Mercury was Isis's father; mythopoeically, Colin has engendered Isis–Mercilla.

The significance of Colin from our point of view becomes clearer when we notice the structural centrality of the tenth canto within the last part of the book. It is at the centre of a processional and recessional movement that begins in canto viii when the cannibals, preparing to sacrifice Serena, flock around her 'like many flies' (st. 40; at st. 41 they view her naked body 'with lustfull fantasyes'). This scene could have been conjured up by Archimago, and it reminds us that we are once again in the world of the depraved imagination, black magic's opposite of the vision afforded by Colin. At stanza 45 the priest approaches Serena with 'murdrous knife' (the dissecting equivalent of Colin's integrative pipe) and begins 'mutter close a certaine secret charme, / With other divelish ceremonies met', his infernal counterpart to Colin's Mercurian music. If Colin's music is the ultimate answer to this grotesque ceremony, however, we attain to it only by stages. Cannibals yield to shepherds in canto ix, where Calidore himself abandons his armour for shepherd's garb and his spear for 'a shepheards hooke' (ix. 36) in an attempt to approach the Mercurian shepherd-god archetype, for the 'shepheards hooke' supersedes the salvage's wand and anticipates Colin's pipe. In the

relevant iconography of the nature god Pan, Pan's 'rod or sheepe hooke
. . . meaneth the rule and governement which he carrieth over all things'
and complements Pan's 'pipe of seven reeds [which signifies] the musical
melodie of the heavens'.[133] This is perhaps the closest we can get, in the
language of prose, to the meanings of Spenser's Mercurian vision in
Book VI. The Mercurian monarch and poet are equal, and they are one
at the level of their primitive origin in the shepherd and goatherd world
of pastoral.

Serena, whose sacrificial altar has been 'deckt . . . all with flowres' at
viii. 44 becomes, in this next canto, transposed into Calidore's (and
Coridon's) beloved Pastorella, who wears 'a crowne / Of sundry flowres'
(ix. 7). Both are Flora figures anticipating Colin's beloved, 'she to whom
the shepheard pypt alone' at x. 15 in the centre of the other circling
maidens, the supreme Flora of the book to complement her Mercury. She
is

> Crownd with a rosie girlond, that right well
> Did her beseeme. And ever, as the crew
> About her daunst, sweet flowres, that far did smell,
> And fragrant odours they uppon her threw. . . . (st. 14)

At the end of canto x the recessional movement begins. From Colin
Calidore 'backe return[s] to his rusticke wonne' (st. 32) and to Pastorella,
but the canto concludes with the abduction of the shepherd community
by 'theeves and *Brigants* bad'. In a tableau that matches the depiction of
the captivity of Serena we see Pastorella and the others imprisoned in an
infernal cave in which the frail light of Mercurian reason yields again to
dark fantasy: it 'Ne lightned was with window, nor with lover, / But with
continuall candlelight, which delt / A doubtfull sense of things, not so
well seene, as felt' (x. 42). Hamilton detects an allusion to the calling
down upon the Egyptians of 'darkenesse that may be felt' as a punishment
for holding the Israelites captive (Exodus 10: 21). He is probably right,
and this would confirm a suspicion that the phrase 'doubtfull sense'
recalls ambivalent Egyptian Proteus and that the world of fantasy here,
which complements the world conjured into being by the cannibals in
canto viii, suggests that other and more evil Egyptian, Busirane.[134]

Calidore rescues Pastorella in canto xi, but only, we are to understand,
because he has been initiated by Mercurian Colin:

> In such discourses they together spent
> Long time, as fit occasion forth them led;
> With which the Knight him selfe did much content,

> And with delight his greedy fancy fed,
> Both of his words, which he with reason red;
> And also of the place. . . . (x. 30)

Words and reason are the province of Mercury. And when Calidore
redeems Pastorella from the cave, scattering the brigands like flies (xi.
48), he almost literally restores her to life: 'So her uneath at last he did
revive, / That long had lyen dead, and made againe alive' (st. 50). The
brigands led her to the hellish cave (x. 43); Calidore, instructed by Colin,
adopts one of the roles of Mercury to lead her, as psychopomp, back to
the light.[135]

It is, finally, no accident that in this most subtly Mercurian of books
the main evil principle should be embodied in the Blatant Beast, whose
name (from Latin *blatire*) means Babbling Beast,[136] and who has 'a
thousand tongues', bestial and reptilian, including 'The Tongues of
Serpents with three forked stings' (xii. 28). Clearly he represents the
abuse of Mercurian eloquence as well as the principle of discord,
displacing as he does the entwined serpents of the god's caduceus with his
poisonous snakes that signify the destruction of language. Moreover, he
abuses 'Kesars [and] Kings', we are told in the same stanza. Calidore's
mastery of the beast, one of whose parents is Typhon, again reminds us
that Mercury made Typhon's sinews produce music, eliciting concord
from discord. The binding of the beast, however temporary, at the end of
this pastoral book thus re-establishes for our consideration a Mercurian
world in which caesars and kings can still hold sway.

[ix] *The Hermetic afterword*

Colin's role is Mercurian. And yet Mercury is not named again
specifically in *The Faerie Queene* (he was last mentioned in Book IV)
until the fragment that Spenser left us of Book VII, the *Two Cantos of
Mutabilitie*, where he appears as the intermediary between Jove and
Mutability to prevent the dethroning of Cynthia (vi. 8 ff.):

> Yet nathemore the *Giantesse* forbare:
> But boldly preacing-on, raught forth her hand
> To pluck her downe perforce from off her chaire;
> And there-with lifting up her golden wand,
> Threatned to strike her if she did with-stand. (st. 13)

The wand is appropriate to Mutability as the embodiment of the
chthonic powers of black magic (she is associated with Hecate in stanza
3) and as a pretender to sovereignty. Indeed, she is the ultimate threat to

Cynthia–Elizabeth, and so inevitably she is countered by Mercury, patron of the Mercurian monarch, who has been sent by Jove to discover if Cynthia is being molested 'with charmes or Magick' (st. 16). Mercury halts 'the *Titanesse*' for a moment when

> he on her shoulder laid
> His snaky-wreathed Mace, whose awfull power
> Doth make both gods and hellish fiends affraid. . . . (st. 18)

She then tells Mercury that she is claiming all the gods' kingdoms. He reports back to Jove, who holds a council. But while the gods are still in disarray she herself ascends 'To *Joves* high Palace . . . / To prosecute her plot' (st. 23). Jove has already announced that her threat marks a resurgence of the old battle between the giants and the gods (st. 20), and there are inevitable suggestions here of Bruno's *Expulsion of the Triumphant Beast*. Spenser's Jove (albeit less aged and disillusioned than Bruno's) has 'Doubt[ed] least *Typhon* were againe uprear'd, / Or other his old foes' (st. 15), and his opponent is Mutability. Bruno's Jove, who once 'chained presumptuous Typhoeus', now in his old age sees his universe overcome by Fortune. His 'most noble oracles, shrines, and altars [have been] torn down and most unworthily profaned. . . . All of this has been brought about by the outrage of our enemy, Fortune'.[137] Fortune and Mutability were frequently identified.[138] Moreover, Bruno's Jove calls his council for the anniversary of the Gigantomachia to signify that the victory over the vices achieved here will be even greater than the original victory over the giants.[139] The defeat of Spenser's Mutability is an equivalent victory ('So was the *Titanesse* put downe and whist, / And *Jove* confirm'd in his imperiall see'; vii. 59). Retrospectively, from Orgoglio, through Argante and Ollyphant, the giant with his balance at the beginning of Book V, and Disdain, we see that *The Faerie Queene* has been concerned with the defeat of the giants and its Brunian corollary, the replacement of the vices by the virtues.

In canto vii, 'at the time that was before agreed, / The Gods assembled all on *Arlo* hill' (st. 3). The only deities to be excluded are 'th'infernall Powers'. In this assembly, which is reminiscent of Colin's evocation of the maidens and Graces on mount Acidale, Dame Nature 'With goodly port and gracious Majesty' acts as judge of Mutability's case (st. 5). She is a mysterious figure, and one of the mysteries that she embodies, in her veiled sexual ambiguity, is that of the Venus Hermaphroditos of the tenth canto of Book IV. It is a partly Mercurian Nature, then, who confirms Jove's sovereignty.[140] The gathering of the gods is compared to another hill gathering, as well:

> Was never so great joyance since the day,
> That all the gods whylome assembled were,
> On *Hæmus* hill in their divine array,
> To celebrate the solemne bridall cheare,
> Twixt *Peleus*, and dame *Thetis* pointed there. . . . (st. 12)

We are back with Eris and the golden apple of discord which, however, led to the founding of Troynovant and the glory of Gloriana.[141] Just so does sovereign and Mercurian Dame Nature subsume Mutability's discord into a greater order which includes the seasons and the months, each of the latter identified by its appropriate zodiacal sign (recalling Bruno's constellations and the related Hermetic constellational scheme that we noticed in connection with Busirane's castle).

Towards the end of this procession come Day and Night. The latter 'held in hand a mace, / On top whereof the moon and stars were pight'; the former 'did beare, upon his scepters hight, / The goodly Sun, encompast all with beames bright' (st. 44). We now remember Isis and Osiris (and Isis's victory over Typhon): lunar Isis with her white wand; solar Osiris with his sceptre surmounted by an eye.[142] With them, too, we remember their surrogates in the poem, Una and Redcrosse, Britomart and Artegall, and the alchemical queen and king. It is fitting that the poem as we have it should end with this suggestion of Egyptian mythology and an allusion to Bruno's *Expulsion* with its emphasis on the restoration of the pure Egyptian religion. And it is fitting that it should end with an admission by Mutability of the 'secret powre' of the gods as 'Kings' (st. 49), reminding us as it does of the poem's theme of monarchs' power over the occult, a power that is manifested through the sceptre–caduceus and that also asserts control over the kingdom as well as the psychological and moral health of the subject. The judgement against Mutability is an affirmation of the return of the springlike Golden Age (Nature is accompanied by Flora's flowers at vii. 10) and at the same time a rejection of the demons of the mind, the infernal false gods, the 'unruly fiends' who are banished from the council. Their name is Legion; but they are now replaced, in a magnificent assertion of angel magic, by the multiplicity of the heavenly host: 'O that great Sabbaoth God, graunt me that Sabaoths sight' (viii. 2). This is Spenser's last supplication on behalf of his Mercurian monarch.

Notes

1 Frank Kermode, '*The Faerie Queene*, I and V', in *Shakespeare, Spenser, Donne: Renaissance Essays* (London: Routledge and Kegan Paul, 1971), p. 48.

2 See James C. Nohrnberg's monumentally exploratory *The Analogy of 'The Faerie Queene'* (Princeton, N.J.: Princeton U.P., 1976). On methods of approaching allegory consult also Angus Fletcher, *Allegory: the Theory of a Symbolic Mode* (Ithaca, N.Y.: Cornell U.P., 1964); Michael Murrin, *The Veil of Allegory: Some Notes toward a Theory of Allegorical Rhetoric in the English Renaissance* (Chicago, Ill.: University of Chicago Press, 1969), and his *The Allegorical Epic: Essays in its Rise and Decline* (Chicago, Ill. and London: University of Chicago Press, 1980).

3 Frances A. Yates, *Astraea: the Imperial Theme in the Sixteenth Century*, p. 4. Essential for an understanding of the concept of the world emperor and the *renovatio mundi* is Marjorie Reeves's *The Influence of Prophecy in the Later Middle Ages: a Study in Joachimism* (Oxford: Clarendon Press, 1969).

4 John Nichols, *The Progresses and Public Processions of Queen Elizabeth*, new edn, 3 vols. (London, 1823), I. 62.

5 E.g., a Sibyl at the Kenilworth entertainment for Elizabeth prophesied: 'But Peace shall governe all your daies, encreasing subjects love. / You shall be called the Prince of Peace, and peace shall be your shield' (*ibid.*, 486–487).

6 Frances Yates links Spenser and Bruno in her *The Occult Philosophy in the Elizabethan Age*, pp. 104–105, though her main interest in the Spenser chapter is to assert the influence of Francesco Giorgi's blend of neo-Platonism and Christian cabbalism on *The Faerie Queene*. Yates's argument from the astrological evidence presented in the poem (pp. 99 ff.) is incomplete and in many ways unconvincing, however, though the spirit of her interpretation is clearly right. I have preferred to emphasise the Agrippan elements in *The Faerie Queene* and to suggest that it is, too, a deeply Brunian work. An earlier exploration of Bruno's influence on Spenser, A. M. Pellegrini's 'Bruno, Sidney, and Spenser', *SP*, 40 (1943), 128–144, states baldly: 'Assuming that Spenser read Bruno, is there any evidence in the former's work that it was materially influenced by the thought of the latter? The answer is a simple negative ...' (p. 137). Angus Fletcher suggests that Bruno's *Expulsion* and *Heroic Frenzies* 'may have directly influenced Spenser' but does not pursue Hermetics in the poem rigorously or at length: see his *The Prophetic Moment: an Essay on Spenser* (Chicago, Ill. and London: University of Chicago Press, 1971), p. 124 etc.

7 *Faerie Queene* quotations are from A. C. Hamilton's edition for the Longman Annotated English Poets series (London and New York, 1977).

8 Compare Yates, *Occult Philosophy*, p. 107; and for Catholicism and the black arts, see D. Douglas Waters, *Duessa as Theological Satire*

(Columbia: Univ. of Missouri Press, 1970), as well as Frank Kermode, 'The Faerie Queene, I and V', pp. 44–45 (n. 1 above). Nichols, *Progresses ... of Queen Elizabeth*, II. 555 reprints James Aske's *Elizabetha Triumphans* (1588), which includes the lines 'This Pope doth send Magitians to her land / To seeke her death, by that their devillish arte'. Additional comments can be found in Keith Thomas, *Religion and the Decline of Magic*, pp. 78–79 and 325.

9 Ernst Kantorowicz, *Frederick the Second, 1194–1250*, tr. E. O. Lorimer (London: Constable, 1957), pp. 258 ff.

10 'Now I deny that any measure of understanding, in *naturall Magick* ... to be a prying into those *Hidden Secrets*, which *God* would have concealed and ranked among the number and nature of those things he has prohibited us to search into. ... And this is fully manifested from *Adam*, who before his *Fall* was so absolute a *Philosopher*, that he fully understood the true and pure knowledge of *Nature* (which is no other then what we call *Naturall Magick*) in the highest degree of Perfection ...': Elias Ashmole, *Theatrum Chemicum Britannicum* (London, 1652), p. 445.

11 Thomas Hobbes, *Leviathan*, ed. C. B. Macpherson (Harmondsworth, Middx.: Penguin Books, 1968), IV. xliv, pp. 627 ff. For flies as symbols of the deluded imagination, see Raymond Klibansky, Erwin Panofsky, Fritz Saxl, *Saturn and Melancholy* (London: Nelson, 1964), p. 302 n. For Agrippa Beelzebub is 'the prince of wickedness', ruler over 'Mammon and the prince of this world and rulers of darkness' (*Three Books of Occult Philosophy*, tr. J. F. (London, 1651), III. xviii, p. 400).

12 Simon Magus appears in Acts 8: 9 ff. Nohrnberg, *Analogy*, pp. 246 ff. considers in detail the relationship between Archimago and Simon Magus.

13 *Ibid.*, pp. 198 ff. and esp. p. 226.

14 Hobbes, *Leviathan*, II. xxvi; ed. cit., p. 333.

15 Similarly, the Douai marginal note to Exodus 7: 11 reads 'Iannes and Mambres'.

16 D. P. Walker, *Spiritual and Demonic Magic*, pp. 111 and 162, discusses Pomponazzi's and Erastus's interpretations of the serpents respectively. Ashmole, *Theatrum Chemicum Britannicum*, p. 446, makes the connection between Moses's magical power and his governorship of the Jews: 'God in constituting *Moses* to be a *Governor* over his owne people, seemed as willing to make choyce of such a one for that high *Office* as was learned in all the *Sciences*, then in request with the *Egyptians*, among whom *Magick* was the chiefe'. The Douai commentary on Exodus 7, involving the relationship of miracle to magic and making the connection with Simon Magus, is worth quoting at length: 'True miracles, being above the course of al created nature, can not be wrought but by the powre of God. ... Other strange things done by enchanters, false prophetes, and divels, are not in deede true miracles, but either sleights, by quicknes and nimblenes of hand, called legier-demain ...; or false presentations deceiving the senses, and imaginations of men, by making

things seme to be that they are not; or els are wrought by applying natural causes knowen to some, especially to divels; who also by their natural force can do great thinges, when God permitteth them. And so *by enchantments and certaine secrecies* [Exodus 7: 11], these sorcerers either conveyed away the roddes, and water, and brought dragons, and bloud, in their place . . .; or els by the divels using natural agents turned roddes into serpentes . . .; al which might be done naturally in a longer time, & by the divel in a short time. . . . It is further to be observed, that whensoever anie have attempted to worke miracles to prove fals doctrin, they have failed, and by Gods providence bene confounded. . . . God . . . for a time suffered Simon Magus to make shew of miracles [and then confounded him]. . . . Al the danger is when in dede wonders are done that may seeme to be miracles. Against such therfore Gods providence more particularly assisteth his servantes divers wayes. . . . God suffered not the Enchanters of Ægypt, nor Simon Magus long. . . .': *The Holie Bible Faithfully Translated into English* (Douay, 1609); vol. I (Ilkley and London: Scolar Press, 1975). For Moses, 'learned in all the wisedome of the Egyptians' (Acts 7: 22), see further Keith Thomas, *Religion and the Decline of Magic*, p. 323, and E. M. Butler, *The Myth of the Magus* (Cambridge: C.U.P., 1948), I. ii, 29–34. The wand/serpent had provided opportunity for legerdemain in the mystery plays: L. B. Wright, 'Juggling Tricks and Conjury on the English Stage before 1642', *MP*, 24 (1926–1927), 271–272.

17 E.g., Gerard Reedy, S.J., 'Mystical Politics: the Imagery of Charles II's Coronation'. In Paul Korshin (ed.), *Studies in Change and Revolution: Aspects of Intellectual History 1640–1800* (Menston, Yorks: Scolar Press, 1972), pp. 19–42.

18 Nichols, *Progresses . . . of Queen Elizabeth*, II. 468–469.

19 The Geneva gloss on Exodus 7: 9, 'it shalbe turned into a serpent', is '*Or, dragon*'. Simon Magus reputedly changed himself into a dragon: see Nohrnberg, *Analogy*, p. 249 and n.

20 From the additional point of view of the Hermetic argument I shall be offering later it is worth noting that in Bruno's *Expulsion of the Triumphant Beast* the brazen serpent is identified with Thoth/Hermes Trismegistus: ed. Imerti, p. 242.

21 *Paracelsus: Selected Writings*, ed. J. Jacobi, tr. N. Guterman. Bollingen Series, 28 (New York: Pantheon Books, 1951), p. 213.

22 Agrippa, III. v, p. 356.

23 For spirit in this sense, see Walker, *Spiritual and Demonic Magic*, ch. I.

24 On this compromise, see E. F. Rice, *The Renaissance Idea of Wisdom* (Cambridge, Mass.: Harvard U.P., 1958). For Contemplation as Saturnian melancholic, see D. Brooks-Davies, *Spenser's 'Faerie Queene': a Critical Commentary on Books I and II* (Manchester and Totowa, N.J.: M.U.P. and Rowman and Littlefield, 1977), pp. 99 ff.

25 III. xxxi–xxxii in a manuscript version of 1510, describing the melancholic fury or frenzy through which the soul is illuminated by demons. The relevant passages are translated by Klibansky *et al.* as

follows: 'As physical cause of this frenzy, the philosophers give the "humor melancholicus", not, however, that which is called the black bile . . . [but] rather that which is called "candida bilis et naturalis". Now this, when it takes fire and glows, generates the frenzy which leads us to wisdom and revelation, especially when it is combined with a heavenly influence, above all with that of Saturn. . . . Aristotle says in the *Problemata* that through melancholy some men have become divine beings, foretelling the future like the Sibyls and the inspired prophets of ancient Greece, while others have become poets . . .; and he says further that all men who have been distinguished in any branch of knowledge have generally been melancholics. . . . Moreover, this "humor melancholicus" has such power that they say it attracts certain daemons into our bodies, through whose presence and activity men fall into ecstasies . . . this occurs in the three different forms, corresponding to the threefold capacity of our soul, namely the imaginative, the rational, and the mental. For when set free by the "humor melancholicus", the soul is fully concentrated in the imagination, and it immediately becomes an habitation for the lower spirits, from whom it often receives wonderful instruction in the manual arts. . . . But when the soul is fully concentrated in the reason, it becomes the home of the middle spirits; thereby it attains knowldge and cognition of natural and human things. . . . But when the soul soars completely to the intellect ("mens"), it becomes the home of the higher spirits, from whom it learns the secrets of divine matters, as, for instance, the law of God, the angelic hierarchy, and that which pertains to the knowledge of eternal things and the soul's salvation; of future events they show us, for instance, approaching prodigies, wonders, a prophet to come, or the emergence of a new religion . . .' (*Saturn and Melancholy*, pp. 355–357). For the three grades of melacholy in tabular form, see *ibid.*, p. 359, briefly summarised as: grade 1, achieved through lower spirits operating on the imagination leading to success in the mechanical arts and relating to the prophecy of natural events; grade 2, achieved through middle spirits operating on reason (*ratio*) leading to knowledge in the areas of the natural sciences, politics, etc. and relating specifically to political prophecies; grade 3, achieved through higher spirits operating on mind (*mens*) leading to knowledge of divine matters (angelology, theology) and prophecy of new religions, etc.

26 Cf. stanza 6 of William Backhouse's 'The Magistery', in Ashmole, *Theatrum Chemicum Britannicum*, p. 342 (reprinted above, p. 27); also *ibid.*, p. 354: 'By bathing and balning the Dragon cometh to light; / Evermor drowned in the bottome of his Well, / Tyl all his Leprousie will no longer dwell, / In his owne Nature he altereth cleane / Into a pure substance . . .'. Additional material on the dragon can be found in E. J. Holmyard, *Alchemy* (Harmondsworth, Middx: Penguin Books, 1968), pp. 159 ff., Charles Nicholl, *The Chemical Theatre* (London, Boston, and Henley: Routledge and Kegan Paul, 1980), pp. 91 ff., and especially C. G. Jung's *Psychology and Alchemy*, tr. R. F. C. Hull, Bollingen Series,

20 (New York: Pantheon Books, 1953), index, *s.v.* dragon, and his *Alchemical Studies*, tr. Hull (Princeton, N.J.: Princeton U.P., 1967), index, *s.v.* dragon(s), serpent.

27 Ashmole, *op. cit.*, sigs A3^V–B, writes of Adam, Abraham, Moses, and Solomon as alchemists; Nicholl, *op. cit.*, pp. 17–19 notes Queen Elizabeth's 'definite – if somewhat covert – contact with alchemy' through her reign. At pp. 20–21 Nicholl also notes the Holy Roman Emperor's obsession with alchemy (citing R. J. Evans, *Rudolf II and His World* (1973)), to which we might suppose Elizabeth's alchemical inclinations are a Protestant imperial answer. Yates, *Occult Philosophy*, p. 87, comments on John Dee's combined interest in Agrippan angel magic and alchemy. Elizabeth's relationship with Dee might be an important clue to the alchemical patterns in *The Faerie Queene*, therefore. On Dee in the poem, see below, n. 87.

28 On 'our Mercury' in its various meanings, see Jung, *Alchemical Studies*, sect. IV, pp. 193 ff. It is both philosophers' stone and prince in Ashmole, *op. cit.*, pp. 123, 198 (where it is 'most royall, and richest of all *Singulorum*'), and 272 ff. Cf. Introduction, above, on Mercury in Dee's *Hieroglyphic Monad*, and plate 1.

29 Nicholl, *passim*, discusses these and other symbols, as does Holmyard, *Alchemy*, ch. VII; and see the quotation from *Dastin's Dreame*, below. An indispensable survey is contained in Jung's alchemical works mentioned in n. 26 above.

30 The first quotation is from Sir George Ripley's *Compound of Alchymie* (Ashmole, *op. cit.*, p. 107); the second is from Thomas Norton's *Ordinall of Alchimy*, ch. V (Ashmole, *op. cit.*, p. 90).

31 See I. vi. 19; John Steadman, 'Una and the Clergy: the Ass Symbol in *The Faerie Queene*', *JWCI*, 21 (1958), 134–137; and D. Brooks-Davies, *Spenser's 'Faerie Queene'*, pp. 65–67. Also n. 142 below.

32 Cf. *The Shepherd's Calendar*, *April*, ll. 68–69, in which Elizabeth mingles the two roses in her one person (and E. K.'s note on this stanza). Holmyard, *Alchemy*, plates 14 and 21, illustrates the alchemical joining of red and white roses.

33 A. D. S. Fowler, *Spenser and the Numbers of Time* (London: Routledge and Kegan Paul, 1964), ch. VIII.

34 The early Tudor solar Arthur is discussed by Sydney Anglo, *Spectacle, Pageantry, and Early Tudor Policy* (Oxford: Clarendon Press, 1969), pp. 77 ff. Spenser's solar Arthur bears a tantalising resemblance, incidentally, to the description of the king-stone in Thomas Charnock's *Ænigma ad Alchimiam* (1572): 'Me thought he was a Prince off honoure, / For he was all in Golden armoure; / And on his head a Crowne off Golde . . .' (Ashmole, *op. cit.*, p. 303).

35 Nohrnberg, *Analogy*, pp. 40 ff., making the connection with Aaron's zodiacal breastplate (on which see also Robert Eisler, *The Royal Art of Astrology* (London: Herbert Joseph, 1946), p. 249). And see the *Gesta Grayorum*, 1594, where the revels prince has for his 'Crest the glorious Planet Sol, *coursing through the twelve Signs of the* Zodiack' (ed. Greg,

p. 10).

36 E.g., the New Arden *Midsummer Night's Dream*, ed. H. F. Brooks (London: Methuen, 1979), Intro., p. cxxviii. In September 1591 Elizabeth was greeted by 'the Fayery Quene [bearing] an imperiall crowne' and carrying 'a silvered staffe': 'I . . . humbly . . . salute you with this chaplet, / Given me by Auberon the Fairy King. / Bright shining Phœbe, that in humaine shape, / Hid'st Heaven's perfection, vouchsafe t'accept it' (Nichols, *Progresses . . . of Queen Elizabeth*, III. 118).

37 By Abraham Andrewes. In Ashmole, *op. cit.*, pp. 278 ff. (the present quotation is on p. 279). Una is, of course, both solar and lunar (e.g., solar at I. xii. 23; Dianan—lunar at vi. 16), a combination that is clearly alchemical despite the primacy of the Biblical archetype of the 'woman cloathed with the Sun, and the Moone . . . under her feet' (Revelation 12: 1).

38 Ashmole, *op. cit.*, p. 342.

39 *Ibid.*, pp. 267–268.

40 Agrippa, *Three Books*, III. i, p. 346.

41 'Surely, Fathers, there is much greater discord in us. We have around us grievous internal wars, wars more than civil which, if we do not want them, and if we strive for that peace which can carry us up on high so that we may stand among the elevated ones of the Lord, philosophy alone will truly curb and calm in us': Pico, *Oration: on the Dignity of Man*, in S. Davies, *Renaissance Views of Man* (Manchester: Manchester U.P., 1978), p. 73. Jung's comments on alchemical incest and rebirth are invaluable: e.g., *Psychology and Alchemy*, tr. Hull (1953), pp. 396 ff.

42 For Fowler, see n. 33 above. Yates's observation appears in her *Occult Philosophy*, pp. 99–100.

43 The complexities of Chaucer's *chronographiæ* have been unravelled by Chauncey Wood, *Chaucer and the Country of the Stars: Poetic Uses of Astrological Imagery* (Princeton, N.J.: Princeton U.P., 1970), and John North, ' "Kalenderes enlumyned ben they": some Astronomical Themes in Chaucer', *RES*, n.s. 20 (1969), 129–154; 257–283; 418–444.

44 Anglo, *Spectacle, Pageantry, and Early Tudor Policy*, pp. 62 ff., 74, and 80 ff. For the Bear as Charles's Wain, and so carrying further imperial associations with Charlemagne, see ch. III, p. 131 below, and *ibid.*, n. 27.

45 Bruno, *Expulsion of the Triumphant Beast*, ed. Imerti, p. 80. The Bear receives sanction from the Hermetic *Pimander*, where it is the constellation whose circling movements, 'revolv[ing] upon herself, and carr[ying] round with her the whole Kosmos', testify to the power of the Creator and his perfect cosmic plan: *Pimander* V. 4 in *Hermetica*, ed. and tr. Walter Scott, 4 vols. (Oxford: Clarendon Press, 1924–1936), I. 159–161. (*Corpus Hermeticum*, ed. and tr. A. D. Nock and A.-J. Festugière, I (Paris, 1945), p. 61.) It should be noted that Bruno is by no means alone in beginning his symbolic almagest with the Bear: as R. H. Allen observes, 'all early catalogues commenced with the two Ursine constellations' (*Star Names: their Lore and Meaning* (New York: Dover Publications, 1963), p. 419).

46 Ed. cit., p. 80.

47 *Fasti*, V. 535 ff. and *Ars Amatoria*, II. 55. See also Allen, *Star Names*, p. 94.

48 For the scorpion and treachery, see P. Ansell Robin, *Animal Lore in English Literature* (London: John Murray, 1932), p. 116; George Ferguson, *Signs and Symbols in Christian Art* (New York: O.U.P., 1961) p. 24; and Bruno, ed. Imerti, p. 234. Spenser's 'snake' is explained astronomically by the fact that Scorpio is bounded on its northern side by the constellation Anguis.

49 Brooks-Davies, *Spenser's 'Faerie Queene'*, p. 135.

50 II. xxxvii, p. 297.

51 *Expulsion*, ed. Imerti, pp. 257–258.

52 For Bruno Scorpio, Orion's celestial antagonist, is identified in his malevolent aspect with 'Feigned Love' as well as fraud (p. 85), which would assimilate the lustful Acrasia as well as Phædria into the Brunian scheme of Book II.

53 *Aeneid*, III. 517 (in connection, incidentally, with Arcturus and the Bears); cit. Alexander Ross, *Mystagogus Poeticus, or the Muses Interpreter* (London, 1648), p. 334. Belphoebe's androgyny is evident from, e.g., the fact that her legs 'Like two faire marble pillours' at iii. 28 are an attribute of the bridegroom in Song of Solomon 5: 15.

54 Nohrnberg, *Analogy*, pp. 351 ff.

55 *The Basilicon Doron of King James VI* [Edinburgh, 1603 text], ed. James Craigie, 2 vols (Edinburgh and London: Scottish Text Society, 1944), I. 103.

56 *Mystagogus Poeticus*, p. 263.

57 *Ibid.* Cf. Richard Linche, *The Fountaine of Ancient Fiction* (London, 1599), sig. Qiii[r].

58 On one level Elizabeth is here identified as Virgo–Astraea, and the rod is Virgo's *spica* or ear of corn symbolising the plenty brought by Golden-Age justice (so that 'raine' has its astrological sense). Yates's *Astraea, passim*, discusses the prevalence of Elizabethan (and other) Astraean iconography in the sixteenth century. See also our plate 3.

59 For the caduceus with its two entwined serpents symbolising the concordant uniting of discordant souls by 'the wand of Mercury's teaching' (*doctrinae suae virga*), see Pierio Valeriano, *Hieroglyphica* . . . (Lyons, 1602 edn), Book XV, p. 156.

60 Linche, *Fountaine of Ancient Fiction*, sig. Qiii[r]; Agrippa, *Three Books*, II. i, p. 169: 'The . . . *white-rod bearer flies i'th' Aire*'.

61 To these Spenser adds later Isis's white wand at V. vii. 7 (see below, sec. vii).

62 Quoted from *The Manner of the Coronation of King Charles the First of England*, ed. Christopher Wordsworth, Henry Bradshaw Society, vol. 2 (1892), p. 43. My attention was drawn to this liturgy by Stevie Davies, though it has already been quoted in connection with Isis's wand by Angus Fletcher, *The Prophetic Moment* (1971), p. 277.

63 *The Manner of the Coronation* . . ., p. 42.

64 *Mystagogus Poeticus*, p. 335; also Natalis Comes, *Mythologiae* . . . (Venice, 1567 edn), VIII. xii, *De Orione*; facsimile, ed. Stephen Orgel (New York and London: Garland Publishing, 1976).

65 Agrippa, *Three Books*, III. xliii, p. 495.

66 See Fowler, *Spenser and the Numbers of Time*, ch. IX, *passim*.

67 For Mercury as reason see, e.g., Vincenzo Cartari, *Le Imagini de i Dei* (Venice, 1571 edn), p. 329. This explains his and his caduceus's function in Bruno's *Expulsion*, which, as the title page explains, is to 'reveal' the 'expulsion of the triumphant beast'. In the Spenser passage Mercury again, in little, reveals the 'expulsion' of beasts.

68 The Mercurian Palmer vanquishes the spirits/phantoms in the same way that the inhabitant of the second room in the turret of Alma's castle banishes the fantasies of Phantastes (II. ix. 53–54). He is a 'grave personage' embodying 'goodly reason' (thus corresponding to the Palmer); significantly, therefore, his chamber walls displace Phantastes's monsters by depicting 'memorable gestes, / Of famous Wisards, and . . . picturals / Of Magistrates, of courts, of tribunals, / Of commen wealthes, of states, of pollicy, / Of lawes, of judgements . . . / All artes, all science, all Philosophy'. This makes the point, economically enough, about the Palmer as magician and his connection with the government of the kingdom, as well as indicating the direction in which the 'analogy' between Books II and V is to be developed.

69 Agrippa, III. xx, p. 405.

70 *Ibid.*, p. 407.

71 *Ibid.*, III. xviii, p. 399 (noticed by Nohrnberg, *Analogy*, p. 331).

72 Agrippa, III. xxii, p. 410.

73 *Ibid.*, p. 410.

74 *Pace* Hamilton, who in his edn identifies him as a cherub (note to II. viii. 5). This angel is discussed by D. W. Sims, 'Cosmological Structure in *The Faerie Queene*, Book III', *HLQ*, 40 (1976–77), 99–116, an article the spirit of which I am entirely in sympathy with. It is marred, however, by apparent ignorance of the magical traditions which are the concern of the present study. The same is true of Robin Kirkpatrick's fascinating 'Appearances of the Red Cross Knight in Book Two of Spenser's *Faerie Queene*', *JWCI*, 34 (1971), 338–350.

75 According to the theory of grades of melancholic frenzy (see n. 25 above) and their attendant demons, if this angel is supercelestial he is being perceived by the Palmer's intellect; if merely a guardian angel, he is perceived by the Palmer's imagination (the lowest grade). He is, of course, both (possible in a poem if not in the actual world of ceremonial magic), and this confirms the Palmer's Saturnian-melancholic qualities (noted, e.g., by Brooks-Davies, *Spenser's 'Faerie Queene'*, pp. 142 and 144–146). The Palmer's combination of Saturn and Mercury, incidentally, embodies the moderation of extreme, destructive, Saturnian tendencies since Mercury, along with the Sun, Jupiter, and Venus, was regarded by, e.g., Ficino as tempering the more malign aspects of Saturn: *De vita*, Book III (*de vita cœlitus comparanda*), ii, etc. (*Marsilii Ficini*

Florentini ... Opera, 2 vols. (Basel, 1576), I. 533 ff.).

76   Agrippa, III. xxxviii, p. 467. Cf. Edgar Wind, *Pagan Mysteries in the Rennaissance*, rev. edn (Harmondsworth, Middx: Penguin Books, 1967), p. 123.

77   Jean Seznec, *The Survival of the Pagan Gods*, tr. Barbara F. Sessions (New York: Harper and Brothers, 1961), p. 181. The relationship between the Palmer, Mercury, and the angel is discussed perceptively by R. M. Cummings, 'An Iconographical Puzzle: Spenser's Cupid at *Faerie Queene*, II. viii', *JWCI*, 33 (1970), 317–321.

78   Agrippa, III. xxxviii, p. 467.

79   *Aeneid*, IV. 242 ff.; tr. W. F. Jackson Knight (Harmondsworth, Middx: Penguin Books, 1974 edn), p. 104.

80   A fair amount of work has been done in recent years on magic in *The Faerie Queene*, though not (except for Yates) on angel magic, and not in connection with the monarchical aspects of the poem. See, e.g., R. A. Ferlo, *The Language of Magic in Renaissance England: Studies in Spenser and Shakespeare*, Yale Univ. Ph.D., 1979 (*DAI*, 40: 2693-A; reviewed in *Spenser Newsletter*, 12 (1981), 21); and P. G. Cheney, *Magic in 'The Faerie Queene'*, Univ. of Toronto Ph.D., 1979 (*DAI*, 40: 6287-A; reviewed *Spenser Newsletter, ibid,*, p. 19).

81   Wind, *Pagan Mysteries*, ch. VII; Charles Dempsey, '*Mercurius Ver:* The Sources of Botticelli's *Primavera*', *JWCI*, 31 (1968), 251–273; and Martianus Capella, *The Marriage of Philology and Mercury*, I. xxvii ('Mercury the god of Spring'); tr. W. H. Stahl *et al.* in *Martianus Capella and the Seven Liberal Arts*, 2 vols (New York: Columbia U.P., 1977), II. 16.

82   Cartari, *Imagini*, p. 357; Wind, *Pagan Mysteries*, p. 203 and n. As Wind notes (*ibid.*) in Bocchi's *Symbolicae quaestiones* (1555), symbolon cii, Hermes and Athena are joined by Eros, which suggests that Britomart's quest in this book of love is for the true Eros through whom her otherwise divergent selves will be integrated.

83   A parallel observed by Hamilton in his edn, p. 309.

84   Ovid, *Fasti*, V. 183 ff.; Dempsey, '*Mercurius Ver*', pp. 251–253, citing Girolamo Aleandro, Jr., *Antiquae tabulae marmoreae solis effigie ...* (Rome, 1616): 'Mercury is the same as Favonius'.

85   Nohrnberg, *Analogy*, pp. 461 ff.; also Lila Geller, 'Venus and the three Graces: a Neoplatonic Paradigm for Book III of *The Faerie Queene*', *JEGP*, 75 (1976), 56–74 (but with no mention of Mercury). For Mercury and the Graces, see, e.g., Cartari, p. 563 (s.v. *Le Gratie*).

86   Nichols, *Progresses ... of Queen Elizabeth*, I. 414–415. See also H. Syer Cuming, 'On Crystals of Augury', *Journal of the British Archaeological Association*, 5 (1850), 51–53.

87   Angus Fletcher, *The Prophetic Moment*, p. 111 n. connects Merlin and Dee, commenting 'Merlin serves King Ryence, but his powers of foresight are those a ruler requires. ... Dr Dee was self-consciously a prophet of empire, and it seems possible that Merlin's mirror in *The Faerie Queene* is intended to suggest . . . the "monad" of Dee's

[*Hieroglyphic Monad*]'. Dee stressed his Welsh ancestry, which would link him with Merlin and Elizabeth: see P. J. French, *John Dee*, p. 20 n. Mercury was emblematically and mystically important to Dee: *ibid.*, p. 28, pp. 78 ff.; and see, e.g., *ibid.*, pp. 33 ff. for Elizabeth's relationship with Dee. Yates, *Occult Philosophy*, pp. 95 ff. detects Dee's influence on *The Faerie Queene* without, however, identifying him with Merlin. She also makes the crucial point that, although some of *The Faerie Queene* was written before Dee fell from favour, the publication of the first three books in 1590 coincided with his return to England and disgrace (see pp. 89 ff. and 105 ff.). For Dee and the philosophers' stone see C. H. Josten, 'An Unknown Chapter in the Life of John Dee', *JWCI*, 28 (1965), p. 229. For the history of Merlin as received by Spenser (with emphasis on Merlin as 'a figure for the poet'), see William Blackburn, 'Spenser's Merlin', *Renaissance and Reformation*, 4 (1980), 179–198. *The Variorum Spenser*, Book III, p. 227 cites Merritt Hughes to the effect that Spenser, unlike Ariosto in *Orlando Furioso*, III, minimises the influence of Virgil (*Aeneid*, VI) in this episode: to emphasise, presumably, the displacement of Sibylline prophecy by demonic magic.

88 Ashmole, *Theatrum Chemicum Britannicum*, sig. B1^v. Merlin's mirror also possesses some of the powers vulgarly attributed to magic crystals: Keith Thomas, *Religion and the Decline of Magic*, pp. 255 ff. and 486. For the traditionally more limited power of 'learned Merline whom God gave the sprite, / To know, and utter princes actes to cum, / Like to the Jewish prophetes', see *The Mirror for Magistrates*, ed. Lily B. Campbell (New York: Barnes and Noble, 1960), p. 228.

89 Hence Merlin's power over 'Both Sunne and Moone' (III. iii. 12).

90 Nohrnberg, pp. 450 and 781–782, citing Plato, *Symposium*, 202E–203A (love is a demon, one of the order of agencies that transmits mortal things to the gods, and divine matters to mortals).

91 As Hamilton notes in his edn, p. 328.

92 Despite the subduing of the Virgilian source in this canto (see n. 87 above), it is apparent that Spenser proposes a connection between the rod and Aeneas's golden bough, traditionally interpreted as symbolising the secrets of wisdom and knowledge: e.g., Henry Peacham, *Minerva Britanna* (London, 1612), sig. A2^r, dedication to Prince Henry: these emblems are 'for the most part . . . Roially discended, and repaire into your owne bosome (farre from the reach of Envie) for their protection. For in truth they are of right your owne, and no other then the substance of those Divine Instructions, his *Majestie* your Royall *Father* præscribed unto you, your guide (as that golden branch to *ÆNEAS*,) to a vertuous & true happy life'. Servius links it with the Pythagorean Y, offering the choice between vice and virtue (*Servii Grammatici qui feruntur in Vergilii Carmina Commentarii*, ed. G. Thilo and H. Hagen, 3 vols (Leipzig, 1878–1887), II. 31 (on *Aeneid*, VI. 136)).

93 III. xii. 46 (1590 edn) has Scudamour and Amoret embracing so closely that 'Had ye them seene, ye would have surely thought, / That they had beene that faire *Hermaphrodite*, / Which that rich *Romane* of white

marble wrought ...'.

94   T. P. Roche, Jr., *The Kindly Flame: a Study of the Third and Fourth Books of Spenser's 'Faerie Queene'* (Princeton, N.J.: Princeton U.P., 1964), pp. 81 ff. (and see *Variorum Spenser*, Book III, p. 287). A full iconography of Busiris is to be found in John M. Steadman, '*Paradise Lost*: The Devil and Pharaoh's Chivalry. Etymological and Typological Imagery and Renaissance Chronography', in his *Nature into Myth: Medieval and Renaissance Moral Symbols* (Pittsburgh, Pa.: Duquesne U.P., 1979), ch. XIII. *Ibid.*, p. 200 notes that Melanchthon translated 'Busiris' as 'Munitor' (builder of fortifications), which would link him further with Merlin, who lives at Maridunum (i.e. sea-fort: *DNB*, XIII, s.v. Merlin, p. 287). See also Hyginus, *Fabulae*, LVI (ed. H. I. Rose (Lyons, 1933), p. 45).

95   Merlin reveals that the ground has been made unstable because of a submerged pool. ' "Order the pool to be drained," said Merlin, "and at the bottom you will observe two hollow stones. Inside the stones you will see two Dragons which are sleeping" ': a subtle hint, if we remember it, of our serpent-dragon-caduceus theme: Geoffrey of Monmouth, *The History of the Kings of Britain*, tr. Lewis Thorpe (Harmondsworth, Middx: Penguin Books, 1973), IV. vi. 17 ff.

96   E.g. (on Vortigern as the betrayer of the Britons), Geoffrey, *History*, IV. vi. 13 ff., and Michael Drayton, *Poly-Olbion*, VIII. 348 ff. Spenser draws particular attention to the enmity in st. 42: 'Then woe, and woe, and everlasting woe, / Be to the Briton babe, that shalbe borne, / To live in thraldome of his fathers foe ...'. The Vortigern theme in early seventeenth-century drama is discussed from this point of view by R. F. Brinkley, *Arthurian Legend in the Seventeenth Century*, Johns Hopkins Monographs in Literary History, 3 (1932; reprint, London: Frank Cass, 1967), pp. 93–94. But Britomart also represents the reconciliation of Briton and Saxon, since she wears Angela's armour: see Roche, *The Kindly Flame*, p. 62. Spenser's emphasis in this canto on 'political *concordia*' is also detected by Harry Berger, Jr., 'The Structure of Merlin's Chronicle in *The Faerie Queene* III(iii)', *SEL*, 9 (1969), 39–51.

97   For an almost definitive history of Proteus lore, see A. Bartlett Giamatti, 'Proteus Unbound: Some Versions of the Sea God in the Renaissance', in Peter Demetz, Thomas Greene, and Lowry Nelson, Jr. (eds.), *The Disciplines of Criticism: Essays in Literary Theory, Interpretation, and History* (New Haven, Conn. and London: Yale U.P., 1968), pp. 437–475. D. M. Murtaugh analyses Proteus's shape-shifting from the point of view of the posturing lover in 'The Garden and the Sea: the Topography of *The Faerie Queene*, III', *ELH*, 40 (1973), 325–338.

98   Agrippa, *Three Books*, III. xviii, p. 400.

99   Ross, *Mystagogus Poeticus*, p. 371, and see Giamatti, 'Proteus Unbound', p. 437 (citing Sir Thomas Elyot's *Bibliotheca Eliotae* (1559)), and Roche, *The Kindly Flame*, pp. 152 ff.

100 A point noted by Fowler, *Spenser and the Numbers of Time*, p. 186 n., and see Cartari, *Imagini*, pp. 202 ff. (s.v. *La Gran Madre*).

101 Again noted by Fowler, *ibid.*, pp. 174–175, and citing Valeriano, *Hieroglyphica*, XV, p. 156 on the caduceus as *Minae paxque*. Spenser's identification of Mercury with Cybele is explained by Valeriano, *ibid.*, analysing the caduceus this time as earth (*terra*), and citing Macrobius (*Saturnalia*, I. xix. 14–17) where statues of Mercury in the form of a square block 'the only features being the head and the male member erect' are described, and interpreted as follows: the head is Mercury as the sun, 'the head of the universe and the father of the world'; the quadrate represents 'either the four quarters of the world or the four seasons of the year'. In paragraph 17 Macrobius considers the caduceus as the Egyptian emblem of 'the generation, or "genesis" as it is called, of mankind; for [the Egyptians] say that four deities are present to preside over a man's birth: his Genius, Fortune, Love, and Necessity. By the first two they understand the sun and the moon; for the sun ... is the creator and the guardian of a man's life and is therefore believed to be the Genius, or god, of a newborn child; the moon is Fortune, since she has charge of the body [these are the two serpents]; the kiss of the serpents is the symbol of Love; and the knot [the middle part of the entwined serpents' coils] is the symbol of Necessity'. Earth and 'genesis' thus link Mercury with Cybele; while the identification of the two serpents as male and female, sun and moon (on which see also Robert Eisler, *The Royal Art of Astrology*, plate 16c) suggests another Mercurian link with the poem's alchemical symbolism. For Macrobius I have used *The Saturnalia*, tr. P. V. Davies (New York and London: Columbia U.P., 1969).

102 For Neptune and Troy, see Comes, *Mythologiae*, II. viii (*De Neptuno*). At the Kenilworth entertainment of 1575 Elizabeth was greeted (on Monday 18 July) by a mermaid and '*Triton, Neptune's* blaster, whoo ... as her Majesty was in sight, gave soound very shrill and sonorous, in sign he had an ambassy to pronoouns ... [on behalf of] the supreame salsipotent Monarch *Neptune*, the great God of the swelling seas, Prins of Profunditees, and Sooverain Segnior of all lakez ...' (Nichols, *Progresses*, I. 457).

103 The legal aspects are discussed by W. Nicholas Knight, 'The Narrative Unity of Book V of *The Faerie Queene*: "That Part of Justice which is Equity" ', *RES*, n.s. 21 (1970), 267–294. Florimell's relationship with Queen Elizabeth is hinted at by William Blissett, who suggests that 'Florimell' echoes Florence, the queen of faerie's protégée in the late medieval *Arthur of Little Britain*: 'Florimell and Marinell', *SEL*, 5 (1965), 102.

104 In his edn, p. 516.

105 '*She was the daughter of the River* Inachus ...': Ross, *Mytagogus Poeticus*, p. 206. Thames is like Cybele; Isis was identified with Cybele: see plate 6.

106 On the hermaphroditic Venus see Wind, *Pagan Mysteries*, pp. 128 ff., 200, and 211 ff. Pp. 128 ff. are particularly interesting, since they consider Ficino's commentary on Plotinus's *Enneads* III. v. 9 in relation

to the combination of Venus–Mercury as an expression of the most perfect form of Venus, the conjoining of soul and mind, lover and philosopher.

107 The snake as the emblem of the cosmic cycle is found in Macrobius, *Saturnalia*, I. ix. 12: 'the Phoenicians in their sacred rites have portrayed [Janus] in the likeness of a serpent coiled and swallowing its own tail, as a visible image of the universe which feeds on itself and returns to itself again' (ed. cit., p. 67). Janus presides over the bridge gate which leads to the temple (IV. x. 12). It is significant in view of the Isis symbolism in the book, that Osiris *'was figured with a Basket upon his head, in the which was a serpent with three heades, holdinge the Tayle in his Mouth'*, emblematic of 'the mutuall accord of consanguinity in evills, which as the Serpent devouring herselfe, by beginninge with her tayle, so are divers Kindomes, by oppressinge cõmõ Wealthes, made weake, and brought to confusion': Stephen Batman, *The Golden Booke of the Leaden Goddes* . . . (London, 1577), p. 16. As Batman goes on to note, however, although Osiris was killed by his brother, Typhon, 'to obtayne the kingdome', Isis 'revenged her husbandes death, by hanging *Typhon* on a Gallowes'.

108 E.g., the entertainment for the Duke of Anjou at Antwerp, 1581–1582: before the Maiden of Antwerp 'sate Concord . . . bearing a target upon hir arme, wherein was painted a crowned scepter, with two little snakes; and under them two dooves, all closed in with a garland of olife, betokening commendable Governement with Providence': Nichols, *Progresses*, II. 368.

109 At st. 22 we are told that Ate's cave contains, among others, 'the name of *Nimrod* strong', the first tyrant (Geneva glosses on Genesis 10: 8–9 read: 'a cruell oppressor and tyrant. His tyrannie came into a proverbe as hated both of God and man . . .'). The Mercurian monarch is unfolded in Book IV, then, to banish tyranny. For Nimrod as a giant (which links him with the giant-rebellion theme of the poem), see R. O. Iredale, 'Giants and Tyrants in Book Five of *The Faerie Queene*', *RES*, n.s. 17 (1966), 373–381.

110 On these concerns see Frank Kermode, *'The Faerie Queene*, I and V', in *Shakespeare, Spenser, Donne* (1971); T. K. Dunseath, *Spenser's Allegory of Justice in Book Five of 'The Faerie Queene'* (Princeton, N.J.: Princeton U.P., 1968); Jane Aptekar, *Icons of Justice: Iconography and Thematic Imagery in Book V of 'The Faerie Queene'* (New York and London: Columbia U.P., 1969).

111 Boccaccio, *Genealogia deorum*, XII. lxii (facsimile of Venice, 1494 edn: New York and London, Garland Publishing, 1976). Hamilton's edn rightly notes an echo, in Mercilla's clouds, of Psalm 97:2: 'Cloudes and darkenesse are round about him: righteousnesse and judgement are the foundation of his throne'. Aptekar, *Icons of Justice*, p. 72, compares emblems of Jupiter seated in a cloud.

112 Wind, *Pagan Mysteries*, pp. 123–124.

113 Plutarch, *De Iside et Osiride*, 351D; Loeb *Moralia* (14 vols.); vol. 5, tr. F. C. Babbitt (London and Cambridge, Mass.: Heinemann and Harvard

U.P., 1936), p. 7. Angus Fletcher, *The Prophetic Moment*, pp. 146 ff. is excellent on the monarchical aspects of Book V.

114   The three *Litae* who attend on Mercilla (st. 31–32) confirm her Mercurian role: they were frequently conflated, as here, with the *Horae* (e.g. Aptekar, p. 20; Hamilton's edn, p. 593) and the *Horae* with the Graces (Cartari, s.v. *Le Gratie*, pp. 556 ff; Nichols, *Progresses*, III. 108). So that Mercilla is Mercury as leader of the Graces again. D. A. Northrop, 'Mercilla's Court as Parliament', *HLQ*, 36 (1972–73), 153–158 is a useful reminder of the practical realities underlying what I see as Spenser's magical politics.

115   Apuleius, *Golden Ass*, XI. 3 ff. and Plutarch, *De Is. et Os.*, 354C ('I am all that has been, and is, and shall be, and my robe no mortal has yet uncovered'); also *ibid.*, 352A (Loeb, p. 11); *ibid.*, for Isis as the daughter of Mercury, and 355F–356. Diodorus Siculus, I. xxvii. 4 has Isis taught by Hermes. On Isis's name, see *De Is. et Os.*, 351F (Loeb, p. 9). In Apuleius, *Golden Ass*, XI. 11 the image of Isis is heralded by Anubis/Mercury, messenger of the gods, with his caduceus. For an iconography of Isis, see plate 7.

116   Plutarch, *De Is. et Os.*, 359C, p. 53. Macrobius's seasonal interpretation of the myth, in which Isis mourns for Osiris as the earth for the sun and as Venus for Adonis (*Saturnalia*, I. xxi. 11, tr. Davies, p. 142), should be noted: it means that the seasonal myths of Books III and IV find their Egyptian fulfilment in Book V.

117   Angus Fletcher, *The Prophetic Moment*, p. 277.

118   On the crocodile, see Aptekar, pp. 90 ff., noting its connection with Osiris's serpent; with evil stratagems; with lust; and with Typhon.

119   Plutarch, *De Is. et Os.*, 381B, p. 173. In this respect the crocodile undoes proleptically the verbal evil of Malfont (ix. 26), whose punishment is to have his tongue 'nayld to a post'. See also n. 128 below on silence.

120   *Iamblichus on the Mysteries of the Egyptians, Chaldeans, and Assyrians*, tr. Thomas Taylor (London, 1821), I. i: 'HERMES, the god who presides over language, was formerly very properly considered as proper to all priests; and the power who presides over true science concerning the Gods is one and the same in the whole of things. Hence our ancestors dedicated the inventions of their wisdom to this deity, inscribing all their own writings with the name of Hermes' [i.e., the *Hermetica*]. Fletcher, *The Prophetic Moment*, pp. 274–275 suggests a parallel with the Merlin of Book III.

121   For an expansion of this idea, see Clifford Davidson, 'The Idol of Isis Church', *SP*, 66 (1969), 84–85.

122   Nohrnberg's polymathic *Analogy*, p. 391 notes the hint of alchemical symbolism here, especially in connection with the analogy between the Cave of Mammon and Isis Church. He does not, however, consider the presence of Mercury.

123   The iconography of Echidna is explored definitively by John M. Steadman in 'Spenser's *Errour* and the Renaissance Allegorical Tradition', *Neuphilologische Mitteilungen*, LXII (1961); reprinted as ch.

XI of *Nature into Myth* (1979).

124 Ross, *Mystagogus Poeticus*, p. 209; cf. Plutarch, *De Is. et Os.*, 354C, pp. 23–24. For evil aspects of the sphinx, see, e.g., Comes, *Mythologiae*, IX. xviii and Hamilton's edn, p. 606, citing Beryl Rowland, *Animals with Human Faces: a Guide to Animal Symbolism* (Knoxville, 1973), p. 148.

125 Yates, *Giordano Bruno and the Hermetic Tradition*, pp. 42–43, and French, *John Dee*, p. 67. The pavement is reproduced as the frontispiece to Scott's edn of the *Hermetica*, vol. I, and to Yates's *Bruno*.

126 Tr. Imerti, pp. 241–242. Cf. *Asclepius*, III, 24A–26A (*Hermetica*, ed. Scott, I. 339 ff.: ed. Nock and Festugière, II. 325 ff.).

127 See R. Bernheimer, *Wild Men in the Middle Ages: a Study in Art, Sentiment, and Demonology* (Cambridge, Mass.: Harvard U.P., 1952).

128 The sovereign implications of the central position were first explored by A. D. S. Fowler, *Triumphal Forms: Structural Patterns in Elizabethan Poetry* (Cambridge: C.U.P., 1970). The *silencing* of Colin attains to the ideal of silence as eloquence/truth, discussed by, e.g., H. A. Hallahan, 'Silence, Eloquence, and Chatter in Jonson's *Epicoene*', *HLQ*, 40 (1976–77), 117–127, esp. p. 119; and Raymond Waddington, 'The Iconography of Silence and Chapman's Hercules', *JWCI*, 33 (1970), 248–263. See particularly p. 259 for its association with Hermes Trismegistus.

129 For the poet at court and the relationship between poetry and monarchy, culminating in a study of *Faerie Queene*, VI, see Daniel Javitch, *Poetry and Courtliness in Renaissance England* (Princeton, N.J.: Princeton U.P., 1978).

130 Cartari, *Imagini*, pp. 335 ff.; Linche, *Fountaine of Ancient Fiction*, sig. Riii.

131 Plutarch, *De Is. et Os.*, 373C–D, p. 133.

132 Mercury received his caduceus from Apollo in exchange for his lyre and/or musical pipe: Comes, *Mythologiae*, V. v; so that the two are mythologically interchangeable.

133 Linche, *Fountaine of Ancient Fiction*, sig. Ki. Mercury's tortoiseshell lyre was sometimes supposed to possess seven strings to signify the harmony of the seven planetary orbits: see Martianus, *Marriage of Philology and Mercury*, tr. Stahl, p. 18.

134 Hamilton's edn, p. 695. On Proteus, compare *FQ*, III. iv. 37, where he is 'father of false prophecies'. Busirane is ominously present because of the brigands, since Busiris sent pirates to capture the Hesperides, daughters of Atlas: Diodorus Siculus, IV. xxvii. 2.

135 Humphrey Tonkin perceptively compares Calidore's role here to that of Orpheus: *Spenser's Courteous Pastoral: Book Six of 'The Faerie Queene'* (Oxford: Clarendon Press, 1972), pp. 215–216. He also observes, via Wind's *Pagan Mysteries*, a parallel between the Mount Acidale episode and Botticelli's *Primavera* (though without noting the relevance of Mercury): see *ibid.*, p. 233; also p. 312, n. 57 for a passing identification of Pastorella with Flora.

136 See *OED*, s.v. *Blatant*; and cf. *Blatter*. If there is a punning relationship

with *bleat*, then he relates on a parodic level to Mercury as shepherd god. For other meanings of 'blatant', see Hamilton's note to V. xii. 37, and Nohrnberg, *Analogy*, pp. 688 ff.

137 *Expulsion*, ed. Imerti, pp. 99–100.

138 See Nohrnberg, pp. 745–746 for documentation. Pellegrini, 'Bruno, Sidney, and Spenser' (see n. 6 above) noted an absolute difference between Spenser's Mutability and Bruno's Fortune and observed no other similarities between the two writers, thus answering R. B. Levinson's more favourable view of Spenser's possible indebtedness in 'Spenser and Bruno', *PMLA*, 43 (1928), 675–681.

139 Ed. Imerti, p. 79.

140 Not surprisingly, when we recall Mercury's identification (via his caduceus) with earth: see n. 101 above. Nature's hermaphroditism was first noted (without emphasis on Mercury) by J. W. Bennett, 'Spenser's Venus and the Goddess Nature in the *Cantos of Mutabilitie*', *PMLA*, 30 (1933), 165 ff. See *ibid.*, p. 173 and n. for the identification of Venus/Nature with Cybele, the 'great mother'.

141 See VI. ix. 36.

142 For the iconographical relationship between Isis and Night, see Linche, *Fountaine of Ancient Fiction*, sig. Hiv: 'The Ægyptians . . . worshipped the Moone under the name of Isis, and her they depicted covered with a black and sable vesture, in token that of her selfe shee giveth no light'. (Cf. Una at I. i. 4, white but covered in 'a black stole' and plate 7. Una is connected with Isis in n. 31 above.) For Osiris's sceptre and eye, see Plutarch, *De Is. et Os.*, 354F–355A and 371E; also Macrobius, *Saturnalia*, I. xxi. 12.

II

Hermetic conservatism:
the court masque

Stephen Orgel and Roy Strong insist on the 'scientific' nature of the court masque: it 'is the form that most consistently projects a world in which all the laws of nature have been understood and the attacks of mutability defeated by the rational power of the mind'.[1] And yet it would be a mistake to underestimate the magical background to this enclosed genre, the sole function of which was to affirm the monarch's virtue and supremacy. Inigo Jones relates, through John Dee, to the tradition of the Vitruvian theatre. And the emphasis, which Jones was responsible for developing, on mysterious machines and the spectacle of wonder is a magical one, while the masque's essential pattern, the calling-down of virtues to attest to the monarch's supreme virtue, again suggests the magician's summoning of the celestial 'virtues'.[2] Moreover, the constant victory over vice that the masque celebrates recalls Bruno's *Expulsion of the Triumphant Beast*, as Carew seems to have recognised when he based his elaborate and in many ways climactic *Coelum Britannicum* (1634) on that work. In this chapter I survey magical symbolism in the court masque, noting particularly the emergence of the Mercurian monarch, an image which, whatever its independent origins, seems to have been indebted to Spenser's elaborate pioneering work in *The Faerie Queene*. As in Spenser, too, the seventeenth-century Mercurian monarch's world is often that of Arthur's and Aeneas's western land: magic is integral to the British myth.

[i] *Masques for the reign of James (excluding the 1613 Wedding)*

Samuel Daniel's *The Vision of the Twelve Goddesses* (8 January 1604) was the first Stuart epiphany masque. There was an earlier Tudor epiphany masque tradition,[3] but the fact that it became a custom under James is scarcely accidental. The magi, those eastern king magicians who were star-led to the infant Christ, were an apt emblem of the British magician king; while epiphany itself, as a January festival, carried with it not only vague general suggestions of a new year and renewed solar cycle but, more specifically, of Janus, whose two faces symbolised 'the foresight and shrewdness of the king, as one who not only knew the past but would also foresee the future' and who reigned with Saturn in the Golden Age, as Evander tells Aeneas after his arrival in Latium.[4]

Much of this is suggested by Daniel, the scene of whose masque is the Temple of Peace. The British theme is evident, since the goddesses have abandoned Greece and Asia, which are now given over to barbarism, for 'this western mount of mighty Brittany' (l. 259),[5] just as James has now, Aeneas-like, taken over his western kingdom. In addition, the device – Sibylla explaining the attributes of the goddesses whom she sees in the 'prospective' which she is given by Iris, 'the messenger of the Goddesses' – recalls Aeneas's entry into the underworld, guided by the Sibyl and protected by the golden bough, to encounter the prospect of the future Roman empire. The dedication to Peacham's *Minerva Britanna* (1612), as we have seen, told the young Prince Henry that the emblems in his book 'are of right your owne, and no other then the substance of those Divine Instructions, his *Majestie* your Royall *Father* præscribed unto you, your guide (as that golden branch to *ÆNEAS*,) to a vertuous & true happy life'. He refers here to the *Basilicon Doron* as the golden bough, which was traditionally the key to hidden knowledge, a symbolism related to the interpretation of Mercury's caduceus as *doctrinae virga* (the rod of Mercury's teaching and eloquence).[6] Daniel's Sibylla gazes into a 'prospective' that recalls Merlin's and John Dee's crystals; but she has been given it by Iris (to whom is also given the masque's closing speech), because Iris, as messenger of Juno, is Mercury's female counterpart.[7] *The Vision* was presented 'by the Queen's Majesty and her Ladies' and accordingly it introduces the magician monarch theme into the new reign through the female Mercury.

The theme is not only fused with allusions to the *Aeneid* and British myth, however, but with the question of the relationship between magic and imagination as well. For the world of *The Vision* is a dream world in which the characters are called up by Night and her son Somnus. Somnus has two wands, one black (for confused dreams, ll. 134–135, 245) the other white, to produce 'significant dreams' (ll. 141 ff.), and this is the wand that operates in the masque.[8] Daniel insists in his prefatory letter to Lucy, Countess of Bedford, that the visions conjured up in the masque are but shadows: 'these apparitions and shows are but as imaginations and dreams that portend our affections'. Nevertheless, this first Stuart epiphany masque, announcing a new creation and so beginning with the first things (Night, born of Chaos), intends a significant correlation between shadow and substance. The monarch embodies the magical power which Somnus invokes for him with his white wand by summoning the goddess-virtues, thus banishing the chthonic forces of black magic (the black wand) and, in Spenserian terms, Archimagean deception. The masque's culmination in the dance of the goddesses 'consisting of divers strains framed unto motions circular, square, triangular, with other proportions exceeding rare and full of variety', as the prefatory letter explains, reminds us of the inseparability of mathematics, motion, and magic:

> The Doctrines of Mathematicks are so necessary to, and have such an affinity with Magick, that they that do profess it without them, are quite out of the way, and labour in vain, and shall in no wise obtain their desired effect. For whatsoever things are, and are done in these inferior naturall vertues, are all done, and governed by number, weight, measure, harmony, motion, and light.[9]

Clearly, James's hatred of witchcraft and the black arts was no hindrance to the resurgence of the cult of the monarch magus in his reign.

The hieroglyphic content of Jonson's early masques has been too well analysed by others for me to need to pause over them here.[10] The muted talismanic aspects of *Blackness* and *Beauty* become more overt, however, in Jonson's second marriage masque, *Haddington* (1608), in which James is Aeneas with shining crown 'whose Scepter here doth grow / . . . . A Prince, that drawes / By th'example more, then others doe by lawes' (ll. 213 ff.).[11] Venus, who has descended to earth to find her missing son Cupid, is prevailed upon to return to heaven by Vulcan's gift of a silver globe, certain features of which '*were heightned with gold . . . the* Zodiake *was of pure gold*'. Vulcan describes it thus:

> It is a *spheare*, I'have formed round, and even,
> In due proportion to the *spheare* of heaven,
> With all his *lines*, and *circles*; that compose
> The perfect'st forme, and aptly doe disclose
> The *heaven of marriage*: which I title it.
> Within whose *Zodiack*, I have made to sit,
> In order of the *signes*, twelve sacred powers,
> That are præsiding at all *nuptiall* howers. . . . (ll. 276 ff.)

The globe is at once a cosmic model in the line of Achilles's and Aeneas's shields and a statement of alchemical fusion (silver and gold, lunar and solar). While ostensibly celebrating a specific marriage the masque in fact celebrates James's magical power as reconciler of opposites and solar lord of the zodiac, whose powers as monarch he has been able to draw down.

In *The Masque of Queens* (February 1609), on the other hand, we are introduced to the monarchical–magical command of stellar power through its chthonic opposite, since it begins with the antimasque in which the chief witch and her eleven companions, manifesting 'all the power attributed to witches by the *Antients*' (ll. 207–208), attempt to undo proleptically the twelve virtues of the end and, retrospectively, the zodiacal virtues of *Haddington*. (Jonson's preface refers to the '*Anti-Masque* of Boyes' in *Haddington*, and adds that he has now 'devis'd that twelve Women, in the habite of *Haggs*, or Witches, sustayning the persons of *Ignorance, Suspicion, Credulity*, &c. the opposites to good *Fame*, should fill that part . . .'. *Haddington's* twelve boys, companions of Cupid, had been the antimasque to the zodiac's masque.) When the twelve virtues do appear in *Queens*, moreover, after the banishing of the witches and their hell, they are 'discoverd . . . sitting upon a Throne triumphall, erected in forme of a *Pyramide*, and circled with all store of light' in the House of Fame (ll. 361 ff.). They are embodied in the figures of twelve queens, eleven ancient and one modern, '*Bel-anna*, Royall *Queene* of the *Ocean*; of whose dignity, and person the whole *scope* of the *Invention* doth speake throughout'; so that she subsumes the eleven and infolds twelve in one. There is no explicit zodiacal symbolism, and yet the description of the House of Fame with its '*Freezes*, both below, and above, [which] were filld with severall-coloured Lights, like *Emeralds, Rubies, Saphires, Carbuncles,* &c. The reflexe of which, with other lights plac'd in ye concave, upon the *Masquers* habites was full of glory' (ll. 695 ff.), calls to mind a celestial globe. Chaucer's description, upon which Jonson models his own, directs us to a lapidary. If we follow this clue and read Jonson's named gems as embodying astrological virtues, the emeralds and saphires would be venerean, appropriate to Anne as a woman, and the rubies and carbuncles solar, to celebrate her as queen and ruler. And since the masque is about the banishing of the powers of darkness it is more than relevant that 'the Carbuncle which shines by night, hath a vertue against all aiery, and vaporous poison'.[12]

There is more elaborate magical suggestiveness in *Prince Henry's Barriers* (6 January 1610). James, in himself and through begetting

Henry, has restored the Golden Age and 'a strength of empire fixt /
Conterminate with heaven' (ll. 340–341):

> Onely the house of *Chivalrie* . . . decayd
> Or rather ruin'd seemes; her buildings layd
> Flat with the earth; that were the pride of time
> And did the barbarous *Memphian* heapes out-clime.
> Those *Obelisks* and *Columnes* broke, and downe,
> That strooke the starres, and rais'd the *Brittish* crowne
> To be a constellation. . . . (ll. 31 ff.)

The emphasis on St George (ll. 136, 141, 313) reminds us that the Order
of the Garter in its Tudor and Stuart form is a religious and chivalric
force greater and more splendid than the achievements of the
Egyptians[13] but that nevertheless the chivalric revival depends on an
Egyptian past. As in *The Faerie Queene*, this motif fuses with the
Arthurian myth: Merlin and the Lady of the Lake testify to Henry's
valour, and the Lady summons down the stellified Arthur:

> I, thy ARTHUR, am
> Translated to a starre; and of that frame
> Or constellation that was called of mee
> So long before, as showing what I should bee,
> ARCTURUS, once thy King, and now thy starre. (ll. 65 ff.)

He goes on to disclose that he can reveal himself now because Merlin's
'misticke prophesies'[14] have been fulfilled, for Britain is united and so its
monarch can claim Arthur's 'scepter and [his] stile' (l. 77). Jonson has
reverted to the Tudor Arcturus myth; and, as we saw earlier, Arcturus,
although properly 'a starre sette behynde the tayle of the synge that
hyght Ursa major',[15] was frequently identified with Ursa Major itself,
whose seven stars were understood by St Gregory as signifying the
Universal Church, the gifts of the Holy Spirit, and the life of the virtuous
Christian. Jonson presumably intends all this for James, who now
'*claimes* ARTHURS seat' (l. 20).[16] But the compliment is aimed more
particularly at Prince Henry, since he and '*his sixe assistants*' who are
'*discovered*' at line 131 embody the relevant total of seven. It is no
accident that Arthur refers to Henry as the 'knight . . . that by the might
/ And magicke of his arme [will] restore / These ruin'd seates of vertue'
(ll. 82 ff.). He is the magical prince who has, like the St George knight
before him in the tenth canto of *The Faerie Queene*, Book I, brought
Arthurian stellar virtues down to earth. Perhaps we should remember
Bruno, too; for the expulsion of Bruno's beast begins when the old Ursa

of deformity, falsity, hypocrisy, and imposture is replaced by the reformed Ursa of Truth.[17] And we may suspect that the allusion continues into *Oberon* (1 January 1611) where Henry, as the fairy prince, appears *'in a chariot . . . drawne by two white beares'* (ll. 295–297), especially as his palace 'show[s] / Like another *Skie* of lights' (ll. 143–144).

So far as I am aware, the Mercurian theme makes its first explicit appearance in James's reign in connection with Henry. This is in Richard Davies's *Chester's Triumph in Honour of her Prince* (St George's day, 1610),[18] where Fame summons Mercury with his 'charming rod' as 'Tongue's man of the Universe' to celebrate 'this Day' (that is, St George's day and the arrival of the prince as symbolic St George). The Chorus's song invoking Mercury identifies god and prince in an unsubtle ambiguity: *'Welcome, O welcome to Earth, / Jove's dearest darling. / Lighten the eyes, thou great Mercurian Prince, / Of all that view thee'*; while in *London's Love to the Royal Prince Henry* (May 1610) the British and Arthurian–Cornish themes merge with the following assertion of the monarch's command of angel magic (a direct consequence, it would seem from the evidence of *The Faerie Queene*, of the tradition of the Mercurian magician king). Here Corinea tells of the citizens' love for Henry:

> let me humbly entreate you to accept their boundlesse love, which is like to Jacob's ladder, reaching from Earth to Heaven; whereon their hourelie holie and devoute desires (like to so many blessed angelles) are continually ascending and descending, for their Royall Soveraigne your Father, his Queene your peerlesse Mother, your sacred selfe, and the rest of their illustrious race, that unpolluted soules may be ever about yee, false hearts or foule hands never come neere yee, but the Hoaste of Heaven alwayes to defend yee![19]

It is, not surprisingly, Jonson's *Mercury Vindicated* (performed before the king and queen, January 1616) that first establishes James as the Mercurian monarch. Mercury emerges from Vulcan's furnace as alchemical Mercury, 'their Crude, and their Sublimate; their Præcipitate, and their unctuous; their male and their female; . . . their *Hermaphrodite*' (ll. 51 ff.). Vulcan and three alchemists try to capture him while *'he defends himselfe with his* Caducæus' (l. 116) and eventually, when Vulcan can produce only an 'Antimasque *of imperfect creatures*' in an attempt to justify and demonstrate alchemical– Paracelsan creative power, he and his works are banished by Mercury and *'the whole Scene chang[es] to a glorious bowre, wherein*

Nature *was placed, with* Prometheus *at her feete*' accompanied by the twelve masquers (ll. 196 ff.). The movement from dark to light symbolises a new creation under the power of the monarch, whose emblem here is a Mercury who transcends the Mercury of the alchemists. And yet his summoning up of Nature and Prometheus, presumably by his caduceus, is still a magical act, for Prometheus was the first sculptor, and he had the power to make living statues (present in the form of the masquers as they move from stasis into dance). As we shall see, the art of making statues come to life was a preoccupation of the 1613 wedding masques for Elizabeth and Frederick, where it seems to have Hermetic significance. Jonson displaces the alchemical magus by a Mercurian monarch whose art derives, we are to infer, from true magical communion with the gods.[20]

It is likely, therefore, that Mercury's role as presenter of the masque in *Pleasure Reconciled to Virtue* (6 January 1618) has a similar meaning. It is Mercury who crowns Hercules (Virtue; l. 166) and announces that the time of reconciliation has come: 'how / by un-alterd law, & working of the stars, / there should be a cessation of all jars / 'twixt Vertue, & hir noted opposite, / Pleasure' (ll. 187 ff.). It is he, too, who announces the arrival of the masquers led by Prince Charles (whose first masque this was), 'cheif . . . of the bright race of *Hesperus*' (ll. 204–205), where Hesperus is Arthur, king of the western land identified with the garden of the Hesperides (ll. 209–210).[21] The masquers then appear led by Daedalus, and it is Mercury's function to act as hermeneut as Hercules asks him 'Who's this that leads?' and he replies: 'A Guid yt gives them Lawes / to all yeir motions: *Dædalus* ye wise' (ll. 242 ff.).[22] Daedalus is the master of the labyrinthine dance and arch-statuary or image-maker. Agrippa summarises a commonplace when he notes, in a passage following the one I quoted earlier in this chapter on the affinity of mathematics to magic, that mathematics enable the magus to simulate living things: 'such as were those which amongst the Ancients were called *Dedalus* his Images, and *automata*, of which *Aristotle* makes mention, *viz.* the threefooted Images of *Vulcan*, and *Dedalus*, moving themselves . . .'.[23] *Pleasure Reconciled* complements *Mercury Vindicated* as a panegyric on the Mercurian and magical monarch. In both, we are to understand, Mercury is the key figure since he possesses and, in the case of *Mercury Vindicated*, transcends the knowledge of the artificer himself.

Mercurian and Hermetic allusions became more frequent as James's reign approached its end. If jokes at the expense of Agrippa and the new sect of Rosicrucians suggest a deliberate attempt to isolate James from the more extreme forms of magical esotericism (see *News from the New World Discovered in the Moon*, 1620), this does not prevent Jonson from magical mystification in the midsummer masque for James's birthday, *Pan's Anniversary*, that same year.[24] It is appropriate that this solstitial masque should celebrate James as Pan, '*that faire Fount of light*' (l. 164), since, according to Macrobius, Pan is the sun god, his horns and beard being 'symbols of the nature of the light by which the sun illumines the expanse of the sky above and brings brightness to the parts that lie below', his 'pipe and wand' respectively indicating the winds (which 'derive their properties and essential nature from the sun') and 'power of the sun, which controls all things'.[25] As we have already seen, though, Pan's pipe also signifies 'the musical melodie of the heavens'. We encountered it in the hands of Spenser's Mercurian Colin in a pastoral interlude somewhat similar to Jonson's here.[26] As musician and dancer as well as shepherd god Pan is a greater Mercury, a fact recognised in the first hymn celebrating the god when we are told that '*Of* Pan *we sing, the best of Leaders*, Pan, / *That leads the Naiad's, and the Dryad's forth*; / *And to their daunces more then* Hermes *can*'. From one point of view James as Pan recalls Plotinus's description of God, in the vision of whom 'is our attainment and our repose and the end of all discord, God in his dancers and God the true Centre of the dance'.[27] He is the one who is also the many, the ultimate assertion of the neo-Platonic doctrine of self-transcendence that Pico expressed in one of his Orphic *Conclusions* that Edgar Wind has helped to make so familiar:[28] 'He who cannot attract Pan approaches Proteus in vain'. This is the apotheosis of James as Mercurian monarch.

More specifically Hermetic is the masque prepared for Charles's return from Spain, *Neptune's Triumph for the Return of Albion* (1624 but not performed). The opening debate finds the Cook saying to the Poet, 'O, you are for the *Oracle* of the *Bottle*, I see; Hogshead *Trismegistus*: He is your *Pegasus*. Thence *flowes* the spring of your *Muses*' (ll. 77–79). Jonson's note directs us to Book V of Rabelais's *Gargantua and Pantagruel*, in the final chapters of which Panurge and Friar John visit the island of lanterns whose queen gives them the best lantern by which they are then led to their 'desired island' where they will find the oracle of the bottle. It seems that the allusion is slightly more than a mere joke. As the masque proper opens, the prince's return is symbolised in the joining of a floating island to the mainland shore; so that the Rabelais chapters offer a commentary on this, and it is a

Hermetic one. Britain is the 'desired island', James is the object of the quest (Trismegistan and oracular), and Whitehall Banqueting House, where the masque was to have been performed, is the Bacchic temple into which Panurge and Friar John are led by the priestess Bacbuc (as Charles–Albion has been brought back by divine power from Spain). Rabelais's temple is entered through a Bacchic triumphal arch, has the motto 'in wine, truth' over the door, and contains tapestries of the god's followers and of his victories, especially his conquest of India.[29] Since mythologically this conquest signified the establishment of law, the allusive compliment is to James as lawgiver as well as Bacchic god of perpetual youth: seated in his palace-temple he is the inspired Bacchic–Hermetic oracle of truth.[30] (This, of course, is to presume little or no satiric intent on Jonson's part. Milton's vision of a Bacchic monarch in *Comus* will be very different and somewhat more historically accurate.)

The Fortunate Isles, and Their Union (January 1625), Jonson's last masque for the court of James, is a reworking of *Neptune's Triumph* with a new antimasque and minor alterations to the masque itself to emphasise the Golden-Age glories of Britain under James. Britain is the alchemical western kingdom, the island of the blest:[31]

> That point of Revolution being come
> When all the Fortunate Islands should be joyn'd,
> MACARIA, one, and thought a Principall,
> That hetherto hath floted, as uncertaine
> Where she should fix her blessings, is to night
> Instructed to adhere to your BRITANNIA:
> That where the happie spirits live, hereafter
> Might be no question made. . . . (ll. 443 ff.)

As James sickened the masque world affirmed its affinity with the ideal. Proteus, in a speech not found in *Neptune's Triumph*, tells of this land where '*is no sickness, nor no olde age knowne / To man*', and Saron reveals that the '*old* Musitians' Arion, Amphion, Apollo, and others are there, '*sing[ing] the present* Prophecie *that goes / Of joyning the bright* LILLIE, *and the* ROSE'. In a sense, then, this is also a prothalamic masque. While celebrating British power and prosperity, a Golden Age resulting from James's peace-pursuing policies, it invokes Venus and the Graces and the Flora motif: '*See! all the flowres / That spring the banks along, / Do move their heads unto that undersong*' (ll. 545 ff.). And it does this in the end not so much to celebrate the king's magical ability to restore the *aurea aetas* and summon the spirits of the blest to his kingdom

as to celebrate the forthcoming marriage of Charles and Henrietta
Maria. The rose, however, has more than simply patriotic and dynastic
associations. In conjunction with the French lily it presumably carries
with it overtones of the alchemical union of white and red,[32] and (a
related symbolism) it suggests the red rose of the Rosicrucians.

This is clear enough from the new antimasque. The antimasque to
Neptune's Triumph had merely mentioned Hermes Trismegistus. Now
Jonson introduces his masque with elaborate Rosicrucian satiric
paraphernalia:[33]

> His Matie being sett,
> Entreth in, running, JOHPHIEL, an aëry spirit, and .
> (acording to the *Magi*) the *Intelligence* of *Jupiters* sphere . . .
> JOHPHIEL.
> Like a lightning from the skie,
> Or an arrow shot by *Love*,
> Or a Bird of his let fly;
> Bee't a Sparrow, or a Dove:
> With that winged hast, come I,
> Loosed from the Sphere of *Jove* . . . .

Johphiel then encounters Merefool, a melancholic in the Ficinan mould,
the magician child of Saturn. He is in despair because he has been denied
his vision: 'What meane the Brethren of the *Rosie-Crosse* / So to desert
their votary!' (ll. 34–35). But Johphiel tells him that he has been sent by
the founder of 'The Castle in the aire, where all the Brethren /
Rhodostaurotick live' to give him his vision, and although he cannot
summon up any of the ancient magi and philosophers that Merefool asks
for (Zoroaster, Hermes Trismegistus, Pythagoras, etc.) he can manage
'skipping *Skelton*' and 'morall *Scogan*' along with the antimasquers.
With their appearance Merefool believes he has just received 'the first
grace / The Company of the *Rosie-Crosse* hath done [him]' (ll. 428–429).
Johphiel disabuses him by telling him that it was the 'company of
Players';[34] and he then turns to address the true magus, James: 'Great
King . . . Heare now the message of the Fates, and *Jove*, / On whom those
Fates depend, to you, as *Neptune*, / The great Commander of the Seas,
and Iles'.

Jove thus speaks, through his demon, to the true magician, and it is in
the king's masque, as opposed to the antimasque, that we find the true
rose, Charles, to displace the rose given to Merefool by Johphiel (l. 155,
marginal note), just as we here find the monarch's sceptre to displace the
Rosicrucians' 'divine rods' (l. 138). Jonson does not divorce the court

from its magical context and roots. On the contrary, he is saying that
there is no need for this new order of the Rosy-cross because we have our
old order of the Red Cross in the Garter Knights of St George presided
over by the magical power of the monarch. If to become a Rosicrucian is
to be

> Principall Secretarie to the Starres;
> Know all their signatures, and combinations (ll. 136–137)

then the magician king has known all this, and more besides, for a long
time, because he is the descendant of the priest king Thoth–Hermes.
Moreover, he possesses his knowledge and power without becoming the
life-denying Saturnian melancholic. Jonson here delicately compliments
the sick and ageing James by emphasising an astrological alternative to
aged Saturn and the inappropriately too-youthful Mercury, restorer of a
spring-like Golden Age and leader of the dance of Venus and her Graces.
Venus and the Graces do indeed dance in the masque, but under the
auspices of James as Jupiter, the more solemn god of governors,
magistrates, and magicians.[35] And yet Jupiter has connotations of youth,
too, presiding as he does over the spring-like first age of man and of the
world, thus complementing Mercury as god of spring and directly
opposing melancholy Saturn.[36] In this way does Jonson banish, or
attempt to banish, old age from James while at the same time offering
him the supreme magical tribute in the form of Johphiel. Herford and
Simpson are surely right to point out that Johphiel is a suitably
Hebraic–cabbalistic transcription of 'Jovial'.[37] As they also point out,
though, the Abbot Trithemius (followed by Agrippa) names
Zachariel/Zadkiel as the presiding intelligence or demon of Jupiter.[38]
What they do not notice is that Johphiel is not just a 'jovial' nonce name.
He is in fact the angelic manifestation in the intelligible world (open to
the highest grade of melancholy) of the zodiac in the celestial world
(middle grade). He appears to the Saturnian Merefool as a joke but to
James in earnest. Johphiel corresponds in the intelligible world to the
cherubim in the heavenly hierarchy, contemplators of god. He opens the
way, in other words, to the angels and to the prophecy of new prophets
and a new religion.[39] The zodiacal theme of earlier masques receives its
ultimate restatement here as James is elevated to the status of supreme
visionary magician king.

[ii] *The alchemical wedding of 1613*

The masques for the marriage of Princess Elizabeth and Frederick, Count Palatine, form a thematically homogeneous group and in many ways confirm — indeed exaggerate — the thematic tendencies that we have been tracing. There is particularly strong emphasis on alchemy and the living statue Hermetic themes that relate as much to Bohemia, as Frances Yates has demonstrated, as to courtly conventions at home.[40]

A basis for the alchemical theme is evident from the description of the wedding with its emphasis on silver (or white) and gold:

> ... the Palsgrave [entered] from the newe-built Banquetting-house, attired in a white sute, richly beset with pearle and gold. . . . After came . . . the Lady Elizabeth, in her virgin-robes, clothed in a gowne of white sattin . . .; upon her head a crown of refined golde, made Imperiall by the pearles and diamonds thereupon placed, which were so thicke beset that they stood like shining pinnacles upon her amber-coloured haire, dependantly hanging playted downe over her shoulders to her waste; between every plaight a roll or liste of gold-spangles, pearles, rich stones, and diamonds. . . .[41]

The wedding was on Shrove Sunday, 14 February 1613. That night Campion's *Lords' Masque* was performed; Chapman's *Middle Temple* masque was performed on the Monday. Beaumont's *Masque of the Inner Temple and Gray's Inn*, intended for the Tuesday, was postponed until 20 February. *The Lords' Masque* has similarities with Campion's earlier *Lord Hay's Masque* (1607), performed before the king and celebrating 'the Lord HAYES, and his Bride. Daughter and Heire to the *Honourable the Lord* DENNYE',[42] and so it seems sensible to consider them together here.

Lord Hay's Masque opposes the house of Night and bower of Flora with a hill between on top of which was 'a goodly large tree . . . supposed to be the tree of *Diana*'. The masque opens with Flora and her sylvans, together with Zephyrus, scattering flowers. When a song in praise of marriage is ended, 'the whole veil is sodainly drawn, [a] grove and trees of gold, and the hill with *Dianas* tree are at once discovered' (p. 66). The gold trees are the nine knights of Apollo, metamorphosed by Cynthia–Diana because they tried to seduce her maidens (p. 67). Apollo has already been established at p. 63 as 'the father of heat and youth, and consequently of amorous affections'. But, in accordance with its epithalamic function, the masque's theme is reconciliation, the coming-together of Day and Night and their respective planets sun and moon. With her wand Night enables the golden trees to resume their 'native forms', and the knights then have to make a gesture of reconciliation:

> *Phoebus* is pleas'd, and all rejoice to see
> His servants from their golden prison free.
> But yet since *Cinthia* hath so freendly smilde,
> And to you tree-borne Knights is reconcild,
> First ere you any more worke undertake,
> About her tree solemne procession make,
> *Dianas* tree, the tree of Chastitie. . . . (p. 72)

The alchemical king and queen make their appearance here, then, as indeed they do even more splendidly in *The Lords' Masque*, the magical context for which is explicit from the beginning when Orpheus and Entheus (Divine Inspiration) invoke Prometheus and his 'lights', '*eight Starres of extraordinarie bignesse, which so were placed, as that they seemed to be fixed betweene the Firmament and the Earth*' (p. 92).[43] In accordance with the tradition that we have already encountered in Jonson's *Mercury Vindicated* Prometheus is again a sculptor, for the stars are transformed into eight masquers clad in gold and silver: '*The ground of their attires was massie Cloth of Silver, embossed with flames of Embroidery; on their heads, they had Crownes, Flames made all of Gold-plate Enameled*' (p. 94). These knights are subsequently complemented by eight silver statues of ladies which, through the power of Jove (who thus reverses his original punishment of Prometheus), now 'have life and move' (p. 95). The two sets of eight produce the epithalamic number sixteen and dance together in affirmation of alchemical union.[44] The spectators join in the dance, too, '*and first of all the Princely Bridegroome and Bride*' (p. 97).

This might have been the end of the masque. But the climax was still to come, for a Sibyl enters, drawing by a gold thread '*an Obeliske, all of silver . . . on the side of [which], standing on Pedestals, were the statues of Bridegroome and Bride, all of gold*'. The Egyptian obelisk of immortality (p. 98) celebrates the alchemical union of Frederick and Elizabeth and their kingdoms and presents us with a final reversal of the Prometheus myth. These statues, after all, do not have to be metamorphosed: once they have been honoured, the masquers can turn to the living figures who are already present and who demonstrate 'how heavenly natures far above all art appear'. As I suggested earlier, and as Frances Yates has already noticed, the statue theme here and elsewhere at this period, whatever its other mythological analogues, seems to allude to the Hermetic *Asclepius*, the passages in which Hermes tells Asclepius of the Egyptians' ability to make gods in imitation of 'the Father and Master [who] made the gods of heaven eternal'. These gods are statues, 'but statues living and conscious, filled with the breath of life, and doing many mighty works . . .'.[45] We recall Spenser's statue of Isis in his book of Justice, which deals with the restoration of the Golden Age through the new religion. The theme is the same in Campion's masque, in which the royal marriage actually restores the Golden Age and simultaneously asserts political and religious renewal.[46] If one of the statue passages in the *Asclepius* is followed by the lament for an Egypt gone astray, then the lament yields to a vision of renewal. The gods, having fled from earth to heaven, will return; God 'will bring back his world to its former aspect'.[47] There is no direct allusion to the lament in *The Lords' Masque*, but the theme of renewal is there and so are the living statues, culminating in the god-like Frederick and Elizabeth themselves.

Chapman's *Middle Temple and Lincoln's Inn Masque* is Hermetic in the broadest sense: spectacular rather than subtle in argument like Campion's, it is avowedly alchemical. The masque's argument concerns the power of Honour to make Plutus, god of riches, see, since he is 'by Aristophanes, Lucian, etc. presented naturally blind, deformed, and dull-witted'.[48] In other words the argument is built on the assertion that alchemical gold is not common gold, a point underlined by the setting for the action, which is a rock 'in the undermost part craggy and full of hollow places':

> All this rock grew by degrees up into a gold colour, and was run quite through with veins of gold. On the one side thereof, eminently raised on a fair hill, was erected a silver temple of an octagonal figure, whose pillars were of a composed order, and bore up an architrave, frieze, and cornice, over which stood a continued plinth, whereon were advanced statues of silver; above this . . . was written in great gold capitals, HONORIS FANUM. . . . For finishing of all upon a pedestal was fixed a round stone of silver, from which grew a pair of golden wings, both feigned to be Fortune's. (O and S, I. 257)

The progression from bottom of rock to temple mimes the alchemical progression from *prima materia* to the achieved work symbolised in the fusion of silver and gold, lunar and solar, a symbolism already asserted in the procession of masquers.[49] Fortune fixes herself on Honour's temple to show that she will never abandon Great Britain (O and S, I. 257, 258); so that the alchemical wedding of Elizabeth and Frederick provides the great occasion for the fixing of mutability, achieved in another way at the end of the masque when Honour's silver-robed priest Eunomia (Law) tells the sun-worshipping Virginian princes, the Phoebades, to abandon their adoration of the planetary sun for a greater, immutable, sun:[50]

> Virginian princes, you must now renounce
> Your superstitious worship of these suns,
> Subject to cloudy dark'nings and descents;
> And of your fit devotions turn the events
> To this our Briton Phœbus, whose bright sky
> (Enlightened with a Christian piety)
> Is never subject to black Error's night. . . . (O and S, I. 261)

Mutability is 'fixed' in another way too by the banishing of the antimasque figure of Capriccio, born from the rock with a pair of (alchemical) bellows on his head, with the name of the philosophers' stone in his mouth, and announcing himself as 'a second Proteus' (O and S, I. 258).[51]

Statues reappear in Beaumont's *Masque of the Inner Temple*. First of all 'the Statues which wise Vulcan plac'd / Under the altar of Olympian Jove', are called up by Mercury to 'dance for joy of these great nuptials', and he presumably represents alchemical Mercury since these statues *'were attired in cases of gold and silver close to their body, faces, hands and feet, nothing seen but gold and silver, as if they had been solid images of metal'*. This is the first antimasque. In the main masque different but symbolically related statues are revealed on Jupiter's altar, which is *'gilt, with three great tapers upon golden candle-sticks burning upon it: and the four Statues, two of gold and two of silver, as supporters'*. Also revealed are *'fifteen Olympian knights'* dressed predominantly in silver, who are invited by Apollo's priests to 'Shake off your heavy trance, / And leap into a dance / Such as no mortals use to tread, / Fit only for Apollo / To play to, for the moon to lead'.[52] In view of what has been said above about Campion's masque, the statues and the solar–lunar mythology of this final masque for the marriage of February 1613 require no further comment. All three masques confirm the commanding presence of Hermes–Mercury at James's court and, with greater or lesser degrees of explicitness, the magical implications of his rule.[53]

[iii] *Caroline Mercury*

The neo-Platonism of the court of Charles and Henrietta Maria was not simply a cult of love, and the masques from their reign reveal a preoccupation with Hermeticism and related traditions. Partly this is because the obsession with purgation continues: the court represents an ideal Brunian–Hermetic world amid a larger Egypt whose people are being led astray by evil angels; partly it is because the mystical adoration of Charles and Henrietta Maria gave new impetus to the Mercurian symbolism which we have been tracing.

Jonson's last two masques, *Love's Triumph through Callipolis* and *Chloridia* (both 1631), exemplify some of these features. They are respectively the king's Christmas and queen's Shrovetide masques, and are complementary in ways that no masques had been previously. The king with his fourteen nobles is answered by the queen with her fourteen ladies; the king in his masque represents heroic love in contrast to love's furies who fail to understand the true nature of love and beauty, while the queen's masque is about love's fury (the rape of Chloris) becoming heroic love (the legitimation of Chloris as Flora and the consequent stellification of the earth with flowers to make it a second heaven). Moreover, in the king's masque Euclia sings 'an applausive song, or Pæan of the whole, which shee takes occasion to ingeminate in the second *Chorus*' (ll. 150–152). The device of doubling or ingemination suggests the zodiacal sign Gemini, whose symbolism was to be developed in later Caroline masques.[54] Gemini's tutelary god was Mercury, a point Jonson requires us to remember at the end when he compares the union of king and queen, rose and lily, in its peace-bringing qualities, to the caduceus: '*But to* Brit[t]aines Genius / *The snaky rod, and serpents of* Cyllenius / *Bring not more peace, then these, who so united be / By* Love' (ll. 214 ff.). Charles and his queen unite to become the Mercurian monarch,[55] and it is no accident that Jonson should have based *Love's Triumph* on Bruno's *De gli eroici furori*, for the Bruno of the *Heroic Frenzies* is little different from the reforming Bruno of *The Expulsion of the Triumphant Beast*. Both works date from his brief London period (1583–1585), and Jonson like Bruno implies the action of renewal through love and, in the purging of the diseased lovers from the city (ll. 84 ff.), an equivalent to the banishing of the vices in *The Expulsion*.[56] And so *Chloridia* celebrates the Mercurian spring world of a new creation, a world that is stellified after violent action (rape) and one which banishes the mischiefs released by a disgruntled Cupid who tries to unleash infernal spirits, tempests, and so forth, '*against the Earth, and the Goddesse* Chloris' in the antimasque. The image of a world purged of evil spirits is explicitly magical and prepares the way for *Coelum Britannicum* with its Brunian–Hermetic vision of a new world emerging after necessary violent reform. Mercury dominates *Love's Triumph*; Zephyrus participates in *Chloridia* and Iris, his female counterpart, is revealed towards the end, accompanying Juno, 'and above them many *aëry spirits*'. If Orgel and Strong are right in seeing thwarted Cupid's forces as images of civil war, then it is important that the spectators should see them banished by the power of the magician monarch.[57]

Even in Townshend's *Albion's Triumph* (8 January 1632), where the British theme dominates, the Hermetic–alchemical is well to the fore. The ostensible subject, the education of Charles–Albanactus into the nature of true love so that he might see his queen, Alba, is transparently metaphorical: Albanactus's city, Albipolis, suggests Virgil's 'Alban cities' in 'Latium, the Hesperian land' (*Aeneid*, VII. 601–602), and the western land itself tends to fuse mythologically, as in Spenser and Drayton, with the alchemical Hesperidean garden.[58] Alba is the white or silver goddess, complemented by Albanactus who, though dressed partly in silver, is mostly solar and golden: '*in a cuirass of yellow satin . . ., on his breast an angel's head embossed of gold . . ., on his head . . . an artificial wreath of laurel*' from which issued '*rays of gold*' (O and S, II. 456).[59] Once again we are with the alchemical king and queen whose union is the beginning and end of the alchemical quest. It is no surprise that the masque opens with Mercury, who approaches Alba after he has called up Orpheus, Amphion, and others with '*his charming rod*' (so that the whole masque is again given a Mercurian context); nor is it a surprise that it should end with a triumph of peace which is seen to be the effect of '*Hymen's twin, the Mary-Charles*' (O and S, II. 457), the true alchemical hermaphrodite.[60]

Magic is the theme of the queen's shrovetide masque *Tempe Restored*, the subject of which is the vanquishing of Circe who 'voluntarily delivers her golden rod to Minerva. So, all the enchantments being dissolved, Tempe, which for a time had been possessed by the voluntary beasts of Circe's court, is restored to the true followers of the muses' (O and S, II. 480). This is the expulsion of the triumphant beast,[61] so that it was almost inevitable that within two years Carew should have written his *Coelum Britannicum* (18 February 1634) to support, with the mysteries of Brunian Hermeticism, Charles's threatened absolutism.[62]

Before considering *Coelum Britannicum*, however, we should pause over James Shirley's *The Triumph of Peace* (3 February 1634), commissioned to celebrate the birth of James, Duke of York. Although it contains no Brunian Hermeticism it does once more present us with an alchemical setting: a first antimasque of projectors (the second, third, and fourth of whom possess alchemical or magical powers) symbolically anticipates the alchemical theme of the masque proper which is announced by the appearance of '*a chariot feigned of goldsmiths' work*' bearing Irene (Peace) dressed like Flora '*in a flowery vesture like the spring*' (O and S, II. 551). She calls on Eunomia and Dicē–Astraea, thus initiating the manifestation of true gold in the form of the Golden Age. Irene's golden chariot, together with Eunomia's silver chariot and Dicē's '*white robe* ... [*and*] *coronet of silver pikes*', recall the alchemical conjunction of sun and moon, perhaps symbolised also in the 'rose and lily', which, as Eunomia says, addressing Irene, 'thou strowest / All the cheerful way thou goest' (O and S, *ibid.*). The 'rose and lily', emblems of the king and queen, mark the flowering of the Golden Age, and the masque culminates in the figure of '*a Genius or angelical person, with* ... *a small white rod in his hand*' (O and S, II. 552), to whom is entrusted the final speech in which he presents 'the sons of Peace' to the royal pair. As champion of peace and with his white, caduceus-like, rod Genius gives a Mercurian cast to *The Triumph of Peace*, acting out as he does the 'hieroglyphic' implications of the '*caduceus* with an olive-branch' depicted in a compartment on the proscenium arch (O and S, II. 547).

Shirley's alchemical and Mercurian masque, which has Dicē, confronted with the dazzling splendour of Charles and Henrietta Maria, expressing doubts as to whether she is 'in earth or heaven' (O and S, II. 551), is the last logical step, after the Circe myth of *Tempe Restored*, to the Brunian Hermetics of *Coelum Britannicum* where Carew portrays a king and queen so powerful in their love that their example persuades Jove to reform heaven. Just as Bruno's Jove in his old age purges heaven of the stellar-embodied vices on the anniversary of the Gigantomachia so, according to Carew's Momus (taken over as a key figure from *The Expulsion*), the Jove of *Coelum Britannicum* 'grown old and fearful, apprehends a subversion of his empire, and doubts lest Fate should introduce a legal succession in the legitimate heir by repossessing the Titanian line' (O and S, II. 572). Bruno's *Expulsion* aimed at a reformed pan-Christian empire of love;[63] *Coelum Britannicum*, after identifying the forces of rebellion with the giants and Titans (as had Spenser in his Brunian *Cantos of Mutabilitie*), locates the centre of this reformed empire in '*Windsor Castle, the famous seat of the most honourable Order of the Garter*' and the pattern of love offered by Charles and Henrietta Maria:

> But O you royal turtles, shed,
> When you from earth remove,
> On the ripe fruits of your chaste bed,
> Those sacred seeds of love,

Which no power can but yours dispense,
Since you the pattern bear from hence.

Then from your fruitful race shall flow
Endless succession. . . . (O and S, II. 580)

More than any other single masque Carew's embodies the themes that are the subject of this book, not only in its Hermetic (Brunian) framework[64] but in the primacy it gives to Mercury, its preoccupation with astronomical/astrological compliment, and its acknowledgement of the alchemical basis of the Charles–Maria cult. The opening '*Description of the Scene*', for instance, directs attention to the two royal *imprese*, the king's 'lion with an imperial crown on his head' and that of 'the Queen's majesty, a lily growing with branches and leaves, and three lesser lilies springing out of the stem' (O and S, II. 570). Heraldically, the lion recalls the Trojan founder of Britain, Brutus, depicted, for example, at the top left of the frontispiece to Drayton's *Poly-Olbion* (1612) bearing on his shield '*In a Golden field the Lion passantred*':[65] this is to be a masque about the restoration of the ancient British virtues in the way that Bruno's *Expulsion*, following the *Asclepian* lament, is about the restoration of the old Egyptian religion. As in Spenser, too, restoration means a return to the pristine virtues and religion, except that whereas in *The Faerie Queene* the Egyptian theme had prominence in Carew, as in Drayton, there is a characteristic seventeenth-century predilection for Druidism. As I shall argue in Chapter IV, for royalists and republicans alike the Druids became a symbol of the Golden-Age religion and ancient liberties, a domestic version of the Brunian nostalgia for the lost Egyptian religion. Carew's masque is fascinating because it is, so far as I know, the only work of the period in which explicit Brunian Hermetics combine with the British myth and a significant appearance of Druids to confirm the mysterious and magical nature of the modern British kingdom.

Emblematically, of course, Charles's lion suggests the imperial virtues of prudence, clemency, and fortitude;[66] yet it is also astrological, identifying Charles as Leo and the just sun king of righteousness,[67] complemented by his lily-white queen. The alchemical sun and moon thus preside once more over this masque.[68] They are, as we discover at the end when Charles and Henrietta Maria, together with those who 'with industrious steps / In the fair prints [their] virtuous feet have made, / Though with unequal paces, follow [them]' are stellified and elevated to the vacant eighth sphere, the 'lights in the firmament of the heaven' of

Genesis 1: 14 ff. bringing light to darkness and announcing the new creation that is in a very real sense the subject of *Coelum Britannicum*.[69] The end of the masque reminds us yet again of Charles's solar supremacy and of the 'let there be light' of Genesis when the Chorus of Druids and Rivers announces

> We see at once in dead of night
> A sun appear, and yet a bright
> Noonday springing from starlight. (O and S, II. 578)

'Noonday' inevitably recalls the *sol iustitiae* and Bruno's *Expulsion*, whose Jove meditates the reform of the heavens (that is, internal as well as external reform) 'not after supper and during the Night of Inconsideration, and without the Sun of Intelligence and Light of Reason . . . [but] around noon, or at the point of noon, that is, when Hostile Error least outrages us and Friendly Truth most favours us, during the period of a more lucid interval. Then is expelled the triumphant beast, that is, the vices which predominate and are wont to tread upon the divine side . . .'.[70] Hence, too, the elaborate banishing of the solstitial sign Cancer in *Coelum Britannicum*:

> Look up and mark where the bright zodiac
> Hangs like a belt about the breast of heaven;
> On the right shoulder, like a flaming jewel,
> His shell with nine rich topazes adorned,
> Lord of this tropic, sits the scalding Crab;
> He, when the sun gallops in full career
> His annual race, his ghastly claws upreared,
> Frights at the confines of the torrid zone
> The fiery team, and proudly stops their course. . . . (O and S, II. 573)

Not only does Cancer stop the sun; it makes the planet retrograde, and so the second antimasque '*is danced in retrograde paces*' to signify the grave political implications of solar retrogression. The Crab is deposed by Mercury 'from his lofty throne' because he threatens the throne of the sun king, while in Brunian terms its deposition signifies the advent of 'Righteous Conversion, Repression of Evil, [and] Retraction from the false and iniquitous'.[71]

From one anthropomorphic point of view the solstices can be seen as a hubristic attempt to stop time and reverse it. This appears to be the view adopted by Carew, since he supplies in this masque the divine alternative in the legitimately time-stopping figure of Eternity, '*bearing in his hand a serpent bent into a circle, with his tail in his mouth*' (O and S, II. 579). We have met the ouroboros before, entwined round the legs of

Spenser's hermaphroditic Venus, and we recall Macrobius's remark that it symbolised universal cycles.[72] Here, since Eternity extols the virtues of the 'royal pair, for whom Fate will / Make motion cease and time stand still', we must presumably extend the application of the serpent emblem to Charles and Henrietta Maria themselves. They are the eternal hermaphrodite whose emblem has to be the serpent because, in addition, they now take on the aspect of Mercury's caduceus. This last point is announced, significantly, by Concord (Homonoia; traditionally associated with Mercury), who says of the royal couple: 'And as their own pure souls entwined, / So are their subjects' hearts combined' (O and S, II. 579), which suggests that they are the entwined serpents of the caduceus become one and cancelling out the *serpents' tongues* of sceptical and satirical Momus (O and S, II. 571).[73] Mercury, with his caduceus, had disappeared from the action at line 881, as attention moved from him, as virtuous banisher of vices, to the masque's complementary embodiments of virtue, the king and queen. He and his rod embodied potentially, in emblem, the pacific and other powers that the king and queen make real. We should, too, regard Mercury as being associated with the *'young man in a white embroidered robe . . . holding in his hand a cornucopia filled with corn and fruits, representing the genius of these kingdoms'*. For the commonplace of the burgeoning of the earth in times of peace was a Mercurian *topos*: Cartari discusses the notion of 'peace the friend of Ceres' under the heading 'Mercury'.[74]

When he descends at the beginning of the masque, accompanied by his traditional cockerel[75] and carrying his caduceus, Mercury approaches the king and queen: 'From the high senate of the gods to you / Bright glorious twins of love and majesty, / . . . Come I, Cyllenius, Jove's ambassador' (O and S, II. 571). 'Twins' immediately establishes the couple as Gemini. And yet, since they embody virtue and the original twins were the result of Jove's rape of Leda, Charles and Henrietta Maria may represent a purified Gemini even before heaven's purification is announced by Mercury.[76] Indeed, they are the cause of it, as Mercury reveals in Carew's most outrageous hyperbole: 'When in the crystal mirror of your reign / [Jove] viewed himself, he found his loathsome stains' and so decided to embark on his programme of reform. Moreover, Mercury (and hence the Mercurian monarch) imposes peace. This ties in neatly with Bruno's scheme in *The Expulsion* where the malign aspects of constellations are banished and the benign preserved, for Bruno identifies the malign particularly with martial wrath and the benign with temperate and redemptive love.[77] The tableau at the opening of *Coelum*

Britannicum, then, is Brunian in its revelation of the monarchs of love triumphant over 'warlike nations' (l. 47), but it is Brunian Hermeticism modified to accommodate the tradition of the Mercurian monarch that the Stuarts inherited from Spenserian monarchical panegyric.

The climax of the masque comes with '*the prospect of Windsor Castle*' and the stellification of the masquers (including the king) into '*a troop of fifteen stars*' (O and S, II. 579). Elizabeth's Garter Festivals had taken place in London on April 23, and their emphasis had been on public spectacle. For Charles Garter ceremonial was more a religious than a public matter and became an instrument of High Anglicanism.[78] A 1629 medal celebrated the Order with the motto 'The glory of an ancient order augmented', suggesting a return to and reform of the church's ancient strengths.[79] As Carew celebrates it, however, it becomes the Order of Hermetic reform, its members the stellified virtues who inhabit the eighth sphere of spiritual rebirth.[80] While the total of fifteen stars does not just signify the king and his fourteen nobles (the usual number of masquers), but is the Ptolemaic total for the constellation Aquila (Eagle), as Carew would have known from *The Expulsion* if from nowhere else. Aquila is the Brunian 'symbol of Empire', 'a divine and heroic bird' (it is, after all, the bird of Jupiter).[81] It is clear from this how Carew wishes us to view the renewed Garter. It supersedes 'Prince Arthur, or the brave / Saint George himself' (ll. 1030–1031), who are themselves seen to symbolically depend upon the choric Druids, to realise the secular and religous empire that even Elizabeth had only half achieved, and the alchemical symbolism in the masque states in addition the Garter's superiority to the celebrated Burgundian Order of the Golden Fleece with its inevitable alchemical overtones.[82] It is for this reason in part that Carew employs the familiar motif of gold and silver (or white) and of Britain as the Hesperides: 'These are th' Hesperian bowers, whose fair trees bear / Rich golden fruit, and yet no dragon near' (O and S, II. 578).[83] The dragon-beast has been expelled astrologically from heaven's 'azure concave' by Mercury near the beginning (O and S, II. 573). We are now to understand its complete expulsion through the Order of dragon-killing George, which then releases the 'Rich golden fruit' of spiritual and imperial renovation. Alchemically, of course, the destroyed dragon is the emblem of putrefaction from which new life emerges. The dragon of corruption and the dragon of renewal are often shown embracing or intertwined in a manner recalling the serpents on Mercury's caduceus.[84] It is not unlikely that Carew offers this analogy, too, to imply the ultimate complexity of his vision of his Mercurian-alchemical-Garter sovereign.

Davenant's remaining masques for the Caroline court eschew Carew's Hermeticism for a simpler assertion of royal virtue. Nevertheless, emphasis is still placed on magic as a key to monarchical power, as in *The Temple of Love* (February 1635), in many ways a supreme expression of Caroline neo-Platonism. Here Divine Poesy, who has obscured the Temple of Chaste Love so that it cannot be abused by certain black magicians, announces that the time has come for the revealing of the Temple and its establishment in Britain through the beauty of Indamora, the queen of Narsinga, who arrives, like Venus on a scallop shell, in a maritime chariot. Her arrival is prepared for by Orpheus, who is accompanied by Brahmins. In *The Triumph of Peace* (February 1634) Shirley had, in familiar fashion, opposed false Fancy and Mercurian Genius. Davenant turns this into an opposition of ancient philosophical wisdom (the *prisci theologi*) and black magic, combining it with the theme of the Mercurian monarch when, at the Temple of Chaste Love, Sunesis and Thelema (Understanding and Will) 'unite [to] become one virtuous appetite' and an emblem of Chaste Love, the 'pattern of [whose] union' may be seen in the king and queen 'in yonder throne' (O and S, II. 604). This is the alchemical hermaphrodite again, since the male Sunesis, dressed in cloth of gold, represents Charles in his solar role as divine intelligence, while the female Thelema represents the lunar principle, '*in a robe of changeable silk . . . and great leaves of silver about her shoulders*'. Together they embody the achieving of the alchemical work through contemplation of the divine, in opposition to the false alchemists of the fourth antimasque entry and the black magicians of sensuality and voluptuousness. In terms of the monarch–magus theme, the latter symbolise the self-deception and ignorance which the hermaphrodite vanquishes through contemplative wisdom; so that the revelation of the Temple of Chaste Love with its enthroned Mercurian hermaphroditic twins marks the end of the black magicians' sovereignty which has itself, we realise, been a claim to Mercurian sovereignty. As the second magician asks the third magician near the beginning: 'art / Thou not within thy circle still a sovereign prince? / When thou dost lift with magic power thy white / Enchanted sceptre thus, do not the thin / Unbodied people bow and obey?' (O and S, II. 601); a question which, in drawing attention to the whiteness of the rod, indicates that he has appropriated Mercury's traditionally white caduceus. These magicians are vainly devoted to perpetuating those very clouds of moral and spiritual obfuscation that it is the function of Mercury and his caduceus to dispel and that are dispelled in the coming together and fusion of Sunesis and Thelema, king and queen.[85]

Similar themes are present in *Britannia Triumphans* (17 January 1638), which celebrates the royal twins in its concluding 'Valediction' in which every lady dreams she has 'stolen a beam' from 'that chief beauty', the queen, and every lover that he has stolen the king's 'vigour, love, and truth'; and since the king acts the part of Britanocles, 'the glory of the western world' (O and S, II. 662), we are – albeit implicitly – in the realm of the alchemical Hesperidean monarch who controls the chaos of ocean through the magical power of his trident, maritime equivalent to the sceptre of terrestrial empire.[86] Moreover, Britanocles also dispels the 'clouds of error' to become the Mercurian monarch with sceptre-caduceus:

> O thou our cheerful morning, rise
> And straight those misty clouds of error clear,
> Which long have overcast our eyes,
> And else will darken all this hemisphere:
>
> What to thy power is hard or strange?
> Since not alone confined unto the land,
> Thy sceptre to a trident change,
> And straight unruly seas thou canst command! (O and S, II. 666)

The masque's main argument is the assertion of the permanence and validity of virtue and wisdom and its flowering in Charles's court. The protagonist is Action and the antagonist Imposture, who attempts to prove that 'imposture governs all, even from / The gilded ethnic mitre to the painted staff / O'th'Christian constable' (O and S, II. 662). Merlin soon enters, '*in his hand a silvered rod*' (the masque is evidently an exposition of the variety of staffs of office and their interrelationships), to see 'how nature's face is changed / Since his decease'. Imposture uses his magic power to summon up the spirits of 'the great seducers of this isle', who follow in six infernal antimasques terminating in '*rebellious leaders in war*', Cade, Kett, and Jack Straw. These yield to the traditionally virtuous Bellerophon, dispeller of the illusive chimaera and the first bridler of horses.[87] As dispeller of illusions he takes on a quasi-Mercurian role, as his subsequent identification with Mercurian reason makes clear when he is angered by Imposture's 'cunning disguise [of his] sense / In reason's shape' (O and S, II. 664). The conflict, as in earlier masques, is between heaven-sent reason (Bellerophon is riding Pegasus) and the clouds of error and ignorance. Only when the intellect is dulled can the phantoms of black magic flourish within the individual and the demons of civil war proliferate in the realm. We note that '*the ornament that enclosed the scene*', and so mutely commented on the action throughout, included the figure of Right Government holding a book and sceptre, '*his foot treading on the head of a serpent*' (O and S, II. 662). For government depends on right reason and contemplation (the book), and this personification's Mercurian qualities again reflect on Charles–Britanocles, one of the culminating emblems of whose reign is the Palace of Fame, in which is Science, '*on her head a band with little wings like those of Mercury, and a scroll of parchment in her hand*' (O and S, II. 666). She suggests the time-worn theme of the monarch as custodian of the liberal arts, of which Mercury is patron,[88] and cancels out Merlin, Imposture's magician, with his 'mysterious books'. But, as we saw in connection with Book III of *The Faerie Queene*, Merlin is an ambiguous figure, to be used for ill or good. To have identified him completely with Imposture would have been to dissociate Charles from the Arthurian roots of the Britanocles–western kingdom myth.[89] And so at the end a '*chorus of our own modern poets*' is 'raised to life by Merlin's might' to sing the queen's praises. The masque's simple narrative and thematic structure reveals a continuing preoccupation with the Mercurian magician king.

The last court masque, *Salmacida Spolia* (21 January 1640), again articulates its theme, the quelling of civil discord by the king's 'secret wisdom' (O and S, II. 730), through the paraphernalia of magic. Discord is announced by darkness, storms, uptorn trees, a tempestuous sea, and a globe (image of the world), which, having burst into flames, '*was turned into a Fury, her hair upright, mixed with snakes. . . . In her hand she brandished a sable torch*'. If the world is given over to discord, she says, why should Britain, this 'over-lucky, too-much-happy isle' not succumb? And she promptly invokes a 'horrid sullen brood / Of evil spirits [to] displace the good' (O and S, II. 731). The Fury is based on Virgil's Allecto (*Aeneid*, VII. 324 ff.), who is released against Aeneas by Juno though, significantly, she knows that even the forces of hell cannot prevent Aeneas's accession to the throne of Latium, the long-sought western land. Davenant's Fury's torch, an attribute of Allecto, is perhaps the parody sceptre of this masque, equivalent to the black magician's wand; while her poisonous snakes are the chthonic antitype to Resolution's serpent wound round her sword blade, who features on the masque's frontispiece. She is thus the mute Mercurian comment on the masque's action as Right Government had been in *Britannia Triumphans*, her serpent-encircled sword recalling the caduceus as well

8 Royalist soldier as Mercury

as the serpent of prudence and wisdom (the king's 'secret wisdom').[90]

This last of the court masques, then, fuses magic and *Aeneid*-western-land themes as it anticipates and tries to fend off the threat of civil strife. Allecto's speciality is civil war (*Aeneid*, VII. 335 ff.), and in the *Aeneid* the bloody consequences of her infernal magic will not easily be quelled. In *Salmacida Spolia*, on the other hand, they are immediately dispelled:

> ... *the scene changed into a calm; the sky serene; afar off Zephyrus appeared breathing a gentle gale; in the landscape were cornfields and pleasant trees sustaining vines fraught with grapes, and in some of the furthest parts villages, with all such things as might express a country in peace, rich and fruitful.*

Pax Cereris amica: another assertion of the monarch's Mercurian power. For Zephyrus, we recall, often doubled for Mercury in his role of spring god. A silver chariot next appears, bearing the Mercurian virtue of Concord and the Good Genius of Great Britain, which have their visual and thematic counterpart towards the end of the masque when the solar monarch[91] is revealed in '*the Throne of Honour, his majesty highest in a seat of gold*', to be joined by his queen who is identified with the moon in the fourth song (O and S, II. 733):

> But what is she that rules the night,
> That kindles ladies with her light
> And gives to men the power of sight?

The opening stanza of this song advises astronomers 'that so wisely studious are / To measure and to trace each star' to turn their telescopes to earth since the chief stellar influences have descended there – a last hint, via Carew, of the Brunian descent of the constellations.

I have, however, omitted the most obvious pointer to the masque's alchemical–magical preoccupations. After Genius and Concord have lamented the present 'sullen age, / When it is harder far to cure / The people's folly than resist their rage' (O and S, II. 731), there is a second antimasque, the first and most elaborate entry of which presents '*Wolfgangus Vandergoose, spagyric, operator to the Invisible Lady styled the Magical Sister of the Rosicross*' (who appears herself in entry 10, at the sovereign centre of the twenty antimasque entries). Vandergoose brings with him '*receipts ... to cure the defects of nature and diseases of the mind*'. We are back with the apparent anti-Rosicrucian satire of Jonson's *Fortunate Isles* which had celebrated the forthcoming union of Charles and Henrietta Maria. Here as there the 'new' Rosicrucianism can be mocked because it is an unworthy imitation of the true bearer of the rosy cross, the Garter sovereign with his divinely ordained magical power. Royal magic, the 'secret wisdom' of the Mercurian king, is the only permissible wisdom; all other kinds are mere pretenders to wisdom. And yet the alchemical Mercurian monarch seems to have retained such a hold even on the imagination of Puritans that they perpetuated him almost in spite of themselves. Thus John Harris's short-lived Leveller newspaper, the *Mercurius Militaris* of 1648, reformulated the concept only slightly when it stated in its first issue that the 'King is an Alchemist, and the Lords are his Mercury'.[92]

Notes

1 Stephen Orgel and Roy Strong, *Inigo Jones: the Theatre of the Stuart Court*, 2 vols. (London, Berkeley and Los Angeles: Sotheby Parke Bernet and Univ. of California Press, 1973), I. 13. See also Orgel's *The Illusion of Power: Political Theater in the Renaissance* (London and Los Angeles: Univ. of California Press, 1975), p. 56: 'when magic appears in the masques, it is regularly counteracted not by an alternative sorcery, black magic defeated by white magic, but by the clear voice of reason, constancy, heroism'. This view is in many ways right but has led to underestimation of the magical content of the masques. For Bacon's tantalising affinities with magic see, e.g., Harold Fisch, *Jerusalem and Albion: the Hebraic Factor in Seventeenth-Century Literature* (London: Routledge and Kegan Paul, 1964), ch. VI; Frances Yates, *The Rosicrucian Enlightenment* (St Albans: Paladin edn, 1975), ch. IX; and Paolo Rossi, *Francis Bacon: from Magic to Science*, tr. S. Rabinovitch (London: Routledge and Kegan Paul, 1968).

2 The background has been indispensably filled in by Frances Yates, *Theatre of the World* (London: Routledge and Kegan Paul, 1969). Agrippa, *Three Books*, II. i discusses the relationship between magic and the mechanical arts and the power to produce wonder; and see also Peter French, *John Dee*, p. 58.

3 E.g., Orgel, *The Jonsonian Masque* (Cambridge, Mass.: Harvard U.P., 1965), pp. 26–28, 32–33.

4 Macrobius, *Saturnalia*, I. vii. 19–26 (tr. Davies, pp. 58–59). For Janus's solar attributes, see *ibid.*, I. ix. 9–10 (p. 67). The *Aeneid* reference is to VIII. 357–358. The symbolism of renewal was accentuated by the fact of James's accession on 24 March 1603, the day before the spring new year date of 25 March, a point that did not escape the notice of his panegyrists: e.g., Thomas Goodrick's congratulatory poem 'Upon occasion offered by the Time and Season of the Yeare, when the Crowne by due descent fell unto our most gratious and Soveraigne Lord the King'; reprinted from *Sorrowes Joy* (1603) in John Nichols, *The Progresses, Processions, and Magnificent Festivities, of King James the First*, 4 vols. (London, 1828), I. 6. For 25 March as a new year date, see R. L. Poole, 'The Beginning of the

Year in the Middle Ages', *Proceedings of the British Academy*, 10 (1921–23); and for the interchangeability in this respect of January and March (with a defence of January), the 'generall argument' to Spenser's *Shepherd's Calendar* (1579). For March as the month of the creation of the world, see *New Calendar of 1561*, cit. Alexander Dunlop, 'The Unity of Spenser's *Amoretti*', in A. D. S. Fowler (ed.), *Silent Poetry: Essays in Numerological Analysis* (London: Routledge and Kegan Paul, 1970), p. 167, n. 5. It is worth noting that an Egyptian Mercury 'with two heads like Janus' featured in Charles IX's 1571 Paris entry: V. E. Graham and W. McAllister Johnson, *The Paris Entries of Charles IX and Elisabeth of Austria 1571* (Toronto and Buffalo: Univ. of Toronto Press, 1974), p. 140.

5   Quotations from the edn by Joan Rees in T. J. B. Spenser and Stanley Wells (eds), *A Book of Masques* (Cambridge: C.U.P., 1970), pp. 19–42. My comments on the masque complement Geoffrey Creigh's 'Samuel Daniel's "The Vision of the Twelve Goddesses" ', *Essays and Studies*, n.s. 24 (1971), 22–35.

6   See ch. I, n. 59 above.

7   Linche, *Fountaine of Ancient Fiction*, sig. Qii^{v}: Mercury is 'the messenger of the gods: of which office also there were two sorts held and observed . . . the one was executed by Mercurie, and the other by Iris' (cf. Cartari, *Imagini*, pp. 310–312).

8   In Philostratus, *Imagines*, I. xxvii the god of dreams 'carries a horn, showing that he brings up his dreams through the gate of truth' (i.e. the gate of horn); tr. Arthur Fairbanks, Loeb edn (London: Heinemann; New York: Putnam's, 1931), p. 107. Mercury is linked with Night and Sleep because the ancients held it 'an odious thing . . . to spend the whole night in sleepe and drowsie cogitations. And therefore Mercurie was often taken for that light of knowledge, & spirit of understanding, which guides men to the true conceavement of darke and engimaticall sentences. And yet notwithstanding, naturall and seasonable rest and repose was altogether also in those times allowed as the refresher of mens wits' (Linche, sigs. Ri^{r}-^{v}).

9   Agrippa, *Three Books*, II. i, p. 167.

10 For example, D. C. Allen, 'Ben Jonson and the Hieroglyphics', *PQ*, 18 (1939), 290–300; E. W. Talbert, 'The Interpretation of Jonson's Courtly Spectacles', *PMLA*, 61 (1946), 454–473; and D. J. Gordon's brilliant series of articles: 'The Imagery of Ben Jonson's *The Masque of Blacknesse* and *The Masque of Beautie*', *JWCI*, 6 (1943), 122–141; '*Hymenæi*: Ben Jonson's Masque of Union', *JWCI*, 8 (1945), 107–145; and 'Ben Jonson's "Haddington Masque": the Story and the Fable', *MLR*, 42 (1947), 180–187. Also M.-T. Jones-Davies, *Inigo Jones, Ben Jonson et le Masque* (Paris: Didier, 1967), ch. V; J. C. Meagher, *Method and Meaning in Jonson's Masques* (Indiana: Univ. of Notre Dame Press, 1966); and Mary Chan, *Music in the Theatre of Ben Jonson* (Oxford: Clarendon Press, 1980), chs. V and VI. A sympathetic and informed account of Jonson's ridicule of occultism is J. S. Mebane's 'Renaissance Magic and the Return

of the Golden Age: Utopianism and Religious Enthusiasm in *The Alchemist', Renaissance Drama*, n.s. 10 (1979), 117–139.

11   Quotations from *The Works of Ben Jonson*, ed. C. H. Herford and P. and E. M. Simpson, 11 vols. (Oxford: Clarendon Press, 1925–52). The masques are in vol. VII (1941).

12   Chaucer, *House of Fame*, III. 1352; Agrippa, I. xxviii, p. 59 for venerean emeralds and saphires; *ibid.*, ch. xxiii, pp. 51–52 on ruby and carbuncle. For the Burgundian–Tudor tradition of such houses/palaces, see Gordon Kipling, *The Triumph of Honour: Burgundian Origins of the Elizabethan Renaissance* (The Hague: Leiden U.P., 1977), pp. 106–108 and 113–115 (the latter drawing attention to this Jonson-Jones instance).

13   For the Garter, see below, nn. 78 and 82. I follow the views of Roy Strong ('Inigo Jones and the Revival of Chivalry', *Apollo*, 88 (1967), 102–107) and Frances Yates (*Shakespeare's Last Plays: a New Approach* (London: Routledge and Kegan Paul, 1975), ch. I) on the chivalric revival surrounding Prince Henry. For reservations concerning Jonson, see Norman Council, 'Ben Jonson, Inigo Jones, and the Transformation of Tudor Chivalry', *ELH*, 47 (1980), 259–275.

14   The most convenient guide, with bibliography, to these prophecies which originate with Geoffrey of Monmouth, *History*, VII. 1–4, is Keith Thomas's *Religion and the Decline of Magic*, ch. XIII.

15   R. H. Allen, *Star Names*, p. 101 citing John of Trevisa. For Ursa–Arcturus symbolism, see above, ch. I, sec. iii.

16   For the anagram Charles James Steuart-Claims Arthurs seat, see William Camden, *Remains concerning Britain* (London, 1870 edn), p. 185, and R. F. Brinkley, *Arthurian Legend in the Seventeenth Century* (London: Frank Cass, 1967 edn), ch. I.

17   *Expulsion*, ed. Imerti, p. 80. We should also recall Diodorus Siculus's comment (V. xxi. 6) that Britain lies under Ursa Major. See ch. IV, sec. iii below.

18   Text from Nichols, *Progresses . . . of King James*, II. 291 ff. There is a useful discussion in D. M. Bergeron, *English Civic Pageantry 1558–1642* (London: Edward Arnold, 1971), pp. 92–94. Bergeron's juxtaposition of quotations reminds us implicitly that one of the masque's topics is the vanquishing of Envy's snakes by the peaceful snakes of Mercury (cf. the opening of ch. I, sec. vii above). There is a possible earlier instance of the Mercury theme in Jonson's *Highgate* entertainment: see below, ch. III. But if I am right in suspecting that the Mercurian theme developed under Elizabeth, it is understandable that it should have been associated with Henry, since he remained a posthumous symbol of Protestant reform as late as 1624: e.g., Margot Heinemann, *Puritanism and Theatre: Thomas Middleton and Opposition Drama under the Early Stuarts* (Cambridge: Cambridge U.P., 1980), pp. 130–131. Mercury's potency under Elizabeth and potential in connection with Henry show good reason for his adoption by James and then by Charles, who modified him into a symbol of Anglo-Catholicism.

19   Nichols, *Progresses . . . of King James*, pp. 320–321. The 1610 works

celebrate Henry's creation as Prince of Wales.

20 A detailed analysis of the alchemical symbolism of this masque is given by E. H. Duncan, 'The Alchemy in Jonson's *Mercury Vindicated*', *SP*, 39 (1942), 625–637. See esp. p. 633 on the caduceus as ' "the gold of the philosophers" and the entwining serpents [as] the male and female . . . principles. The caduceus becomes thus a symbol for the stone itself and for the power over the ordinary processes of nature the alchemists believed possession of the stone would give them'. For Vulcan, see Paracelsus, *Selected Writings*, ed. Jacobi, tr. Guterman (1951), p. 218: 'Alchemy is a necessary, indispensable art. . . . It is an art, and Vulcan is its artist'; for Prometheus as 'the first Statuary or Image-maker, which expressed a man to the life, as if he had animated it with Cœlestial fire', see Ross, *Mystagogus Poeticus*, p. 368, and Olga Raggio, 'The Myth of Prometheus: its Survival and Metamorphoses up to the Eighteenth Century', *JWCI*, 21 (1958), 44–62, esp. p. 47 and plates (Prometheus and Vulcan, Prometheus and Mercury) and p. 52 and plate 7d for Prometheus as sculptor and magus. From the Hermetic/Egyptian point of view, Raggio's citation of Diodorus Siculus, I. xix. 1 on Prometheus as an Egyptian governor at the time of Osiris is significant. Leah S. Marcus notes the identification of James as 'Favonius, father of the spring' in *The Vision of Delight* (1617) but without making the further connection with Mercury as spring god: ' "Present Occasions" and the Shaping of Ben Jonson's Masques', *ELH*, 45 (1978), 212.

21 For Arthur–Hesperus see Anglo, *Spectacle, Pageantry, and Early Tudor Policy*, pp. 79–81 where, however, the connection between Hesperus and Mercury is not noticed (on this see *The 'Anticlaudian' of Alain de Lille*, tr. W. H. Cornog (Philadelphia, Pa. 1935), II. iii, p. 68, and IV. vi, pp. 100–101). There may be implications of Hesperus–James's identification with ultimate Justice, described as 'beautiful beyond the beauty of Evening' in Plotinus, *Enneads*, I. vi. 4 (tr. Stephen MacKenna, 4th edn, rev. B. S. Page (London: Faber, 1969), p. 59).

22 '. . . that power from which comes speech has received the name Mercury; and, since speech is the expression of inward thoughts, this god is appropriately called Hermes, from the Greek word *Hermēneuein*, to put into words': Macrobius, *Saturnalia*, I. xvii. 5 (tr. Davies, pp. 114–115); Diodorus Siculus, I. xvi. 2.

23 *Three Books*, II. i, p. 168; Aristotle, *Politics*, 1253B (I. ii. 5).

24 *Works*, ed. Herford and Simpson, X. 604.

25 *Saturnalia*, I. xxii. 4 and xxi. 9 (pp. 147 and 142).

26 Linche, *Fountaine of Ancient Fiction*, sig. Ki, and see ch. I, sec. viii above.

27 Plotinus, *Enneads*, VI. ix. 8, as cited by Wind, *Pagan Mysteries*, p. 209.

28 Wind, p. 191; Pico della Mirandola, *Opera omnia*, facs, of Basel, 1572 edn, ed. Eugenio Garin, 2 vols. (Turin, 1971), I. 107 (Frustra adit naturam & Protheum, qui Pana non attraxerit).

29 I have used the Urquhart–Motteux transln, Everyman edn, 2 vols. (London and New York, 1949–1950). The identification of Bacchus with Osiris gives a subdued Egyptian cast to this masque: Plutarch, *De Is. et*

Os., 356A–B, noting that Osiris civilised Egypt and the rest of the world, giving laws 'without the slightest need of arms' (Loeb edn, p. 35). See also Diodorus Siculus, I. xiii. 5. *Ibid.*, I. xvi. 3 notes that Osiris left Hermes with Isis as a counsellor-substitute for himself when he left Egypt. (At I. xv. 16 we are told that Osiris consulted with Hermes on every matter.) On Rabelais and the *Hermetica*, see, e.g., M. A. Screech, *Rabelais* (London: Duckworth, 1979), pp. 90 ff. Other appearances of the oracular bottle in Jonson are listed by Huntington Brown, 'Ben Jonson and Rabelais', *MLN*, 44 (1929), 6–13.

30 For Bacchus as eternal youth, see, e.g., Ovid, *Metamorphoses*, IV. 18 (Tu puer aeternus). It is possible that Hermeticism underlies the Egyptian theme of *The Gypsies Metamorphosed*, so ably discussed from other points of view by D. B. J. Randall, *Jonson's Gypsies Unmasked: Background and Theme of 'The Gypsies Metamorphos'd'* (Durham, N.C.: Duke U.P., 1975).

31 Greek *makaria* = bliss, felicity (hence isles of the blest). Macaria appears as the goddess of felicity complete with caduceus in Daniel's *Vision of the Twelve Goddesses* and is the name of the ideal land 'not far distant from Utopia' in More's *Utopia*. For its importance as the name of the ideal Christian society with Hartlib and others, see Yates, *Rosicrucian Enlightenment*, pp. 191 n., 195, and 217, also *Giordano Bruno*, pp. 185 ff., 233, 370 ff. For the background to the tradition, see J. W. Bennett, 'Britain among the Fortunate Isles', *SP*, 53 (1956), 114–140.

32 See above, ch. I, n. 32. For the alchemical queen holding lilies, see S. K. Heninger, Jr., *The Cosmographical Glass: Renaissance Diagrams of the Universe* (San Marino, Calif.: Huntington Library, 1977), pp. 183–184, and Jung, *Psychology and Alchemy*, pp. 272 ff.; and for the lily and rose motif celebrating the royal wedding, Roy Strong, *Van Dyck: Charles I on Horseback* (London: Allen Lane, 1972), pp. 70–71 and 104 n.76.

33 There is earlier anti-Rosicrucian satire in *News from the New World discovered in the Moon* (1620) and *The Masque of Augurs* (1622). Jonson's familiarity with Rosicrucian work is discussed by, e.g., Percy Simpson, 'The Castle of the Rosy Cross: Ben Jonson and Theophilus Schweighardt', *MLR*, 41 (1946), 206–207, and Yates, *Rosicrucian Enlightenment*, p. 182, which makes the indispensable point that Jonson's anti-Rosicrucianism should be related to his pro-James and anti-Protestant-extremist attitudes. My argument in this section follows Yates in assuming a connection between Rosicrucianism and the Order of the Garter.

34 For the possibility of calling up the dead, see Agrippa, III. xlii, '*By what wayes the Magicians and Necromancers do think they can call forth the souls of the dead*'.

35 Ptolemy, *Tetrabiblos*, III. xiii.

36 Klibansky, Panofsky, Saxl, *Saturn and Melancholy*, pp. 127, 187, 397, etc.; Jean Seznec, *The Survival of the Pagan Gods*, tr. Barbara F. Sessions (1961), p. 47. Venus too presided over the first age of man (*ibid.*). For Mercury, Jupiter, and Venus moderating Saturn, see ch. I, n. 75 above.

37 *Works*, II. 329.

38 *Ibid.*, X. 670; Agrippa, III. xxiv, p. 415.

39 For the grades of melancholy and the revelations open to them, see ch. I, n. 25. Jophiel [*sic*] is connected with cherubim and the zodiac in Agrippa, II. xiii, p. 214. For the function of cherubim, see Pseudo Dionysius, *Celestial Hierarchy*, 205C, etc.

40 Yates, *Rosicrucian Enlightenment, passim* (but esp. ch. I). The living statue tradition of the *tableaux vivants*, utilised especially for royal entries, must not be forgotten: not all such statues are Hermetic, as I am grateful to Alastair Fowler for reminding me. See George R. Kernodle, *From Art to Theatre: Form and Convention in the Renaissance* (Chicago, Ill.: Univ. of Chicago Press, 1944), ch. II, pp. 58 ff.

41 Nichols, *Progresses ... of King James*, II. 542–543.

42 Quotations from *Campion's Works*, ed. Percival Vivian (Oxford: Clarendon Press, 1909). Page references given in text. The present quotation is from the facsimile of the masque's title page on p. 57. David Lindley rightly argues for political symbolism in the masque, but fails to detect alchemical images of union: 'Campion's *Lord Hay's Masque* and Anglo-Scottish Union', *HLQ*, 43 (1979–80), 1–11. See, however, *ibid.* p. 7 n. for a recognition of the presence of talismanic magic.

43 Orpheus's relationship with Hermetic and related traditions is explained in detail by D. P. Walker, *The Ancient Theology: Studies in Christian Platonism from the Fifteenth to the Eighteenth Century* (London: Duckworth, 1972), ch. I and *passim*. See also his earlier 'Orpheus the Theologian and Renaissance Platonists', *JWCI*, 16 (1953), 100–120.

44 Sixteen doubles eight, the number of Juno, goddess of marriage: A. D. S. Fowler, *Triumphal Forms: Structural Patterns in Elizabethan Poetry* (Cambridge: C.U.P., 1970), pp. 151 ff.

45 Yates, *Shakespeare's Last Plays: a New Approach* (London: Routledge and Kegan Paul, 1975), pp. 89 ff.; *Hermetica*, ed. Scott, I. 339; cf. Bruno, *Expulsion*, ed. Imerti, p. 241, and ch. I, sec. vii above. A slightly later passage in the *Asclepius* (ed. Scott, I. 359 ff.) is even more important in discussing statues animated by demons: see Walker, *Spiritual and Demonic Magic, passim*.

46 The Sibyl talks of the one mind and faith that will join the two peoples (of Germany and Britain) and, with perhaps more than a hint of Bruno, of the one religion and simple love (*Utramque iunget una mens gentem, fides. / Deique Cultus unus, et simplex amor*; p. 98). St. 2 of the following song announces the return of the Golden Age (as, indeed, has the Sibyl). The masque thus possesses the politically oriented 'integrity' denied it most recently by A. Leigh De Neef, 'Structure and Theme in Campion's *Lords' Maske*', *SEL*, 17 (1977), 95–103, which is again unaware of alchemical and Hermetic traditions.

47 *Hermetica*, ed. Scott, I. 347.

48 Quotations from the text in Orgel and Strong, *Inigo Jones: the Theatre of the Stuart Court*, I. 256–262 and identified subsequently by volume and page numbers in parenthesis. The blindfolded quester appears in the

right foreground of the Michelspacher engraving referred to in n. 49.

49 In the first triumphal car are the sun-worshipping Virginian priests, the Phoebades (but *Virginia* recalls Elizabeth and the Diana–Phoebe cult); then come the chief masquers dressed in silver and gold. The second triumphal car contains Honour (in blue and silver), her priest Eunomia (white and silver), her herald (silver and gold), and Plutus (gold). For the difference between material and alchemical gold, see Ashmole, *Theatrum Chemicum Britannicum*, sig. A3^V: to make gold etc. by means of the 'Minerall Stone . . . [is] *the lowest use the* Adepti *made of the* Materia. *For they being lovers of* Wisdome *more then* Worldly Wealth, *drove at* higher *and more* Excellent Operations: *And certainly* He *to whom the whole* Course of Nature *lyes open, rejoyceth not so much that he can make* Gold *and* Silver. . . . *as that he sees the* Heavens *open, the* Angells *of* God *Ascending and Descending, and that his own Name is fairely written in the* Book of life'. On the early seventeenth-century alchemical revival, see esp. Charles Nicholl, *Chemical Theatre, passim*. The rock-temple setting of Chapman's masque draws on the castle of knowledge tradition conflated with the Lullian intellectual stairway leading to the house of wisdom (see reproductions in S. K. Heninger, Jr., *The Cosmographical Glass: Renaissance Diagrams of the Universe*, pp. 5, 161). Closest of all, however, is the stairway-cupola enclosed within a mountain (the cupola surmounted by sun, moon, and phoenix) symbolising conjunction and the completion of the work, a common alchemical vision reproduced in this instance by Heninger, p. 183, from Michelspacher's *Cabala, Speculum Artis et Naturae, in Alchymia*.

50 When the Phoebades first sing (at p. 260) to bid the earth open her 'womb of gold' we are told that they sing 'to six lutes (being used as an Orphean virtue for the state of the mines opening)': see p. 257, ll. 149–150. Six is the number of harmony: Martianus Capella, *Marriage of Philology and Mercury*, VII, sec. 737 (tr. Stahl, etc. p. 281): 'the number six is the source and origin of the musical concords. . . . For this reason Venus is said to be the mother of Harmony' (i.e., the daughter of Venus and Mars). Harmony herself, significantly, is Mercurian and appears for the marriage walking between Phoebus and virginal Pallas (*ibid.*, IX, secs 899 and 909). D. J. Gordon detects Orphic elements in the masque and relates it to contemporary preoccupations with Virginia in 'Le "Masque Mémorable" de Chapman', in Jean Jacquot (ed.), *Les Fêtes de la Renaissance*, I (second edn, Paris, 1973), 305–317. For the identification of Mercury with Fortune, see Cartari, *Imagini*, pp. 478–479.

51 Capriccio produces an antimasque of baboons (p. 259), which alchemically complement the Phoebades since they were regarded as lunar creatures (Agrippa, I. xxiv, p. 54) or, occasionally, solar (*ibid.*, I. xxiii, p. 53); or they could be parody alchemists: see the dance of monkey-baboon alchemists in M. Caron and S. Hutin, *The Alchemists*, tr. H. R. Lane (New York and London: Grove Press, Inc., 1961), p. 81. For 'fixing', see e.g. Nicholl's comments on crude mercury in *Chemical Theatre*, pp. 108 ff., etc.

52 It is significant that the first part of the masque is devoted to an elaborate exchange between Mercury and Iris (symbolic doubles for king and queen, bridegroom and bride). Text used is that edited by Philip Edwards in Spenser and Wells (eds), *A Book of Masques*, pp. 127–148.

53 For monarch and alchemy, see ch. I, sec. ii above, and add the prefatory verse to Thomas Norton's *Ordinall of Alchimy* (Ashmole, *Theatrum Chemicum Britannicum*, p. 3): 'This *Art* in such you only finde / As *Justice* love, with *spotless-Minde*. . . . / These had adorn'd the *English-Throne*, / If they had trusted *God* alone: / For he that hereby *Honor* winns, / *Shall change the old for better things.* / And when he comes to *rule* the Land, / *Reforme* it with a *vertuous hand*: / Leaving *examples* of *good deedes* / To every *King* that him *succeedes* . . .'.

54 As it is printed the song, about the creative and chaos-quelling power of love, consists of eighteen lines. The Ptolemaic star total for Gemini is eighteen, and is followed by Bruno, *Expulsion*, ed. Imerti, I. ii (p. 111): 'those two boys . . . who comprise eighteen stars'. The Twins were not necessarily boys, however, but could be boy and girl depicted as a hermaphrodite as in the May miniature to the Duke of Berry's *Trés Riches Heures*. And see A. D. S. Fowler, *Spenser and the Numbers of Time*, p. 167. For Rubens's connection of Henrietta Maria with an angel-Mercury, see Per Palme, *Triumph of Peace: a Study of the Whitehall Banqueting House* (London: Thames and Hudson, 1957), p. 260. Palme's study offers indispensable background for this whole chapter.

55 The appearance at ll. 176 ff. of 'foure new persons, in forme of a Constellation' is probably meant to remind us of the quadrate of virtue as the emblem of Mercury: Cartari, *Imagini*, pp. 315 ff.; Macrobius, *Saturnalia*, I. xix. 15 (tr. Davies, p. 135). For the quadrate of virtue, see Aristotle, *Nicomachean Ethics*, 1100B.

56 In the *Heroic Frenzies* Bruno alludes to the *Asclepian* lament in connection with the Platonic Great Year, the cyclical return to better things symbolised in the Flora mythology of *Chloridia*: see *Heroic Frenzies*, tr. P. E. Memmo, Jr., Univ. of North Carolina Studies in the Romance Languages and Literatures, 50 (Chapel Hill, N.C.: Univ. of North Carolina Press, 1964), II. i, pp. 179–180 (Great Year) and 181–182 (*Asclepius*). The rose and lily of Jonson's l. 212 move beyond love cliché to the Song of Solomon 2: 1; which reminds us not only that the Song is about the marriage of a king and queen but that Bruno constantly draws attention to parallels between his *Frenzies* and the Song: e.g., 'Argument of the Nolan', pp. 62–63, 68, etc. At p. 67 he declares that the ultimate end of the *Frenzies* is the reduction of 'every discord to concord, every diversity to unity' (and cf. p. 77). This is a reforming as well as transcending vision. For general background, see Frances Yates, 'The Emblematic Conceit in Giordano Bruno's *De Gli Eroici Furori* and in the Elizabethan Sonnet Sequences', *JWCI*, 6 (1943), 101–121; her *Giordano Bruno, passim*; and J. C. Nelson, *Renaissance Theory of Love; the Context of Giordano Bruno's 'Eroici Furori'* (New York: Columbia U.P., 1958).

57 *Inigo Jones*, I. 56–57.

58 The Hesperidean apples fuse with the Hesperidean golden sheep in, e.g., Diodorus Siculus, IV. xxvii. 1 (Greek mēlon = sheep or apple) and hence belong with alchemical readings of the Jason myth. The alchemical symbolism of the Hesperidean apples is a main topic of Michael Maier's *Atalanta fugiens* (1618).

59 I.e., Orgel and Strong, *Inigo Jones*, from whose second vol. all subsequent masque quotations are taken.

60 The twin motif has been established earlier when the poets, singing the priaises of Albanactus, have told Alba: 'Th'immortal swans, contending for his name, / Shall bear it singing to the House of Fame' (O and S, II. 454). Symbolically, then, Alba and Albanactus become *twin* swans, the twins born of the swan-father Jove (Gemini) and associated with the constellation Cygnus (Allen, *Star Names*, p. 193). In Bruno's *Expulsion*, Cygnus is associated with Repentance, Purification, and Reform and connected with the royal swans of the Thames (ed. Imerti, pp. 81, 183–184). Equally to the point, perhaps, is the auspicious importance of the constellations Cygnus and Serpentarius (we recall the role of Mercury's serpent–caduceus in the masque) in the early seventeenth century after the discovery of new stars in these constellations in 1604. They were interpreted by 'Rosicrucians', Kepler, Donne, and others: Yates, *Rosicrucian Enlightenment*, pp. 79 n., 129, 302 and n.

61 Confirmed by the possibility that there is an allusion to Bruno's *Heroic Frenzies*, II. v, where Circe-imposed blindness yields to celestial vision (and see 'Argument of the Nolan', Memmo's transln, pp. 73–78).

62 The Brunian influence has long been recognised: *The Poems of Thomas Carew with his Masque 'Coelum Britannicum'*, ed. Rhodes Dunlap (Oxford: Clarendon Press, 1949), pp. 275–276 and n. See also Yates, *Giordano Bruno*, pp. 392–393.

63 Yates, *Giordano Bruno, passim*, but esp. chs. XII ff.

64 *Pace* Orgel and Strong, *Inigo Jones*, I. 66, who regard the debt to Bruno as 'superficial', in which they are followed by Graham Parry, *The Golden Age Restor'd: the Culture of the Stuart Court* (Manchester: Manchester U.P., 1981), p. 186 (though a slightly more sympathetic discussion follows on pp. 194–196). A similar underestimation is made by Lynn Sadler, *Thomas Carew* (Boston, Mass.: Twayne, 1979), ch. VI.

65 *Works*, ed. J. William Hebel, 5 vols. (Oxford: Shakespeare Head, 1961), IV (1961), 'Upon the *Frontispice*'.

66 Guy de Tervarent, *Attributs et Symboles dans l'Art Profane 1450–1600* (Geneva: Droz, 1958), cols 242 ff.

67 See Malachi 4: 1–2 and Erwin Panofsky, *Meaning in the Visual Arts* (Garden City, N.Y.: Doubleday, 1955), pp. 261 ff.

68 Alchemical probably fuses with Biblical to recall the 'woman cloathed with the Sun, and the Moone ... under her feet, and upon her head a crowne of twelve Starres' of Revelation 12: 1 (Geneva gloss: 'A type of the true and holy Church'). The alchemical symbolism offers a poignant hope for the success of the union of Protestant and Catholic in Charles and his queen after the failure of the Protestant alchemical union of Frederick and

Elizabeth.

69 The crowning of the queen 'with Ariadne's diadem' (O and S, II. 571) connects her with March and the creation of the world (see n. 4 above) *via* Ovid, *Fasti*, III. 459 ff. The fact that Ariadne was united with Bacchus–Dionysus (*ibid.*) suggests the further Brunian–Egyptian identification of the queen here with moon–Isis and Charles with sun–Osiris. For Osiris–Bacchus see n. 29 above. A Brunian reading of the constellation is even more significant: Corona Borealis will be bestowed only upon that 'heroic prince [who] will bring back the so-longed-for peace to wretched and unhappy Europe' by overcoming the monster of 'multiform heresy' (*Expulsion*, ed. Imerti, p. 124). Carew presumably intends the compliment to the king and queen's love for each other as an expression of the union of the two religions.

70 Ed. Imerti, pp. 79–80.

71 *Ibid.*, p. 84. The actual stopping of the 'fiery team' to make 'a solstice' occurs in the central lines of Mercury's speech (ll. 9–10 of a total of eighteen: O and S, II. 573) to affirm the maintaining of the true central position of monarchy by the king (on the sovereign centre, see Fowler, *Triumphal Forms*, chs. I–V).

72 Ch. I, n. 107 above.

73 Momus, the reproving son of Sleep and Night (Comes, *Mythologiae*, IX. xx), is crucial to Bruno's reforming scheme in *The Expulsion*, where he is recalled by Jove from his place 'at the tip of Callisto's tail . . . vindicated, [and] restored to his pristine state, and made ordinary and extraordinary herald, with the most ample privilege of being able to reprehend vices without any regard to the title or dignity of any persons' (ed. Imerti, p. 95). As herald he thus becomes, in *Coelum Britannicum*, the antimasque equivalent to the Mercurian monarchs of the masque proper. In the *Hermetica*, Momus, 'a mighty spirit . . . comely and stately to look on, but exceeding fierce and terrible' sees Hermes 'making man' and comments on his potentiality for audacity and inquisitiveness and bids Hermes 'Let their presumptuous eagerness be disappointed of its expectations': *Stobaei Hermetica*, Excerpt XXIII, Isis to Horus (ed. Scott, I. 481 ff.). This might imply a level of Hermetic seriousness in Carew's Momus which we might otherwise overlook. James in the *Basilicon Doron* had advised the young Prince Henry that the monarch must see to it 'so to prop the weale of your people, with provident care for their good government; that justly *Momus* him self may have no grounde to grudge at': ed. cit., ch. I, n. 55 above, I. 93.

74 'Pace amica di Cerere': Cartari, *Imagini*, pp. 316–317. The 'peace and plenty' motif is, of course, a commonplace: for James's reign see Nichols, *Progresses*, I. 240 and 275 (where peace and Ceres are connected by the Recorder of Winchester with James as Justice with his sceptre). In Jonson's *Part of the King's Entertainment in passing to his Coronation*, Eudaimonia (Felicity) holds 'in her right hand a *Caduceus*, the note of peacefull wisedome: in her left, a *Cornucopia* fill'd onely with flowers, as a signe of florishing blessednesse' (*Works*, ed. Herford and Simpson, VII.

99). See Tervarent, *Attributs et Symboles*, cols 58 and 123–124, on the relationship between caduceus and cornucopia.

75 I.e., vigilance and contemplation (Cartari, p. 329) and, in the context of this masque, the dawn bird heralding a new era, complementing Mercury as a solar deity (Cartari, pp. 337 f. following Macrobius, *Saturnalia*, I. xix. 7–18, a passage which also identifies the caduceus's serpents as solar and lunar and which Carew probably has in mind in portraying his hermaphroditic serpent-entwined solar and lunar monarchs). For the solar cock, see, e.g., Agrippa, I. xxiii, p. 53.

76 In Bruno, 'Iniquitous and Perverse Desire' descends with the old Gemini to be replaced by 'Figurative Love, Friendship, and Peace' (ed. Imerti, p. 84).

77 Yates, *Giordano Bruno*, p. 221; *Expulsion*, ed. Imerti, pp. 84, 184 ff., 219–220, 227–228, etc.

78 Roy Strong, *Van Dyck: Charles I on Horseback*, pp. 59 ff. For the Garter, see further, ch. IV below. The authoritative history remains Elias Ashmole's *The Institution, Laws and Ceremonies of the most Noble Order of the Garter* (London, 1672).

79 Strong, *Van Dyck*, p. 102, n. 57.

80 On eight as rebirth, see Pietro Bongo, *Numerorum mysteria* (Bergamo, 1599), pp. 325 ff. and I Peter 3: 20–21.

81 Ed. Imerti, p. 218 (and p. 113 for the star total).

82 For the Garter and Golden Fleece, see, e.g., Strong, above (n. 78); Ashmole, *The Institution . . .*, pp. 115 ff. and 189; Selden's note to *Poly-Olbion*, Song XV, l. 315; Kipling, *The Triumph of Honour: Burgundian Origins of the Elizabethan Renaissance*, p. 65. For alchemy and the Fleece, see, e.g., Nichols, *Progresses . . . of King James*, II. 619 on the Heidelberg festivities for the wedding of Frederick and Elizabeth, and Yates's comments in *Rosicrucian Enlightenment*, ch. I.

83 On gold and silver in the masque, see, e.g., O and S, II. 578, and for additional Hesperidean references, ll. 480, 949. The commonplace of the alchemical meaning of the Hesperidean garden is celebrated by Drayton in his *A Pœan Triumphall . . . To the Majestie of the King* (1604): *Works*, ed. Hebel, I. 480 ff. Hesperides contains an allusion to Hesperus–Mercury: see above, n. 21.

84 See plate 2 and ch. I, sec. ii above. This is possibly implied in Rubens's 1629 painting of Charles as George killing the dragon (Strong, *Van Dyck*, p. 61). The knight killing the dragon of putrefaction is an alchemical commonplace: e.g., Jung, *Psychology and Alchemy*, p. 284, fig. 150.

85 See above, ch. I, n. 60 for the whiteness of the caduceus and *ibid.*, sec. vii for the dispelling of clouds.

86 Cf. the similar though more elaborate symbolism in *Faerie Queene*, IV (above, ch. I, sec. vi). Alchemical allusion is present in the combination of gold and silver in the palace of Fame from which Britanocles emerges (O and S, II. 666). For the alchemical sea king see Jung, *Psychology and Alchemy*, pp. 313 ff.

87 Comes, *Mythologiae*, IX. iii. Bellerophon on Pegasus is a type of Charles I

on horseback not noted by Strong, *Van Dyck*.

88 E.g., Strong, *Van Dyck*, pp. 92–93.

89 The masque coincides with the proliferation of Merlin prophecies as the Civil War approached: Thomas, *Religion and the Decline of Magic*, pp. 486 ff.

90 For the serpent of prudence and wisdom, see Matthew 10: 16 and Cesare Ripa, *Iconologia* (1603), pp. 416 ff., where the serpent is entwined round a spear. This is the serpent that appears on Elizabeth's right arm in the 'Rainbow' portrait (with possible allusion to the Mercurian tradition?): Strong, *Portraits of Queen Elizabeth I*, pp. 84–86 and plate 17. For the sword and serpent, see Nichols, *Progresses . . . of Queen Elizabeth*, II. 368 describing a tableau of Concord: 'a sword with two serpents writhing about it, and holding their tailes to their eares; signifieing discreet governement, and eares stopped against flatterers'.

91 Solar: O and S, II. 733 (ll. 326 ff.). The figure of Genius carries with it a complex background, including a connection with Mercurian serpents: J. C. Nitzsche, *The Genius Figure in Antiquity and the Middle Ages* (New York and London: Columbia U.P., 1975), p. 28 (cf. p. 8).

92 Cit. Margot Heinemann, *Puritanism and Theatre*, p. 253. The proliferation of Puritan *Mercurius* periodicals in general in the 1640s may have been in part an attempt to herald the demise of monarchical Mercury, but they were answered by Royalist Mercuries: see plate 8, the frontispiece to B. Ryves's *Mercurius Rusticus* (London, 1648).

III

The early Milton and the hermetics of revolution: 'L'Allegro' and 'Il Penseroso' and 'Comus'

[i] *Mercury redefined:* L'Allegro *and* Il Penseroso

The young Milton's attitude to the monarchy is a matter open to debate, and at first sight his apparently simple companion poems (probably of 1631) would appear to have little to do with the theme I have been tracing. But if we take as part of their background the Puritan tradition at Milton's college (Christ's), together with its hospitality to cabbalistic studies, and Milton's friendship with Charles Diodati, whose family, in Christopher Hill's words, was 'almost a symbol of international Protestantism', then we perhaps get a clue to their possible revolutionary Hermetic meanings.[1] Hermes Trismegistus is, after all, the, literally, central character in *Il Penseroso*, leading us to suspect that the young Milton's attention might have been turning to the relationship between poetry, Hermetics, and Protestant reform. The old view of a Cavalier *L'Allegro* rejected for a more serious *Il Penseroso* may not be so far from the truth.[2] In these two poems, I shall argue, we find a reforming intention based explicitly on Hermes. *L'Allegro* depicts a corrupt court; *Il Penseroso* espouses a private contemplative ideal as an alternative, while at the same time locating the principle of reform in the possibility of the ultimate British earthly monarch, the returned Arthur.

The opposition of Joy and Melancholy was a common early seventeenth-century theme,[3] but Milton's two poems go beyond mere contrast to develop an argument based on progression (from *L'Allegro* to *Il Penseroso*) which is at once chronological and moral. Above all, and this is an obvious aspect of the poems' background which it is nevertheless easy to overlook, their whole ethos is that of the court masque, as a glance at Jonson's *Vision of Delight* (January 1617) will show. In this masque Delight appears, accompanied by Grace, Love, Harmony, Revel, Sport, and Laughter, and announces:

> Let us play, and dance, and sing,
>   let us now turne every sort
> O'the pleasures of the Spring,
>   to the graces of a Court.
>
> From ayre, from cloud, from dreams, from toyes,
>   to sounds, to sence, to love, to joyes;
> Let your shewes be new, as strange,
>   let them oft and sweetly vary. ....[4]

Night then rises with sceptre and crown, accompanied by the moon, and invokes '*Phant'sie* [to produce] a waking dreame' (ll. 44 ff.) who subsequently presents the spectators with a vision of the bower of Zephyrus which 'showes / As if *Favonius*, father of the Spring, / Who in the verdant Meads, doth reigne sole king, / Had rowsd him here' (ll. 142 ff.). The answer to Wonder's question 'How comes it Winter is so quite forc't hence, / And lockt up under ground' is, of course, 'because of King James', as Phantasy explains:

> Behold a King
> Whose presence maketh this perpetuall *Spring*,
> The glories of which Spring grow in that Bower,
> And are the marks and beauties of his power. (ll. 201 ff.)

James is Mercury–Zephyrus, whose magical power is so great that he can apparently vanquish midwinter, such is his control over the imagination of his subjects. To the monarchical panegyrist the sovereign enjoys, with Moses and Solomon, revelation and magical power. To the sceptic, however, such claims are more like the delusions of a Simon Magus. And so, whereas in Jonson's masque Delight, Night, and Phantasy conspire naively to eulogise the Mercurian monarch, in Milton's two poems the same components appear only to be separated off. The springlike world of monarchical delusion (a perversion of the ideal of the Hermetic philosopher king) is rejected for the visions brought by the contemplative night of the Hermetic philosopher poet.

Critics now recognise in the contrast between *L'Allegro* and *Il Penseroso* an opposition of sanguinic and melancholic temperaments.[5] Equally to the point is the relationship of temperaments and humours to the four ages of man scheme. If we apply this familiar tradition to Milton's poems, *L'Allegro* would deal with the youthful first age, and melancholic *Penseroso* with the third middle age. Since the ages were frequently correlated with moral qualities, Milton might also be opposing youth's irresponsibility against middle age's temperate wisdom.[6] Finally, each age and temperament had its tutelary planetary deities. Jupiter and Venus presided over the first age and the sanguinic temperament, melancholy Saturn over the third. Thus *L'Allegro* and *Il Penseroso* would appear to argue that, although the progression towards age is inevitable, age's intellectual corollary, wisdom, is not. There are many, Milton implies in *L'Allegro* (and his eye is sternly on the court) who, like Spenser's Verdant trapped by Acrasia, wish to remain Bacchic eternal boys. The assumption of the rigours of Hermetic contemplation requires enormous body-destroying effort, but it is just that effort that is required of the dedicated poet and of the dedicated monarch.[7] As I see it, the movement Milton traces from youthful folly to wisdom, from sanguinic to melancholic, from Venus to Saturn, is not only a movement within the individual psyche. It is a plan projected, as later in *Comus*, for the regeneration of Britain by a restoration of the Saturnian Golden Age attained through the summoning up of Hermes Trismegistus and the visions granted to the melancholic contemplative of 'approaching prodigies, wonders, a prophet to come, . . . the emergence of a new religion'.[8] It is the more compelling because of its contrast with the false Mercurian spring of *L'Allegro*.

The invocation to Euphrosyne at the beginning of *L'Allegro*, together with references to Venus and Zephyrus, recalls the iconography of the three Graces, interpreted by neo-Platonists as an emblem of divine love. The further we read, however, the more our reservations about the type of love depicted here develop: it becomes a poem about physical passion and love as frivolous mirth, traditional cure for melancholy. The suggestion that Bacchus and Venus are the parents of the Graces draws attention to Bacchus as god of wine rather than lawgiver[9] and to Venus as the goddess of mirth and youth, while the alternative parentage of lines 17–24, Zephyrus and Aurora, continues some at least of these implications. The tale Milton recounts echoes *Fasti*, V and the rape of Chloris[10] to give us a spring myth appropriate to the first age of man that is confirmed by the 'beds of violets blue, / And fresh-blown roses washed in dew' of lines 21–22, which call to mind Chloris–Flora as queen of flowers.[11] But the displacement of Flora by Aurora, the dawn goddess (whose position with respect to the day corresponds to that of the spring with respect to the year), echoes, as Warton first noticed,[12] the collocation of Zephyrus, Aurora, and Flora in Jonson's Highgate *Entertainment of the King and Queen, on May-day in the Morning*

(1604), where the three, introduced by Mercury, sing the praises of James and his queen. This would appear to be an early Jacobean statement of the Mercurian monarch theme if we regard the male gods, Mercury and Zephyrus, as embodying aspects of the king and the goddesses (Aurora, Flora, together with Maia) as aspects of the queen. By transferring this imagery to the world of Charles's court Milton might already be hinting at the limitations of the old style Mercurian monarch, limitations which were the more apparent because of the Caroline court's affectation of the neo-Platonic love cult in which, I argued in chapter II, Hermeticism played such an important role.[13]

In this context, *L'Allegro*'s cock announces not so much Mercurian vigilance and spiritual illumination[14] as sexual licence ('Stoutly struts his dames before', l. 52), in preparation for the appearance of a sun which suggests the solar iconography of masque, pageant, and other forms of monarchical propaganda ('the great sun begins his state', l. 60). Indeed, it rises in order to shed its light on a pastoral day peopled by the rustic couples Corydon and Thyrsis and Thestylis and Phillis, which leads one to suspect an additional courtly allusion, this time to the predilection for Arcadian pastoral, the wrong-headed escapism of which is confirmed when the poet's roaming eye lights upon

> Towers, and battlements . . .
> Bosomed high in tufted trees,
> Where perhaps some beauty lies,
> The cynosure of neighbouring eyes. (ll. 77 ff.)

The sexual nuance of these lines contrasts with the Elder Brother's allusion to the same constellation in *Comus* when he invokes the virginal moon and then 'a gentle taper['s] . . . streaming light' to 'be our star of Arcady, / Or Tyrian Cynosure' (ll. 330 ff.). Cynosure, or Ursa Minor, is the metamorphosed Arcas, son of the Arcadian Callisto and follower of Diana who bore Arcas after being raped by Jupiter. Callisto was transformed into a bear by Juno and stellified by Jupiter to become Ursa Major: 'As constellations [mother and son] sparkle beside each other'. Ursa Minor is the subject of *L'Allegro*'s lines; Ursa Major, as we shall see, is the subject of the corresponding lines in *Il Penseroso* (ll. 87 ff.).[15] For the moment we may anticipate and suppose that Dianan Callisto offers an Arcadian ideal of virginity and moral rigour diametrically opposed to 'the cynosure' of *L'Allegro*, whose 'beauty' relates to that of the courtly Petrarchan 'ladies, whose bright eyes / Rain influence' in the 'towered cities' of the same poem (ll. 117 ff.). The Arcadia of *Il Penseroso* is not that of *L'Allegro* and the court, but rather, perhaps, the puritan and possibly Brunian world of Sidney's *Arcadia*.[16]

As evening comes and night falls tales of fairy lore are told in *L'Allegro* (ll. 102 ff.). These are the fairies of *The Faerie Queene, A Midsummer Night's Dream*, and Jonson's *Oberon*, not to mention Drayton and others, and they belong to the Elizabethan/Jacobean courtly tradition.[17] They must, though, be displaced by the magical demons of *Il Penseroso*, for they are as illusory as the masques and pageants that are their more sophisticated counterparts:[18]

> Towered cities please us then,
> And the busy hum of men,
> Where throngs of knights and barons bold,
> In weeds of peace high triumphs hold,
> With store of ladies, whose bright eyes
> Rain influence, and judge the prize,
> Of wit, or arms, while both contend
> To win her grace, whom both commend.
> There let Hymen oft appear
> In saffron robe, with taper clear,
> And pomp, and feast, and revelry,
> With masque and antique pageantry. . . . (ll. 117 ff.)

There are suggestions here of *Prince Henry's Barriers*, and of the Elizabethan Accession Day tilts which had provided some of the narrative and thematic substance of *The Faerie Queene*. But all these are, we are told, 'Such sights as youthful poets dream / On summer eves by haunted stream' (ll. 129–130). It is a captivating world – as captivating as the 'soft Lydian airs' that have the power to protect the poet from 'eating cares' a few lines later. The Lydian mode often belonged to Jupiter, one of the gods of sanguinic youth (and astrological complement to Mercury), however, so that the note of regressive escapism is again sounded.[19]

The prelude to *Il Penseroso*, with its rejection of 'vain deluding Joys', insists on the identification of *L'Allegro* with a dream world and hence with the uncontrolled fantasy: 'Dwell in some idle brain, / And fancies fond with gaudy shapes possess'. *Il Penseroso*, on the other hand, concerns the world of contemplating mind. Its subject is the visions of the Saturnian melancholic who is the inspired magus. Appropriately, then, the poem welcomes Saturnian black, the deceptive darkness that, like the Orphic night, conceals the ineffable brightness of wisdom (l. 16), the seventh and last gift of the Holy Spirit, which was traditionally correlated with Saturn and which had as its corresponding beatitude 'blessed are the peacemakers'. *Beati pacifici* had been one of James I's mottoes.[20] The irony directed at the monarchy, implicit in the reference to wisdom, becomes explicit at line 45 with the invocation of 'calm Peace'. *Il Penseroso* is not just about an inner world, the tower of the mind. The peace is not solely internal or (if external) merely conducive to private contemplation. It is the peace of a renewed external world, a world renewed through the visionary power of the melancholic magus. Milton displaces *L'Allegro*'s spring world with its Arcadian courtly associations for a Golden Age, a return to pristine purity as promised in the *Asclepian* lament, restored through Hermetic purgation. Hence the reference to 'Saturn's reign' (the *aurea aetas*) at line 25, and the withdrawal of *penseroso* to groves 'Of pine, or monumental oak / Where the rude axe with heaved stroke / Was never heard . . .' (ll. 135–136), which recall Ovid's description of the Golden Age as a time when pine trees had never yet been cut down.[21]

'Saturn's reign' is mentioned in connection with 'bright-haired Vesta' (l. 23). The epithet would seem to confirm Merritt Hughes's suggestion that her importance for Milton resides in the fact of her elevation to the heavens to inhabit the region of fire, dwelling place of the gods, a point made in one of the Orphic hymns.[22] The Orphic implications fuse, moreover, with other religious associations of Vesta, to whom were dedicated the first oblations in all sacrifices, and who was 'the mother of all the gods'. Indeed, it is not unlikely that for Milton, as earlier for Daniel, Vesta represents Religion itself, 'in a white mantle embroidered with gold flames, with a dressing like a nun, . . . a burning lamp in one hand, and a book in the other'.[23] *The Vision of the Twelve Goddesses* had presented James with a Golden-Age programme for his new reign in which Vesta, Flora, Concordia, Astraea, and others appeared under the auspices of a Sibyl and suggestions of magic. In *Il Penseroso* Milton reworks the theme. Melancholy is the daughter of Vesta (Religion) and Golden-Age Saturn. That is, the melancholy that is the poem's subject is Agrippan prophetic melancholy, allegorically the offspring of Orphic/Hermetic religious asceticism and of the symbol of the purity of the pristine, Golden-Age religion. The Milton of *L'Allegro* and *Il Penseroso* hovers somewhere between the apocalyptic Spenser of *The Shepherd's Calendar* and the later Milton of *Lycidas* and the *Epitaphium Damonis* in his concern for a pristine Christianity and its relationship with the visionary power of the poet. But since his attitude to the monarchy at this period is so difficult to determine it is impossible to locate exactly the kind of reform he visualises and how it is to be put into effect. What we can say with certainty is that *Il Penseroso* rejects the world of *L'Allegro*, a world that is indisputably courtly and recognisably Stuart. Equally certainly, 'the fiery-wheeled throne' (*Il Penseroso*, l. 53) from Ezekiel has monarchical overtones, which may imply the ideal of an earthly Christian sovereign, the monarch-magus who has the power of angel magic. It seems safest to assume that Milton was working towards the idea of a reformed earthly monarchy and that in *Il Penseroso* he sees the poet as the visionary intermediary — an inspired Merlin, perhaps, to the monarchical Arthur.

It is not easy otherwise to account for the presence of the British myth in the poem in the reference to 'the tale of Troy divine' at line 100 and the suggestion of it in Vesta herself, because she was worshipped at Troy and Aeneas took her sacred fire with him to his western land (*Aeneid*, II. 296–297). When Rome was founded the Vestal fire was lit and the goddess invoked (Ovid, *Fasti*, IV. 823 ff.), so that, according to Macrobius, she became the goddess of the new year: Romulus 'dedicated the first month of the year to his father, Mars. . . . Moreover, on the first day of March a new fire was kindled on the altars of Vesta, that the charge to keep a new fire alight might begin with the beginning of the year'. And, since Vesta in her role as Earth (Terra) was decorated with flowers and also had them bestowed upon her as offerings,[24] she becomes the alternative Flora of *Il Penseroso*, displacing *L'Allegro*'s Flora–Aurora and consequently rejecting that poem's Mercury–Zephyrus in favour of her own Mercurian leader of the Graces, 'thrice great Hermes' (l. 88).

Vesta, it is apparent, links all the poem's themes: Trojan–Roman, religious, the themes of rebirth and renewal. Where, then, is Arthur? He is present, as we shall see, in the Bear, at the poem's Hermetic centre:

> . . . let my lamp at midnight hour,
> Be seen in some high lonely tower,
> Where I may oft outwatch the Bear,
> With thrice great Hermes, or unsphere
> The spirit of Plato. . . .

Penseroso here envisages himself enjoying demonic illumination under the power of a melancholic frenzy. But this is a passage that should be read in connection with the poem's concluding lines in which *penseroso* imagines himself, after his ecstasy in the chapel, as an ascetic hermit in his mossy cell,

Where I may sit and rightly spell
Of every star that heaven doth shew,
And every herb that sips the dew;
Till old experience do attain
To something like prophetic strain.

The Hermetic centre with its evocation of elemental demons and its calling-up of the spirits of the dead has, we now see in retrospect, been but a stage in *penseroso*'s arduous journey to understand the relationship between magic and Christianity. Even in wise old age the disciplines of natural and celestial magic (herbs and stars) have to be rehearsed yet again before the final possible move into ceremonial magic. For it is this last that we are to infer from the 'prophetic strain' that *penseroso* hopes to 'attain'. This is the power that is bestowed by the highest spirits 'when the soul soars completely to the intellect . . . from whom it learns [of] approaching prodigies, wonders, a prophet to come, or the emergence of a new religion'.

The 'new religion' is a purified Christianity, a Hermetic Puritanism. How is it to be initiated? This is where the Bear is so important, the Ursa Major which cancels out *L'Allegro*'s Cynosure, or Ursa Minor. To D. C. Allen it is the Bear of the Hermetic *Pimander*; to Frances Yates it is the Great Bear of Bruno's *Expulsion* with which reform begins: 'with the Bear descend Deformity, Falsity, Defect. . . . There, . . . where the Bear was, by virtue of the place's being the most eminent part of the heaven, Truth is placed first, who is the highest and most worthy of all things'.[25] If the Bear announces Hermetic reform it also suggests, albeit in a shadowy hieroglyph, the identity of the reformer. Ursa Major, we recall, was confused with Arcturus and became the astronomical and astrological symbol of the Tudor Arthurian revival.[26] We have encountered the symbolism in *Prince Henry's Barriers*. It reappeared with the death of James and the accession of Charles because of the familiar alternative name for Ursa Major, Charles's Wain:[27]

> Brittaine doth under those bright starres remaine
> Which English shepheardes *Charles his waine* doe name;
> But more this Ile is Charles his waine,
> Since Charles her Royall wagoner became:
> For Charles, which now in Arthures seat doth raigne,
> Is our Arcturus and doth guide the waine.

The Arthurian associations of Ursa Major connect with hints of the Roman-British myth in *Il Penseroso* to record that here Milton identifies the reform of English Christianity with Hermeticism and with the myth of Arthur and his return. As I have said, it is easiest to assume that Milton at this early period envisaged the possibility of reform through monarchy, perhaps through a Mercurian monarch in the sense that I have traced it so far in the book. The rejection of the Caroline court in *L'Allegro* indicates emphatically that Charles is not the Arthur-magician whom Milton seeks. Reform lies elsewhere, in a figure maybe as yet unborn who will unite in himself the power of an Arthur and the combined Hermetic roles of king, priest, and magician. And yet this figure might, we are tempted to speculate, have some symbolic connection with the old Queen Elizabeth. It might, indeed, be her spirit that informs this poem as it informed Spenser's great epic. Why else should Milton allude to Chaucer's *Squire's Tale* as continued by Spenser in the Mercurian fourth book of *The Faerie Queene* (ll. 109 ff.)? Why else should Cassiopeia, 'that starred Ethiop queen', be given prominence at the beginning of the poem (ll. 19–20)? For Cassiopeia was associated with the dead Elizabeth:[28]

> What meanes this shining lustre of the aire,
>   As though our Northern welkin were on fire?
> How is this cloudie night become so faire,
>   Lamping in starrie light and bright attire?
> Some say, the starres from heaven to earth descended,
> I say, a starre from earth to heaven ascended. . . .
>
> The spangled canopie of heaven's vault,
>   Cassiopæa's chaire but late received;
> Astrologers great wonder did assault,
>   To finde the cause; and yet were all deceived.
> Eliza sent to heaven, the heavens had care
> A golden starrie throne for to prepare.

[ii] *Asclepian*-British *Comus*

In *Comus* (1634; 1637), Christopher Hill suggests, Milton tries to infuse 'order into what he saw as the moral chaos that court and papists were bringing upon England'.[29] Hill also detects in it attacks on the cult of court Platonism. A.-L. Scoufos is more precise in connecting the imagery and narrative with Revelation 12, seeing the Lady in conventional Reformation terms as the exiled Protestant church and Comus as the Catholic (and Anglican) Antichrist.[30] In general, however, critical discussion of the masque has centred on the moral or tropological areas of interpretation, avoiding the question of political meanings to which there are two main clues. First, the occasion of the masque, which celebrated on 29 September 1634 the inauguration of the Earl of Bridgewater as Lord President of Wales at his official seat, Ludlow Castle. The Lord Presidency was an important viceregal post, which meant that the essential subject of the masque had to be Wales and its relationship with England. Second, only a few months earlier (18 February 1634) the Earl's two sons, Viscount Brackley and Thomas Egerton, had performed in Carew's *Coelum Britannicum*. They were to play the Elder and Younger Brothers respectively in *Comus*. This fact encouraged Willa Evans to detect structural parallels between Carew's masque and Milton's.[31] Perhaps structural details are less to the point, though, than a thematic correspondence suggested by the Egerton association with both masques: it seems likely that *Comus* might be a Brunian Hermetic exploration of the Cambro-British theme continuing the concerns initiated in *L'Allegro* and *Il Penseroso*.

In *Comus* the Attendant Spirit (in the Trinity manuscript 'A Guardian spirit, or Dæmon'),[32] who has descended from his 'mansion' 'Before the starry threshold of Jove's court', disguises himself as 'a swain' (l. 84) to ally himself with the two youths and the Lady against the evil magician Comus and his bestial followers. Later we learn that Comus inhabits 'a stately palace' in which he tempts the Lady to a *luxuria* which is related to court Platonism:

> Beauty is Nature's brag, and must be shown
> In courts, at feasts, and high solemnities. . . . (ll. 744–745)

The masque contrasts a pure world and an impure world: Jove versus Comus; the celestial court versus the corruptions of an earthly court. If we think of *Coelum Britannicum* and Bruno's *Expulsion* at this point, the possibility of a Brunian *Comus* becomes apparent. For in *The Expulsion* Jove purges heaven and himself by banishing the constellations in their malign aspects and replacing them with the same constellations in their benign, virtuous, aspects. The purging begins with Ursa Major, the constellation which is enthroned at the centre of *Il Penseroso* and which, together with Ursa Minor, is also invoked by the Elder Brother when he is benighted with his Younger Brother in Comus's wood in lines quoted earlier: 'thou shalt be our star of Arcady, / Or Tyrian Cynosure'. Both constellations were used by navigators, and this is a primary reason for their appearance here.[33] Nevertheless, there remains the likelihood of a more specific allusion, via Bruno, to Callisto's rape by Jupiter, for the tale can be seen as a mythological anticipation of the attempted abuse of the Lady by Comus, the antimasque and chthonic opposite of the purified Jupiter of the masque's beginning and his Attendant Spirit. She is bound as Callisto but then released as the still pure Ursa of Truth and the church, to confirm the Revelation *ecclesia* theme already noticed by Scoufos.

Against the Elder Brother's invocation of these northern circumpolar constellations, moreover, we must place Comus's introductory allusion to 'the dusky pole' at line 99 (a phrase modified from 'northren pole' in the Trinity manuscript and 'Northerne Pole' in the Bridgewater manuscript).[34] In conjunction with his 'Roving the Celtic, and Iberian fields' (l. 60; i.e., France and Spain), this makes him the corrupt Catholic opposite of the Lady's Ursine church. Hence he and his followers 'Imitate the starry quire' (l. 112) and include men and women with heads 'changed / Into some brutish form of . . . bear' as well as other creatures (ll. 69–70).

This in turn might lead us to interpret his wood as the godless world of the *Asclepian* lament, which Bruno had quoted at length in the third dialogue of *The Expulsion* and which tells of an Egypt filled with barbarians: 'religion . . . will be threatened with destruction. . . . Darkness will be preferred to light . . . no one will raise his eyes to heaven'. But when all this has occurred, 'God will call back to the right path those who have gone astray; he will cleanse the world from evil, . . . washing it away with water floods . . .'. This will be 'the new birth of the Kosmos; . . . a holy and awe-striking restoration of all nature'.[35] As in *The Faerie Queene* so, I think, in *Comus* the Egyptian theme is fused with the British myth. To anticipate a later stage of my argument, the purgation by water in *Comus* is achieved by Sabrina, the personification of the main Cambro-British river. The Welsh setting with its river celebrates a nonce event and, simultaneously, the true meaning of Milton's commitment to the Arthurian-British myth at this stage of his career. He locates the restored world and revitalised religion in ancient Wales because he sees in Wales a reminder of the British strengths uncorrupted by Saxons or Normans and a domestic equivalent to the Egypt of Hermes Trismegistus and Bruno. These strengths are to be released through the Egerton children by virtue of their father's Lord Presidency, a point which becomes clearer when we understand the Earl's 'Three fair branches' (l. 968) as being assimilated into the three Hesperidean daughters 'That sing about the golden tree' in the Attendant Spirit's epilogue, where we also encounter 'the spruce and jocund Spring, / The Graces . . ., / And west winds' (ll. 980 ff.).

For Wales is the western land, Hesperidean equivalent to the pure Egypt of Osiris and Hermes:

> And all this tract *that fronts the falling sun*
> A noble peer of mickle trust, and power
> Has in his charge, with tempered awe to guide
> An old, and haughty nation proud in arms:
> Where his fair offspring nursed in princely lore,
> Are coming to attend their father's state,
> And new-entrusted sceptre. . . . (ll. 30 ff.; my italics)

With his sceptre the Earl is a Mercurian viceroy, equivalent to Hesperus–Mercury, in one tradition father of the Hesperides.[36] Through his Hesperidean children the Golden-Age world of *Mercurius Ver*, leader of the three Graces, will be released. We now see that the Attendant Spirit's announcement of the arrival of the children at the castle with an allusion to Mercury as leader of the dance ('such court guise / As Mercury did first devise / With the mincing Dryades', ll. 961–963) is a preparation for the resolution of the Mercurian–Hermetic theme, itself a continuation of the dialogue established between *L'Allegro* and *Il Penseroso*.[37]

The real Earl is at best a shadowy presence in the masque, however. And yet he is present in the manifest virtue of his children, and since it is their virtue that calls down the Attendant Spirit, intermediary between heaven and earth (a Mercurian-angelic role), we may assume that the Attendant Spirit's function is to embody the guardian-angelic role of the Mercurian father,[38] itself to be interpreted in a politico-philosophical way rather than as a simple statement about the responsibilities of parenthood. And is it an accident that the Attendant Spirit appears disguised as Thyrsis, 'my father's shepherd' (l. 492)? Mercury was, after all, a shepherd god; and if Milton was also thinking here of the Johphiel of Jonson's *Fortunate Isles*, testament to James's power as magician monarch to summon angels, we might begin to hear the notes of Hermetic revolution sounding again.[39] Maybe the temperate viceregal and Mercurian Earl offers a more acceptable example than the Mercurian Charles, and the Earl's double, Thyrsis, recalls the Mercurian shepherd god to offer (as in *L'Allegro* and *Il Penseroso*) a revisionist version of court pastoralism. On this reading Comus with his 'charming rod' (l. 93), which is the antimasque equivalent of the Earl's 'new-entrusted sceptre', is the present monarch as wizard or black magician (ll. 570, 601, 612–613). Hence his 'stately palace'.

Like Protean Archimago beguiling Redcrosse and Una, he has led the Lady to his false palace rather than 'the cottage, and the safe abode' he promised her (1. 692). Just as Archimago weaves a web of delusion around Redcrosse, so does Comus weave one around the Lady. When she is lost in the wood, 'A thousand fantasies / Begin to throng into [her] memory / Of calling shapes, and beckoning shadows dire' (ll. 204 ff.). She is the woman in the wilderness of Revelation 12; a pure being surrounded by the 'evil angels' of the fallen Egypt of the *Asclepian* lament; and, finally, the particular victim of a black magician. If you yield your will to evil spirits you are 'deposed, and thrust down . . . unto the lowest degree of misery'. 'But evil spirits are overcome by us through the assistance of the good, especially when the petitioner is very pious and devout'.[40] The presence of the Attendant Spirit in *Comus* confirms that Milton is thinking in terms of ceremonial angel magic, the invocation of a good demon to overcome evil demons.

It is significant in this respect that in searching for Spenserian analogues critics relate Comus less to Archimago than to Busirane, drawing particular attention to the parallels between the situations of the Lady and the captive Amoret.[41] As we saw in chapter I, Busirane's castle is particularly imbued with the magical, the Brunian, and the monarchical. Busirane himself is modelled on the tyrannical Egyptian Busiris, symbol of the wrong religion described in terms of black magic, who is vanquished by Mercurian Britomart, champion of the reformed religion. The Spenserian parallel helps establish Comus as representative of the fallen Egypt of the *Asclepian* lament as well as symbol of corrupt monarchy and master of delusion.

But if on one level Comus's black magic is vanquished by white magic's ability to call up demons it is on another, complementary, level undone by alchemy, a clue to the presence of which in the masque lies, in the 1637 version, first in the herb haemony given to the Attendant Spirit by the magician 'shepherd lad' (ll. 618 ff.). There has been considerable controversy over the meaning of this plant,[42] but from our point of view the important factors in the Attendant Spirit's account of it are its name (suggestive of magic through association with Haemonia/Thessaly, invariably connected with magic by the ancients), and his comparison of it to 'that moly / That Hermes once to wise Ulysses gave', which adds yet another Mercurian layer to the Attendant Spirit since he carries his haemony (like a rod?) as a protective talisman ' 'Gainst all enchantments, mildew blast, or damp / Or ghastly Furies' apparition' (ll. 639–640). Although it would be surprising if it did not embody the

Christian meanings many critics have wished for it, the Attendant Spirit's haemony remains obstinately magical – a necessary and elementary decorum, indeed, since Wales was particularly associated with magic.[43]

The plant seems to be alchemical because its 'unsightly root', 'darkish' leaves, and 'bright golden flower' borne 'in another country' call to mind the alchemical tradition of sun and moon herb-trees which usually embrace a colour spectrum that moves from black (to signify putrefaction and the *prima materia* itself) to gold, so that they symbolise the complete alchemical work. The tradition is a common one, but a medieval poem reprinted by Elias Ashmole in his *Theatrum Chemicum Britannicum* offers a useful analogue to Milton's haemony since it, too, describes an alchemical and prophylactic herb with a dark root and shining flowers that is discovered, like haemony, by a shepherd: it is the

> . . . Erbe men calls *Lunayrie*,
> I blesset mowte hys maker bee.
> *Asterion* he ys, I callet alle so,
> And other namys many and mo;
> He ys an Erbe of grete myght,
> Of Sol the Sunne he takyth hys lyght,
> He ys the Fader, to Croppe and Rote. . . .
> A growyth a pon a Mowntayne brym
> Where *Febis* [Phoebus] hath grete dominacion:
> The Sune by day, the Mone by nyght,
> That maketh hym both fayre and bryght,
> The Rote growyth on stonns clere,
> Whyte and Rede, that is so peyre:
> The Rote ys blacke, the Stalke ys red;
> The wyche schall ther never be dede,
> The Lewis ben rownd, as a Nowbel son,
> And wexyth and wanyth as the Mon:
> In the meddes a marke the brede of a peni,
> Lo thys is lyke to owre sweght Lunoyre:
> Hys Flowrys schynith, fayre and cler,
> In all the Worlde thaye have none pere,
> He ys not fownde in no maner wyse,
> But of a Schepeherd in Godis servyse:
> The good Schepeherd that I her mene,
> Ys he that keepeth hys Sowle clene:
> Hys Flowrys ben gret and sum ben small,
> Lyke to hem that growyth in Dale;
> With many a vertu both fayre and cler,
> As ther ben dayes in alle the yere,

> Fro fallyng Ewel and alle Sekenys,
> From Sorowe he brengyth man to Bles. . . .[44]

It is maybe something like this that Milton had in mind, and in view of the alchemical traditions in the court masque it is not going too far to speculate that this mysterious 'bright golden flower' suggests that *Comus* is in part about the achieving of the alchemical quest, the art of Hermes. After all, the Wales of Milton's masque is the western Hesperidean land with its 'golden tree' (l. 982) – itself a symbol for the alchemical work[45] – and when the brothers and the Attendant Spirit 'assault the necromancer's hall' protected by the apparently solary herb with its golden flower (l. 648) they might be alchemically trying to conjoin, perhaps, with the lunar Lady (connected with Diana–luna at ll. 440 ff.).

But the brothers, lacking the Minervan wisdom of a Britomart, fail to capture Comus and release their sister: 'O ye mistook, ye should have snatched his wand / And bound him fast' (ll. 814–815). Instead the Lady is released by the power of Sabrina, mythological and historical prototype of the river Severn called up by the Attendant Spirit. She symbolically possesses her father's sceptre which now displaces Thyrsis-thyrsus as the masque's equivalent to the Lord President's 'new-entrusted' rod of office:

> There is a gentle nymph not far from hence,
> That with moist curls sways the smooth Severn stream,
> Sabrina is her name, a virgin pure,
> Whilom she was the daughter of Locrine,
> That had the sceptre from his father Brute. (ll. 823 ff.)

It is possible, as the *Variorum* editors note,[46] that Milton adds monarchical overtones by recalling Drayton's description of Sabrina as queen–goddess of the Severn:

> Now *Sabrine*, as a Queen, miraculouslie faire,
> Is absolutelie plac't in her Emperiall Chaire
> Of Crystall richlie wrought, that gl001ouslie did shine,
> Her Grace becomming well, a creature so Divine:
> And as her God-like selfe, so glorious was her Throne. . . .

The Severn was the traditional ancient southern boundary between Wales and England. In Drayton's account it becomes an important symbol for his British theme and for his location of British strengths in Wales as the last refuge of the ancient British race against the Saxon invaders. But Drayton also anticipates the return of the Welsh to their former glory. As the original Trojan Britons, descendants of Aeneas,

9 The alchemical plant lunary

they first lost Troy then Britain, as Gerald reports. They now look forward to reoccupying their kingdom:

> It is remarkable how everyone in Wales entertains this illusion. According to the prophecies of Merlin, the foreign occupation of the island will come to an end and the foreigners themselves will be destroyed. The Welsh will then be called Britons once more and they will enjoy their ancient privileges.[47]

The Stuarts, of course, claimed descent from Brutus and were welcomed as the uniters of Britain. In a sense the enthralled Lady in *Comus* becomes the enthroned Severn as Sabrina sprinkles her water on her to release her, bestowing upon her the Cambro-British virtues which she then presents embodied in her own person to the Lord President. As I have said, it is impossible to attribute firm anti-monarchical principles to Milton at this period. But we might suppose that if in *Comus* he had his eye on Jonson's *Pleasure Reconciled to Virtue*, he could also have heard of and borne in mind the new antimasque added by Jonson for the performance of 17 February 1618, *For the Honour of Wales*. Jonson's masque had been Prince Charles's first; *For the Honour of Wales* honoured Charles as Prince of Wales with its comparison of Wales to the Hesperides; its utilisation of the anagram Charles James Stuart — 'Claims Arthurs Seate, which is as much as to say, your Madestee s'ud be the first King of gread *Prittan*, and sit in *Cadier Arthur*, which is *Arthurs Chaire* . . .'; and its further anagram of '*Charles Stuart* [as] *cals true hearts*, that is us, he cals us, the Welse Nation, to be ever at your service'.[48] Here the Stuart utilisation of Arthurian-Cambrian myth had received somewhat vapid expression. In Milton's masque we are given a more prophetic sense of monarchical restoration through that same myth. The Lord President is bringing viceregal power to Wales and, more important, receiving Welsh power in return, the traditional magical power which is bound up with Wales's uniquely Trojan roots and enables it to restore the Lord President's daughter to him as a reborn virginal Sabrina, granddaughter of Brutus.[49] It might be that the Lord President and his children are then required to act as a means for spreading this Comus-banishing ability into England, directing it back into a court in need of reform.

The binding of the Lady 'In stony fetters fixed' (1. 818) is Comus's parody of the cosmic adamantine chain,[50] an assertion of his magical power in the direction of uncreation. It also turns the Lady, potentially at least, into a statue, as Comus himself informs her:

> if I but wave this wand,
> Your nerves are all chained up in alabaster,
> And you a statue. . . . (ll. 658 ff.)

Like Hermione in *The Winter's Tale* she is in effect a statue subsequently brought to life, and the ability to bestow life is Sabrina's only. Promethean on one level, on another Sabrina recalls the god-making ability of the Egyptians before they became corrupted. For the Lady, like Amoret, seems to be one of the 'statues living and conscious, filled with the breath of life' of the Hermetic *Asclepius* that we have already encountered in the Jacobean and Caroline masque.[51] Comus represents the fallen Egypt[52] and Sabrina announces its renewal, the cleansing of 'the world from evil, . . . washing it away with water floods'. Moreover, she actually becomes the land she has renewed when, after the Lady's release, the Attendant Spirit wishes that Sabrina's 'lofty head [may] be crowned / With many a tower' (ll. 933–934), thus identifying her with Cybele and, maybe, with Spenser's turreted Thames.[53] Like them she is a magical monarchical Cybele supported, as in Spenser, by the magical and monarchical power of the sea gods, Neptune with his mace, prophetic Nereus, and Proteus, 'the Carpathian wizard' (ll. 868 ff.).[54] This is Milton's last word on the theme until *Paradise Lost* and Protean Satan with his 'wand', infernal inversion of Moses's magic rod (I. 294, 338), who perverts Mercury's role as guide of the souls of the dead to become the dedicated anti-royalist's type of the Mercurian magician king.[55]

Notes

1 Christopher Hill, *Milton and the English Revolution* (London and Boston, Mass.: Faber, 1979), pp. 30–35. For the magical–prophetic backgrounds to seventeenth-century Puritanism, see, e.g., Thomas, *Religion and the Decline of Magic*, ch. XIII, and P. M. Rattansi, 'Paracelsus and the Puritan Revolution', *Ambix*, 11 (1963), 24–32, relating mid-century English Hermeticism to anti-Aristotelianism. Rattansi's article is implicitly illuminated by J. W. Montgomery's 'Cross, Constellation, and Crucible: Lutheran Astrology and Alchemy in the Age of the Reformation', *ibid.*, pp. 65–86. My reading of *Il Penseroso* is indebted to Frances Yates, *Giordano Bruno*, p. 280, and her expansion of her insight in *The Occult Philosophy in the Elizabethan Age*. The current view of the place of Hermes Trismegistus in Milton's work may be judged from the entry *Hermeticism* in W. B. Hunter *et al.*, eds., *A Milton Encyclopedia* (Lewisburg, Pa. and London: Bucknell U.P., A.U.P., 1978), III.

2 Rejected by W. R. Parker, *Milton: a Biography*, 2 vols. (Oxford: Clarendon Press, 1968), I. 98, and by Kenneth Muir, cited in *A Variorum Commentary on the Poems of John Milton*, ed. A. S. P. Woodhouse and Douglas Bush, II (i) (London: Routledge and Kegan Paul, 1972), p. 258.

3 *Variorum Commentary*, II (i). 231 ff.; Klibansky, Saxl, Panofsky, *Saturn and Melancholy*, p. 382, plate 69, and *passim*.

4 Quoted from *Works*, ed. Herford and Simpson, VII. 463. I offer *The Vision* as an analogue, not a source, since it was not printed until 1640.

5 E.g., *Oxford Anthology of English Literature*, ed. Frank Kermode, John Hollander, *et al.*, 2 vols. (New York, London, Toronto: O.U.P., 1973), I. 1209 and plates 16–19; Rosemond Tuve, *Images and Themes in Five Poems by Milton* (Cambridge, Mass.: Harvard U.P., 1967), p. 29.

6 For the tradition, see refs in ch. II, n. 36 above, and for the moral corollaries of the ages, e.g., Pietro Bongo, *Numerorum mysteria* (1599), p. 216 (identifying the third age with wisdom).

7 The special relationship between monarch and poet is the subject of Daniel Javitch's *Poetry and Courtliness in Renaissance England*: see ch. I, n. 129 above.

8 Agrippa as cited in ch. I, n. 25 above. Cf. Tuve, *Images and Themes*, p. 30. Yates, *Occult Philosophy*, pp. 53 ff. cites the same passage in conjunction with *Il Penseroso*. The interpretation of the poems offered here is consistent with Milton's attitudes to monarchy in the *Commonplace Book*; note especially his reading of Dante's *De Monarchia: Complete Prose Works of John Milton*, ed. D. M. Wolfe *et al.*, 8 vols. (New Haven, Conn. and London: Yale U.P., O.U.P., 1953–1982), I. 438; and see *ibid.*, p. 7.

9 Or the Bacchus of *Epitaphium Damonis*. Agrippa discusses the Bacchus-inspired 'phrensie' in *Three Books*, III. xlvii (it 'divert[s] the soul into the mind, the supream part of it self, and makes it a fit and pure temple of the Gods . . .').

10 *Fasti*, V. 183 ff. Noted by the *Variorum* editors, II (i). 275.

11 Milton quotations are from *The Poems of John Milton*, ed. John Carey and A. D. S. Fowler (London and Harlow: Longmans, 1968).

12 *Variorum, ibid.*

13 Jonson's *Entertainment* was published in 1616. It is worth recalling that Erasmus locates the birth of Folly in the Fortunate Isles where, among other flowers, roses and violets grow, and that she 'was suckled by two jolly nymphs . . . Drunkenness, the daugher of Bacchus, and Ignorance'. One of her 'household servants' is '*Komos*, Intemperance' (*The Praise of Folly*, tr. John Wilson (1668); Ann Arbor, Mich.: Univ. of Michigan Press, 1961 edn, pp. 14–15). This suggests a closer relationship between *L'Allegro* and *Comus* than one may have suspected, and a tantalising possibility of monarchical folly presiding over the former that is confirmed by the rejection of 'deluding Joys [as] / The brood of Folly' in *Il Penseroso*, ll. 1–2. If the phrase 'brood of Folly' deliberately echoes Jonson's *Love Freed from Ignorance and Folly*, l. 274 (*Works*, ed. Herford and Simpson, VII. 367), then this might offer a further lead to the 'Egyptian' theme that I

argue for in this chapter. In Jonson's masque the 'brood of Folly' are the followers of the sphinx of ignorance, opponents of the sun king (l. 304); a simple reversal would give us the sphinx of religious mysteries connected with Hermes Trismegistus, opponent of the false sun king. Hence the summoning of Hermes Trismegistus in the darkness of *Il Penseroso* (on the sphinx see ch. I, sec. vii above).

14 See ch. II, n. 75 above. Cf. Linche, *Fountaine of Ancient Fiction*, sig Ri: Mercury's cock 'meaneth the watchfulnesse and waking studies of learned men. . . . Mercurie was often taken for that light of knowledge, & spirit of understanding, which guides men to the true conceavement of darke and enigmaticall sentences'.

15 Ovid, *Fasti*, II. 189, Loeb edn, tr. J. G. Frazer (London and Cambridge, Mass.: Heinemann and Harvard U.P., 1951), p. 71. Fowler, *Triumphal Forms*, p. 116, notes the arithmetical centrality of the Bear passages in *L'Allegro* and *Il Penseroso*. The presence of the 'triumphal form' would have considerable allusive point if the poems are as concerned with the failure of, and hopes for, monarchy as I take them to be.

16 On Sidney and Bruno, see Yates, *Giordano Bruno*, ch. XII and, for related material, D. P. Walker, *The Ancient Theology*, ch. IV. The ladies might not be just Petrarchan, however, but a court parody of Bruno's *Heroic Frenzies*, II. i. 7, where Cesarino and Maricondo discuss the emblem 'in which we find two stars in the shape of two radiant eyes and the motto, *Mors et vita*' (tr. Memmo, p. 198). Unlike the eyes of *L'Allegro*, these eyes lead one to consider the cabbalistic *mors osculi*, or death of the kiss, the full realisation of love and divinity through death (*ibid.*, p. 200 and cf. p. 127). On the *mors osculi* see also Wind, *Pagan Mysteries*, pp. 154 ff., and p. 157 for the concept in relation to Orpheus, whose unwillingness to die in order to regain Eurydice was, on Plato's authority (*Symposium*, 179D), a sign of his failure in love, revealing to him the shadow rather than the true Eurydice. The relevance of this to the Orpheus of *L'Allegro* with his 'half-regained Eurydice' (l. 150) in contrast to the Orpheus of *Il Penseroso* who 'made hell grant what love did seek' (l. 108) seems clear enough, suggesting an Orphic layer to complement the Hermeticism of these poems. See further below, nn. 20, 22, and for the Orphic background, Walker as in ch. II, n. 43 above, and W. K. C. Guthrie, *Orpheus and Greek Religion* (London: Methuen, 1952 edn). Cf. in addition M. L. Williamson, 'The Myth of Orpheus in "L'Allegro" and "Il Penseroso" ', *MLQ*, 32 (1971), 377–386 and (most informed) Michael Fixler, 'The Orphic Technique of "L'Allegro" and "Il Penseroso" ', *ELR*, 1 (1971), 165–177.

17 The *Variorum Commentary* collects most of the allusions to this area of monarchical literature. To it should be added Archie Burnett's 'Miltonic Parallels: (I) "L'Allegro" and *A Midsummer Night's Dream*, (II) "L'Allegro" and "Il Penseroso" and Theophrastan Character Literature', *N and Q*, 225 (1980), 332–334, and J. M. Taylor, '*Comus* and *The Tempest*', *Shakespeare Quarterly*, 10 (1959), 177–183, which does not, however, follow its findings through to a 'political' reading. Although Milton rejects these aspects of Shakespeare, incidentally, it is tempting to

see his reference to 'sweetest Shakespeare' (*L'Allegro*, l. 133) as an anti-Royalist gesture, since Shakespeare was not particularly in favour at Charles's court: e.g., Margot Heinemann, *Puritanism and Theatre*, p. 255.

18 Fairies belong to the third and lowest order of intelligences or angels, whose concern is with 'those things which are on earth'; whereas the demons 'Whose power hath a true consent / With planet, or with element' (*Il Penseroso*, ll. 95–96) belong to the higher rank of 'Celestiall intelligences ... being appointed besides the Divine worship for the spheres of the world, and for the government of every heaven & Star ...'. Amongst these are 'seventy two, which may rule ... the tongues of men and the Nations, and four which may rule the triplicities and Elements, and seven governors of the whole world, according to the seven planets' which can be duly invoked with talismans, etc. (Agrippa, *Three Books*, III. xvi, pp. 390–392). It is important to recognise the connection of these intelligences with world rule: *Il Penseroso* is far more concerned with a vision of practical political reform than with philosophical withdrawal. The *Variorum Commentary*, II (i). 324–326 usefully summarises the current critical consensus on this tricky passage.

19 On Jupiter and Mercury, see ch. I, n. 75 above. The Lydian mode is correlated with Jupiter in, e.g., the frontispiece to Gafurius's *Practica musice*, reprod. by S. K. Heninger, Jr., *The Cosmographical Glass*, p. 137, and Wind, *Pagan Mysteries*, plate 20. See also Tuve, *Images and Themes*, p. 29. For a different view, which sees the Lydian mode as solemn, see H. F. Fletcher, *the Intellectual Development of John Milton* (Urbana, Ill.: University of Illinois press, 1956), I. 350–357.

20 On the Orphic night, which conceals and reveals ultimate knowledge, see Pico's Platonic *Conclusion*, 6 (Ideo amor ab Orpheo sine oculis dicitur, quia est supra intellectum: love is blind because it is above the intellect), and his Orphic *Conclusion*, 15, identifying Orphic night with the cabbalistic ensoph (infinity): *Opera omnia*, I. 96 and 107. Rosemond Tuve usefully correlated gifts/virtues/vices/beatitudes in *Allegorical Imagery: Some Mediaeval Books and their Posterity* (Princeton, N.J.: Princeton U.P., 1966), appendix. The correlation with planets is documented in Klibansky *et al.*, *Saturn and Melancholy*, pp. 163 ff. For James and *beati pacifici*, see Parry, *The Golden Age Restor'd*, pp. 17–18, and Milton's *In Quintum Novembris*, l. 5 etc.

21 *Metamorphoses*, I. 94–95, a point noted in T.J. Embry's 'Sensuality and Chastity in *L'Allegro* and *Il Penseroso*', *JEGP*, 77 (1978), 526. The groves of oak might be Druidic: see ch. IV below for their implications for the Golden-Age religion. The restoration of the Golden Age, the spring of the world, is of course a return to *Mercurius Ver*. We may suspect an alchemical logic: Saturnian lead (*Il Penseroso*, l. 43; Agrippa, I. xxv, p. 55) yields, through meditation, to Saturnian gold (*ibid.*), which is 'historically' the Golden Age and alchemical Mercury (on which see ch. I, n. 28 above). Druidic lore (in connection with gold- and sun-worship) conjoins with Arthurianism and references to the Bear in *Mansus*, incidentally, which might offer a retrospective gloss on *Il Penseroso*. For Milton and alchemy

see, e.g., Kester Svendsen, *Milton and Science* (1956; New York: Greenwood Press repr., 1969), ch. IV.

22 *Variorum*, II (i). 314 citing Comes, *Mythologiae*, VIII. xix (De Vesta), p. 264. Vesta is the subject of Pico's nineteenth *Orphic Conclusion*, Nihil habebit firmum in opere, qui Vestam non attraxerit: he will have no power [steadfastness with the implication of religious steadfastness?] in his work who has not attracted Vesta to himself (*Opera omnia*, I. 107). In the relevant Orphic hymn to Vesta she is described as 'laughing'; maybe Milton's Vesta replaces *L'Allegro*'s mirth with divine laughter: text in Kathleen Raine and G. M. Harper (eds.), *Thomas Taylor the Platonist: Selected Writings*, Bollingen Series, 88 (Princeton, N.J.: Princeton U.P., 1969), pp. 288–289.

23 Ross, *Mystagogus Poeticus*, pp. 410–411; Daniel's *Vision*, ed. cit. (ch. II, n. 5), p. 27. *Ibid.*, p. 33 identifies Vesta's flames as 'flames of zeal', her white robe as 'purity', her book as revealing 'the soul's sweet comfort', and her lamp as 'the ever-burning lamp of piety'.

24 Macrobius, *Saturnalia*, I. xii. 5–6; tr. Davies, p. 85. For Earth and flowers, see Ovid, *Fasti*, VI. 299, 460, Comes, VIII. xix, and Ross, pp. 410–412. Confirmation for *Il Penseroso* as a vision of political rebirth, undoing the 'Towered cities' of *L'Allegro*, comes from the identification of Vesta with Cybele: e.g., Andrew Tooke, *The Pantheon* (London, 1713 edn), p. 196.

25 Allen, *The Harmonious Vision: Studies in Milton's Poetry* (Baltimore, Md. and London: Johns Hopkins U.P., 1970), p. 13 (and see ch. I, n. 45 above); Yates, *Giordano Bruno*, p. 280.

26 Ch. I, sec. iii; ch. II, sec. i above.

27 'Charles his Waine' in *The Poems of Sir John Davies*, ed. Robert Krueger and Ruby Nemser (Oxford: Clarendon Press, 1975), pp. 231–232. For the connection of the constellation with the future Charles II as early as 1649 (?), see the royalist ballad 'The twelve brave bells of Bow', in H. E. Rollins, ed., *Cavalier and Puritan* (New York: New York U.P., 1923), no. 33 (p. 252). None of these Arthurian connections is noticed by J. D. Merriman, *The Flower of Kings: a Study of the Arthurian Legend in England between 1485 and 1835* (Lawrence, Manhattan, Wichita: Univ. of Kansas Press, 1973), pp. 54 ff. The association of Charles's Wain with Charlemagne is noted by, e.g., Allen, *Star Names*, p. 428.

28 On Mercury in *Faerie Queene*, IV, see ch. I, sec. vi above; the Cassiopeia passage is from Bowle's poem in *Sorrowes Joy* (1603), in Nichols, *Progresses ... of King James*, I. 15–16. We should also recall the Ethiopians of Jonson's *Masque of Blackness*, fair and moon-worshipping (ed. Herford and Simpson, VII. 174, 176–177, etc.). In view of *Il Penseroso*'s rejection of *L'Allegro*'s 'hovering dreams', moreover, it is significant that Jonson should report, via Pliny, *Natural History*, V. viii. 45, that '*Aethiopes* never dreame' (VII. 175).

29 *Milton and the English Revolution*, p. 49; cf. pp. 47, 63, 179–180. I use the title *Comus* for the sake of convenience and to accord with common critical usage.

30 Alice-Lyle Scoufos, 'The Mysteries in Milton's *Masque*', *Milton Studies*, 6 (1974), 113–142. Lyle follows W. B. Hunter and James Taafe in noting the significance of the masque's original performance on Michaelmas night ('The Liturgical Context of *Comus*', *ELN*, 10 (1972–73), 11–15; 'Michaelmas, the "Lawless Hour", and the Occasion of Milton's *Comus*', *ELN*, 6 (1968–1969), 257–262). St Michael is relevant to our Mercury theme, since he was identified with Mercury: Klibansky *et al.*, *Saturn and Melancholy*, p. 355, n.245. A context of Christian reform is convincingly offered by G. B. Christopher, 'The Virginity of Faith: *Comus* as a Reformation Conceit', *ELH*, 43 (1976), 479–499.

31 Willa M. Evans, *Henry Lawes, Musician and Friend of Poets* (New York and London: M.L.A. and O.U.P., 1941), p. 96, convincingly demolished by J. G. Demaray, *Milton and the Masque Tradition* (Cambridge, Mass.: Harvard U.P., 1968), pp. 71 ff. Demaray's interest in Baltasar de Beaujoyeulx's *Balet comique de la Royne* (1581) in connection with Milton usefully, albeit indirectly, points to the relationship between monarchy and magic. Beaujoyeulx's work was in effect translated by Aurelian Townshend for his Circe-based masque *Tempe Restored* (1632) in which, incidentally, two of the Egerton children also performed. In the masque Circe yields her wand to the king and queen, heroic virtue and divine beauty: compare Yates's comment on Beaujoyeulx's original: Circe is 'led in triumph to King Henry III, to whom her magic wand is presented, thus transforming bad Circe magic into good French Monarchy magic' (*Giordano Bruno*, p. 202).

32 John Milton, *'A Maske': the Earlier Versions*, ed. S. E. Sprott (Toronto and Buffalo: Univ. of Toronto Press, 1973), p. 42; cf. Bridgewater MS, p. 43.

33 Cf. *Variorum*, II (iii). 903, citing *Fasti*, III. 107–108.

34 Ed. Sprott, pp. 58–59.

35 Ch. I, sec. vii above, and n. 126; Scott's transln. I. 341 ff. (*Asclepius*, III 24B ff.).

36 On Hesperus–Mercury (and, indeed, Hesperus–Arthur), see ch. II, n. 21 above. For the Welsh as 'proud in arms' and descendants of 'The sons of Aeneas who fought for liberty' (*Aeneid*, VIII. 648; so that Wales becomes, as it were, Aeneas's western land) see Gerald of Wales, *Description of Wales*, I. viii (Penguin edn, tr. Lewis Thorpe (Harmondsworth, 1978), p. 233). For Hesperus as father of the Hesperides, see Comes, *Mythologiae*, VII. vii (p. 216) and Servius on *Aeneid*, IV. 484 (in a context of magic): *Commentarii*, ed. Thilo and Hagen, I. 552–553. For the Hesperides and alchemical gold (and hence the Golden Age), see ch. II, n. 58 above. We should also connect western Wales with the statues–gods passage in *Asclepius*, III, looking forward to the restoration of the Egyptian religion: 'the rulers of the land will be made gods, and their worship will be established in a city . . . which will be founded towards the setting sun, and to which men of every race will speed by land and sea' (*Hermetica*, ed. Scott, I. 361). These 'terrestrial gods' are 'induced . . . by means of herbs, and stones, and scents'.

37 See above, ch. II, sec. 1 on Jonson's *Pan's Anniversary* for Mercury and the dance, an allusion to which Douglas Bush detects here: 'Notes on Milton's Classical Mythology', *SP*, 28 (1931), 263–264.

38 On guardian angels, see ch. I, n. 75 above. The Spirit is conjured up by the Elder Brother's 'divine philosophy' (1. 475), which is explicitly angel magic at ll. 454 ff. ('A thousand liveried angels . . . clear dream . . . solemn vision'). My comments should be read alongside M. H. Nicolson's 'The Spirit World of Milton and More', *SP*, 22 (1925), 433–452 and (with some reservations) Sears Jayne's Platonic reading, 'The Subject of Milton's Ludlow *Mask*', *PMLA*, 74 (1959), 533–543. The most thoroughgoing survey of the traditions available to Milton (though more cautious than I am about how he utilises them) is R. H. West, *Milton and the Angels* (Athens, Georgia: Univ. of Georgia Press, 1955).

39 Angus Fletcher, *The Transcendental Masque: an Essay on Milton's 'Comus'* (Ithaca, N.Y. and London: Cornell U.P., 1971), p. 165, notes the possibility of a pun on Thyrsis/thyrsus (the Bacchic wand), which would make him the law-giving Bacchic opposite of Bacchic Comus with his rod as well as the Mercurian wand-bearing equivalent of the Earl with his sceptre. Cf. John Steadman, 'A Mask at Ludlow: Comus and Dionysiac Revel' (ch. XIV of *Nature into Myth* (1979)) for a formidable account of Bacchic iconography. His plate 12 (from Peacham, *Minerva Britanna* (1612), p. 96) shows a drunken Bacchus holding a serpent-entwined caduceus, emblem of the specious wit bestowed by wine. For Mercury as shepherd god, see ch. I, sec. viii above, and *ibid.*, n. 130. The Mercurian–Hesperidean significance of the Spirit was established at the very beginning of the masque in lines subsequently rejected from the Bridgewater MS and added to the epilogue in Trinity and *1637*: the demon has flown from 'happy Clymes' where he 'suck[s] the liquid ayre / all amidst the gardens fayre / of Hesperus and his daughters three', etc. (ed. Sprott, p. 43; cf. pp. 186–187).

40 Agrippa, *Three Books*, III. xx, p. 407 and xxxii, p. 448 respectively. The Lady invokes Faith, Hope and Chastity at ll. 212 ff. (cf. the Elder Brother at 452 ff.) because Faith, Hope, and Charity (Love) are prerequisites of ceremonial magic: 'Our mind being pure and divine, inflamed with a religious love, adorned with hope, directed by faith . . . doth attract the truth' (Agrippa, III. vi, p. 357). The three theological virtues were associated with the three Graces, companions of Mercury: Ross, *Mystagogus Poeticus*, p. 143; and the Graces were, *inter alia*, identified with the triad Chastity–Beauty–Love (Wind, *Pagan Mysteries*, pp. 73 ff., 118). The asceticism of the white magician included virginity-chastity, a tradition still found in *Le Comte de Gabalis* and followed in *The Rape of the Lock* (below, ch. V).

41 *Variorum*, II (iii). 762, 784, 956; Watson Kirkconnell, *Awake the Courteous Echo* (Toronto and Buffalo: Univ. of Toronto Press, 1973), pp. 46–47.

42 Summarised in *Variorum*, pp. 931–938. See especially J. M. Steadman, 'Milton's *Haemony*: Etymology and Allegory', *PMLA*, 77 (1962),

200–207. Also relevant to my reading would be the etymology from Greek *haimon* (cf. *daimon*) = knowing, skilful, instructive, etc: in other words, the provinces of Mercury (Steadman, pp. 204 ff. but without reference to Mercury).

43 Cf. N. E. Enkvist, 'The Functions of Magic in Milton's *Comus*', *Neuphilologische Mitteilungen*, 54 (1953), 311.

44 Ashmole, *Theatrum Chemicum Britannicum*, pp. 348–349, and see plate 9. On the alchemical herb-tree, see Jung, *Alchemical Studies*, tr. Hull (1967), ch. V and esp. pp. 302 ff. Richard Neuse seems to detect an alchemical hint in 'Metamorphosis and Symbolic Action in *Comus*', *ELH*, 34 (1967), 54; it is of course implicit through the connection Haemonia–Medea–Jason and alchemical readings of the Argonautic myth.

45 E.g., Jung, *Alchemical Studies*, p. 307, and ch. II, n. 58 above.

46 *Variorum*, II(iii). 958; *Poly-Olbion*, V. 1 ff. (ed. Hebel, IV. 97).

47 Southern boundary: Gerald, *Description of Wales*, I. v (p. 225); prophecies of Merlin: *ibid.*, II. vii (p. 265). Critics seem in general to be remarkably reluctant to grant the relevance of Sabrina's Welshness to the masque's meaning. Exceptions include R. Blenner-Hassett, 'Geoffrey of Monmouth and Milton's *Comus*', *MLN*, 64 (1949), 315–318; M. T. Jones-Davies, 'Note sur la légende de Sabrina dans le *Comus* de Milton', *Etudes Anglaises*, 20 (1967), 416–419; Philip Brockbank, 'The Measure of *Comus*', *Essays and Studies*, 21 (1968), 60 n.; and H. M. Richmond, *The Christian Revolutionary* (Berkeley and Los Angeles, Calif. and London: Univ. of California Press, 1974), pp. 73 ff. A complementary reading to my own, relating to the contemporary split between court and country, is offered by J. D. Cox, 'Poetry and History in Milton's Country Masque', *ELH*, 44 (1977), 622–640, esp. 632 ff. on Sabrina.

48 *Works*, ed. Herford and Simpson, VII. 509: ll. 363 ff. (Hesperides); 373 ff., the anagram (on which see ch. II, n. 16 above).

49 Anthony Munday's 1605 Lord Mayor's pageant *The Triumphs of Reunited Britannia* contains an elaborate treatment of the Brutus myth in which James is 'our second Brute'. In their joy at the reunion of kingdoms under James, 'Locrine, Camber, and Albanact ... deliver up theyr Crownes and Sceptres'; then 'Thamesis, as Queene of all Britaine's rivers, begins the triumphal course of solemne rejoysing. Next her, Saverne, that took her name of Sabrina, begotten by Locrine on faire Elstred ...' (Nichols, *Progresses ... of King James*, I. 569). The monarchical–dynastic implications of Sabrina's appearance in *Comus* would, from this and other instances, seem to be ineluctable. The interpretative problem is to decide how revisionist Milton's use of the myth is.

50 On the *topos*, see James Hutton, 'Spenser's "Adamantine Chains": a Cosmological Metaphor', in his *Essays on Renaissance Poetry*, ed. Rita Guerlac (Ithaca, N.Y. and London: Cornell U.P., 1980), pp. 169–191.

51 For Yates's Hermetic reading of Hermione, see *Shakespeare's Last Plays*, pp. 89 ff. For an argued objection which is also an implicit rejection of Yates's approach to Shakespeare, see Gary Schmidgall, *Shakespeare and*

the *Courtly Aesthetic* (Berkeley and Los Angeles, Calif. and London: Univ. of California Press, 1981), pp. 5 ff. and *passim*.

52 He begins his temptation by alluding to 'that Nepenthes which the wife of Thone, / In Egypt gave to Jove-born Helena' (ll. 674–675). Cf. *Odyssey*, IV. 219 ff.

53 Sabrina's association with flower garlands of 'pansies, pinks, and gaudy daffodils' (ll. 847 ff.) identifies her with Flora, Mercury-Zephyrus's spring companion; for Spenser's Thames–Cybele, see ch. I, sec. vi above.

54 Proteus can, of course, be Egyptian, and it is no accident that the Spirit's invocation here seems to echo the procession for the marriage of Thames and Medway in *Faerie Queene*, IV. xi. See esp. st. 13 and 18–19.

55 The case for a monarchical Satan has been argued by Stevie Davies in 'John Milton on Liberty', *Memoirs and Proceedings of the Manchester Literary and Philosophical Society*, 117 (1974–1975), 37–51, 'Triumph and Anti-triumph: Milton's Satan and the Roman Emperors in *Paradise Lost*', *Etudes Anglaises*, 34 (1981), 385–398, and *Images of Kingship in Milton's 'Paradise Lost'* (Columbia, Missouri: Univ. of Missouri Press, 1983).

IV

Druids, Egyptians, and the Norman yoke

The theme that we have been tracing takes a slightly strange turn in the early seventeenth century when it becomes involved in the resurgence of interest in Druidism. A simultaneous revival of interest occurred in France, where again it is connected with Hermeticism. The connection is explained by the fact that the Druids were included in the tradition of *prisci theologi* which D. P. Walker has revealed to us. They were ancient philosophers whose wisdom belonged to the line of Hermes Trismegistus, Orpheus, Pythagoras, the Sibyls, and others. Their specific importance for Britain as for France was nationalistic, for they embodied an antique Celtic wisdom that was equivalent, almost, to the wisdom of the priest king Hermes himself.[1] Druidic Britain, sadly undocumented by any works like the *Hermetica* might, it was thought, have been rather like the Egypt celebrated in the *Asclepius* before its lamented decline – a land of magician-prophet-priest-bards whose religion was of a pristine purity. The last Druids lived in Wales or, more precisely, Anglesey. Destroyed by the Romans they nevertheless lived on in the Wales of the Cambro-British myth, despite the onslaughts of Saxon and other invaders. Being Welsh they are inhabitants of the western land, Hesperia, the land of Hesperus. In this chapter we shall look at how royalist and republican poets utilised the Druids, and how Druidism is interwoven with the Egyptian and Hermetic–Mercurian theme. We have seen how, in *Coelum Britannicum*, Druids form part of a heroic line which includes Arthur and St George and culminates in a vision of the reforming power embodied in the Order of the Garter and the Mercurian monarchs Charles and Henrietta Maria. We have also wondered, in passing, if the oak woods of Hermetic *Il Penseroso* might not be Druidic. It is now time to examine Druidism more carefully as a propagandist phenomenon.

The key works here are Drayton's *Poly-Olbion* (where Druidic, alchemical, and Egyptian images function as a thematic underpinning); Milton's *Lycidas*, with its Druidic and Mercurian reformism; Lovelace's *Aramantha: a Pastoral*, where royalist Druidism fuses with Mercurian mythology; and Marvell's *Upon Appleton House*, the most elaborate exploration of the Druidic–Hermetic and Mercurian themes that I have been able to find.

[i] *The background*

To the royalist, Druids added another strand to the British myth, confirming the magical and priestly role of the king: Druidic oak became identified with royal oak. To the republican, they represented the strengths of an ancient British philosophy and religion, an imagined return to which signified the ultimate overthrowing of the Norman yoke and affirmation of British liberty. Before we can interpret those poems in which Druids make their appearance, however, it is essential to understand the Druidic tradition as it was received by the seventeenth century.

As I have said, their wisdom led to Druids being listed among the ancient theologians. Historically nothing was known of the British Druids, all information being supplied from accounts of the Gallic Druids, who were supposed to have derived from the British Druids. The Druids were priests and philosophers whose wisdom was transmitted orally; they believed in the immortality of the soul; they worshipped in oak groves; they had judicial power. It became a commonplace that they derived from Noah, being the posterity of his son Japhet. Their family line, as fabricated by Annius of Viterbo, is the line that we find, for example, in Holinshed, where we also encounter the identification of Druids as bards as well as priests, philosophers, and seers.[2] Their relation to the British myth was succinctly stated by Anthony Munday in the preface to his 1605 mayoral pageant *The Triumphs of Reunited Britannia*:

> Most writers do agree, that after the deluge Noah was the sole monarch of all the world, and that hee devided the dominion of the whole earth to his three sonnes: all Europe with the isles therto belonging (wherein this our Isle of Brytaine was one among the rest) fell to the lot and possession of Japhet, his third sonne. Samothes, the sixt sonne of Japhet, called by Moses Mesech, by others Dys, had for his portion the whole contrey lying between the ryver of Rhene and the Pyrenian mountains, where he

founded his Kingdom of Celtica, over his people called Celtae, which name, by the opinion of Bale our countreyman, was indifferent to them of Gallia, and us of this Isle of Britaine. This Samothes being the first King over these people, of him came lineally these Kings following: Magus, Sarron, Druis, and Bardus, all ruling severally over the Celts and Brytons, who were not then so called, but Samotheans. . . . Of Bardus, whoe, according to Berosus, was very famous for inventing of musicke and ditties, came an order of philosophicall Poets or Heralds, called Bardi. . . .

Many of these Bards lived among the Britons before the birth of Christ, as Plenedius and Oronius. Since then, Thalestin, the two Merlins, Melkin, Elaskirion, and others. . . .

Thus continued the name of Samothes the space of 310 yeares, till Neptune put his son Albion, the gyant, in possession of this land, who, subduing the Samotheans, called this iland Albion. . . .

The country thus peopled with giantes, and continuing after the name of Albion for 600 yeares: Brute (being directed by a vision in his sleepe, to find out a country situated in the West) with the remaines of Troyan folowers, arived and landed at the haven now called Totnes. . . .

Brutus founded Troynovant 'near to the side of the river Thamesis'.[3] It is the name-link between Isis and Thames (or Thamesis), as we have gathered from *The Faerie Queene*, that seems to have encouraged the domestication of the Egyptian theme. And the chronology so conveniently summarised by Munday here reveals how the Egyptian Hermetic tradition could become conflated in the syncretising mind of the English Renaissance with the traditions of native Druids.

The argument of the present chapter can be more easily sustained by the quotation of one more passage concerning seventeenth-century attitudes to the Druids, this time from Elias Ashmole. Ashmole is anxious to assert the antiquity of the Hermetic philosophy in Britain. Much valuable evidence was destroyed in the anti-magical fury of the Reformation with the dissolution of the monasteries, he claims: '*where a* Red letter *or a* Mathematicall Diagram *appeared, they were sufficient to intitle the* Booke *to be* Popish *or* Diabolicall'. Nevertheless it is possible to trace the broad line of the British Hermetic tradition, including as it does such alchemical adepts as Merlin and Chaucer:

> *Our* English Nation *hath ever been happy for* Learning *and* Learned men. . . .
> *As first, the* Druydæ (*the famous and mysterious* Druydæ) *that were* Priests, Divines, *and* Wise men: *and took their* Originall *and* Name *from* Druys Sarronyus *the* fourth King *of the* Celts (*styled* Sapientum & Augurum Doctor,) *who dyed Anno Mundi.* 2069.

Next the Bardi, *who celebrated the* Illustrious Deeds *of* Famous Men, *which they ingeniously dispos'd in* Heroique Verse, *and sung them to the sweete* Melody *of the* Harpe. . . .

These Philosophers *had their Name from* Bardus Druydus (*the* 5 King *of the* Celts,) *who was the first* Inventor *of* Verses, *as* Berosius *tells us; and dyed* An. Mundi 2138. *Neither of these* Sects *of* Philosophers *used any* writing (*indeed it was not lawfull; for,*) *such was the* Policy *and* Curiosity *of* Elder Ages (*to defend their* Learning *and* Mysteries *from the Injury of* Ignorant Interpretations) *that they delivered them to* Posterity, *by* Tradition *only.*

Cæsar *testifies, (and tis a noble* Testimony) *That the* Learning *of the* Druydi, *was first invented in* Britaine, *and thence transferr'd into* France; *and that, in all his time, those of* France *came over hither to be* Instructed. . . .

As for Magick, Pliny *tells us, It flourished in* Britaine, *and that the* People *there were so devoted to it* (*yea, with all the* Complements *of* Ceremony) *a man would think that even the* Persian *learned his* Magick *thence.* . . .

Nay more, England *was twice* Schoole-Mistris *to* France (*for so saith* Peter Ramus) *viz. First by the* Druydæ (*who taught them their* Discipline) *and afterwards by* Alcunius [*sic*], *in* Charles the Great's *time.* . . .

For the Saxons, *it is not to be denied but that many of them, after their conversion to* Christianity, *were exceedingly* Learned, *and before that, much addicted to* Southsaying, Augury . . . *&c. And tis worth the* Enquiry (*there being more in it than we ordinarily apprehend*) *why they in Generall worshiped* herthus [*i.e. Dame* Earth] *for a Goddesse, and honoured* Mercury *above all the* Gods *of the* Germanes, *whom they called* Wooden, (*hence* Wodensday *now our* Wednesday:) *For, they believed that this Dame* herthus *Intermediated in* Humane Affaires. . . . *And for their* God Wooden *they esteemed him as their* God *of* Battaile, *representing him by an* Armed Man. *Insomuch that wee to this very day retaine the word* Wood *among us, to Signifie* Fierce, Furious, Raging . . .: *So the* Mercury *of the* Philosophers *is shaddowed under the fierce and terrible Name of* Lyon, Dragon, Poyson, *&c.*[4]

In this way the tradition of ancient British learning posited the continuation of the Druids' influence, focussing it eventually on the figure of Mercury and so identifying it with the Egyptian Hermetic tradition. Moreover, since Druids were, according to Dio, monarchical advisers (but in fact so powerful that they ruled through the kings),[5] we may see how they related to the tradition of Arthur and Merlin, king and wizard-adviser, so crucial to *The Faerie Queene* and itself a primary component in the elucidation and development of the myth of the Mercurian magician monarch.

[ii] *Isis and the Druids in Drayton's* Poly-Olbion

Drayton's apparently rambling topographical poem was published in two parts (1612; 1622), the first (Songs I to XVIII) dedicated to Henry, Prince of Wales, the second (Songs XIX to XXX) dedicated to the new Prince of Wales, Charles. Understandably, therefore, it has a Welsh theme. Wales is the refuge of the last of the descendants of Brutus, and this is a poem on the matter of Britain and the fulfilling of 'the *Eagles* prophecies' on the restoration of the British line.[6] James is the second Brutus, restoring to Britain her 'ancient Name', as Drummond was to write in *Forth Feasting* (1617),[7] where he also states that the coming of James had been foretold by 'the *Bards* and mysticke *Sybilles*' (l. 330). 'Bards', in context, could allude to Druidic bards. Drummond's poem begins with the river Nile (ll. 26 ff.) and ends with the Isis. The suggestion of Egyptian symbolism is difficult to avoid, as it is in *The Faerie Queene*, where the river Isis of Book IV becomes the goddess Isis of Book V. Is Drummond saying that with the accession of James, with his Welsh blood (he was a descendant of the last Welsh prince of Wales), to the English throne Britain is restored to her former western-land purity as represented by bardic–Druidic powers which make it equivalent to the Egypt of Hermes Trismegistus and Isis? This seems a possible reading, supported as it is by *Poly-Olbion*.

The themes I wish to trace in Drayton's poem are concentrated in the first part (Songs I to XVIII), and involve the Henrician reformation, alchemy, Druidism, and the climactic river marriage of Tame and Isis. In the reading I offer I assume that Selden's commentary, sceptical though it often is about the myths that Drayton utilises, are crucial guides to the poem's meaning.[8]

Towards the end of the first part, in Song XVII, Thames, offspring of Tame and Isis, sings '*as King of Rivers . . . / The Catalogue of th' English Kings*'. Not surprisingly he emphasises the dynastic union of York and Lancaster which the marriage of his own river parents has, in the poem's chronology, symbolically anticipated. The union produced Henry VIII who, having received the title Defender of the Faith, with a splendid historical irony went and restored the old religion (ll. 315 ff.), as Selden notes in his comment on the passage:[9] '. . . towards the XXV. yeere of his raigne, he began so to examine [Roman Catholic] Traditions, Doctrine, Lives, and the numerous faults of the corrupted Time, that he was indeed founder of Reformation for Inducement of the true ancient faith . . .'.

The union of York and Lancaster is a marriage of flowers, of red and white roses. The marriage of Tame and Isis is a marriage of flower-bedecked rivers. Isis, the female river, is garlanded as with a crown imperial, bedecked (among others) with 'The Red, the dainty White, the goodly Damask Rose' (XV. 174). Her offspring is Thames but also Henry VIII and James. The inference is that James perpetuates the religion purified by Henry, and that Henry's purging of the church was somehow inspired by, or derived from, Egyptian Isis, herself daughter of a river god and intimately bound up with the *Hermetica* and Bruno's *Expulsion of the Triumphant Beast*.[10]

I shall return to the river marriage, for it is the Druids who are important earlier on in the poem. Henry's 'true ancient faith', it is implied, is integrally related to British Druidism. They make their first appearance in Song I, when Drayton asks to be inspired by the 'sacred Bards' and 'those *Druides* . . ., which kept the British rites, / And dwelt in darksome Groves, there counsailing with sprites' (ll. 31 ff.). In fact, they are the muses of a poem that simultaneously considers the myths of Brutus and Arthur and the western land. Indeed, it is in this same first Song that the moon goddess (Cynthia–Diana–Isis) reveals to Brutus 'in dreames, that furthest to the West, / He should discrie the Ile of *Albion*, highlie blest; . . . / Where, from the stock of Troy, those puissant Kings should rise, / Whose conquests from the West, the world should scant suffice' (ll. 409 ff.).[11]

Brutus's empire of the west becomes even more specifically western when related to Cornish Arthur who died, we are told, in the county 'where he had his birth' (I. 191). So western-directed is the poem (the Druids inhabited the western, Welsh-Celtic side of Britain, we recall) that even eastern Kent can become, by virtue of its orchards, western and Hesperidean: 'Whose golden Gardens seeme th'*Hesperides* to mock' (XVIII. 671).

A restored old faith; Druids; Brutus and the western land; Arthur; Hesperides: we are in familiar territory, territory that we have already partly covered in the court masque, that Milton covered in *Comus*, and that was to be so dear to Ashmole. We might suspect that the image of unity and reform underlying *Poly-Olbion* is Hermetic. Drayton's poetic initiative lies in the addition of the Druids.

I say 'Hermetic' rather than 'Mercurian' because the poem's mystical symbolism seems to be essentially alchemical, and it is to the alchemical symbolism that the Druids are related. Selden seems to recognise this in his note on line 29 of Song I where, a few lines before mentioning the Druids, Drayton refers to 'the cold *Ducalidon* [sea], / Amongst whose

Iron rockes grym *Saturne* yet remaines, / Bound in those gloomie Caves with Adamantine chaines'. Selden's note on Jupiter's imprisonment of Saturn reads:[12]

> *Homer* joynes *Japet* with him, living in eternal night about the utmost ends of the earth: which well fits the more Northerne climate of these Islands. Of them (dispersed in the *Deucalidonian* Sea) in one most temperate, of gentle ayre, and fragrant with sweetest odours, lying towards the Northwest, it is reported, that *Saturne* lies bound in iron chaines, kept by *Briareus*, attended by spirits, continually dreaming of *Jupiters* projects, whereby his ministers prognosticate the secrets of Fate. Every thirtie yeares, divers of the adjacent Islanders ... enter the vast Seas, and at last, in this *Saturnian* Isle ... enjoy the happy quiet of the place; some in studies of nature, and the Mathematiques. ... This fabulous relation might be, and in parts is, by Chymiques as well interpreted for mysteries of their art, as the common tale of *Dœdalus* Labyrinth, *Jason* and his *Argonautiques*, and almost the whole Chaos of Mythique inventions.

'Japet' (the Titan Japetus) was identified with Biblical Japhet, progenitor of the Druids; imprisoned Saturn, when released, will restore the Golden Age. He is accompanied by Briareus, the snake-legged Titan who, alchemically, would signify the dragon of putrefaction and regeneration.[13] This same Song, however, tells of the birth and death of Arthur; so that the temperate island of this Saturnian myth recalls Arthur's island resting-place of Avalon, and bound Saturn becomes analogous to the sleeping Arthur. Eventually, over the span of the poem and with the alchemical mysteries as our clue, the western apple-island of Avalon fuses with the alchemical Hesperides to give us an alchemical Britain, 'Queene of all the West' (VI. 199).[14] From this point of view Drayton's insistence on the contribution of the Saxon invaders to British traditions is relevant. Like Ashmole after him Drayton remarks on the descent of the Saxons from Woden–Mercury (XI. 174). Selden amplifies: '*Woden*, in *Saxon* Genealogies, is ascended to, as the chiefe Ancestor of their most Roiall Progenies'.[15] Although largely in favour of the British myth in its pure form, Drayton is also aware of, and occasionally uses, the new debate over the Saxon origins of the race. Here they permit him to introduce Mercury as a founding father of monarchs to whom the poem's Hermetic alchemy can symbolically relate. But Hermetic alchemy historically precedes the Saxon Mercury, as do the British Druids. The restoration of the ancient faith involves a careful recovery and incorporation of all these elements which should, if possible, be seen to unite in a kind of alchemical fusion available, if not to the historian, then at least to the mythologising imagination of the poet. Hence the union of red and white, York and Lancaster, recalls the alchemical marriage of red king and white queen. The product of the union is reforming Henry who, since he succeeded to the throne only because of 'Prince *Arthurs* death (his elder *Brother*)' (XVII. 316), becomes a second Arthur, through his reform restoring the old western Arthurian empire. And when we are told that the original Arthur was buried in an oaken coffin we must, surely, associate him with the poem's Druidic forests, remembering the commonly accepted etymology, perpetuated by Selden, of Druid from Greek *drūs* (oak).[16]

The Welsh theme is crucial because, as Selden again conveniently notes, the descendants of Brutus 'were by incroachment of *Saxons, Jutes, Angles, Danes, . . . Frisians* and *Franks* driven into those westerne parts of the now *Wales* and *Cornwales*' (he has already established that the name Cornwall is 'as if you should say *Corn-wales*; for hither in the *Saxon* conquest the *British* called *Welsh . . .* made transmigration').[17] It was the western Welsh who withstood the invader longest, including the invasion which imposed 'Th'unwieldy *Norman* yoke' (Song IX, l. 282), so that Wales can always tell an overweening England that she is

> the Nurse of all the *British* race;
> And he that was by heaven appointed to unite
> (After that tedious warre) the red Rose and the white,
> A *Tudor* was of [hers], and native of [her] *Mon*,
> From whom descends that King now sitting on her Throane.
>
> (*Ibid.*, ll. 366 ff.)

This makes James – like the Henries before him – an honorary Druid, for Mona (Anglesey) was the last piece of Wales left under the rule of 'Llewelin ap Gruffyth . . . the last Prince of *Wales* of the *British* bloud'. It was also the last refuge of the Druids against the Romans.[18] Moreover, Mona 'Was call'd (in former times) her Country *Cambria's* mother' (l. 390), and there the Druids, 'fearelesse *British* Priests, under an aged Oake, / Taking a milk-white Bull, unstrained with the yoke, / And with an Axe of gold, from that *Jove*-sacred tree / The Missleto cut downe' and performed their sacrificial rites (ll. 417 ff.).[19] The unyoked bull suggests the refusal of the Druids and the Cambro-Britons after them to be subjugated to the Norman yoke. Hence the overthrow of that yoke with the accession of Henry VII (born on Anglesey) who, as it were, revives the spirit of Llewelyn, the last Welsh (or British) Prince of Wales, because of his connection with Anglesey.

It would seem that Drayton sees the Tudors and Stuarts as reborn Druids, with the Druids' religious and racial strengths. The Druids' mythological and dynastic force is strengthened in addition by Selden's comment on the Druidic mistletoe which he associates, as tradition and Virgil's own words permitted him to, with Aeneas's golden bough, that emblem of the secret wisdom that belongs to kings and that was revealed to the progenitor of the British race by the Sibyl herself.[20]

'The *British Druids* took this Isle of *Anglesey* (then well stored with thicke Woods, and religious Groves . . .) for their chiefe residence'; Aeneas discovers the golden bough gleaming 'in [a] shadowy holm-oak tree' protected by an enclosing forest.[21] This is why *Poly-Olbion* is deeply concerned with forests and their fate, a concern that is announced in Song II with a lament on their decay. Drayton implores his muse (who is herself in part Druidic):

> Old *Arden* when thou meet'st, or doost faire *Sherwood* see,
> Tell them, that as they waste, so everie day doe wee:
> Wish them, we of our griefes may be each others heirs;
> Let them lament our fall, and we will mourne for theirs. (ll. 477 ff.)

The death of forests marks the death of Druidism. But there is a hierarchy of forests in which Arden is supreme because of its Druidic associations, and this explains the importance of Arden in the second Song which has earlier concentrated on the New Forest. The New Forest speaks as the sovereign forest of Hampshire and therefore as the sovereign forest of oak trees.[22] But since it was created 'by *Williams* tyrannie' (l. 200), it is a symbol of the Norman yoke and so stands for the appropriation of the ancient British oak by the upstart invaders. Just as, according to 'the *Eagles* prophecies', the British line will be restored (l. 152), and just as, in a tale sung by the river Itchin, Bevis of Southampton, having been sold among the Armenians and after enjoying many victories, was 'Unto his ancient lands and titles . . . restor'd' (l. 380),[23] so will the New Forest herself be superseded by Arden. Indeed, it is presumably a sense of a doom already accomplished (through the succession of Tudors and the house of Stuart) that makes the New Forest, on hearing of Bevis's restoration to his 'ancient lands', cry 'enough' (l. 381), although we are also still in the realm of prophecy. Tudors and Stuart have accomplished much, but there is more to be achieved before the return can be completed.

Arden has supremacy because of its former vastness and because it was the central (sovereign) forest of England:

> Of all the Forrests heere within this mightie Ile,
> If those old *Britains* then me Soveraigne did instile,
> I needs must be the great'st. (XIII. 29 ff.)

It has Druidic associations: 'The *Druids* (as some say) by her instructed were. / In many secret skills shee had been cond her lere' (XII. 501–502). It is even a 'Wisard' (XII. 546). Arden has been despoiled, but Drayton associates it with spring rebirth (XIII. 41 ff.). What is being reborn is the old religion of magic.

When we read of the spoliation of Arden, we recall the heartfelt lament for the death of forests in Song III:

> . . . Ages there shall rise,
> So senselesse of the good of their posterities,
> That of your greatest Groves they scarce shall leave a tree.

This lament follows immediately on from lines about the appearance of angels to Abraham 'upon the *Plaine* of *Mamre*' (l. 143), where the allusion is to Genesis 18:1: 'Againe the Lord appeared unto him in the plain of Mamre as he sate in his tent-doore about the heate of the day'. The allusion can be seen to confirm the poem's mystical message in relation to Druidic forests if we follow the alternative reading *oak grove* for 'plain of Mamre': Abraham entertained angels in an oak grove; *Poly-Olbion* is about the restoration, at least in symbolic terms, of the ancient oak forests, connected as they are with Druids and (we now suspect) angels.[24] Druidism and the Bible are thus again reconciled. It is surely no accident that less than thirty lines later we have our first introduction to '*Isis* setting forth upon her way to *Tame*' (ll. 184–185). In this brief passage of Song III the Biblical, Druidic and Egyptian are gently yet insistently fused.

Isis has Egyptian connotations in part because Drayton chooses to make the river female, thereby, as J. B. Oruch remarks,[25] following Spenser and also, perhaps, to recall Spenser's own Egyptianism. Egyptian Isis has, indeed, already appeared in Song II, which makes the connection more inherently likely. Here Drayton comments on the black coral found round 'the Ile of *Portland*', 'which th'Ancients, for the love that they to *Isis* bare / (Their Goddesse most ador'd) have sacred for her haire' (ll. 43–44), and Selden's note draws attention to the ubiquity of Isis cults:

> You have in *Plutarch* and *Apuleius* such variety of *Isis* titles, and, in *Clemens* of *Alexandria*, so large circuits of her travels, that it were no

more wonder to heare of her name in this Northerne climat, then in
Ægypt: especially, we having three rivers of note synonymous with her.

The same note remarks that '*Osiris* her husband [was] sonne to *Cham*',[26]
that is, brother to Japhet and father of the Druids. Flower-bedecked Isis
evokes Egyptian Isis to identify religious reformation in England with
the restoration of Druidism and the Egyptian mysteries. Having married
Tame, her offspring Thames (Thamesis) comes to Windsor,

> To that supreamest place of the great English Kings,
> The *Garters* Royall seate, from him who did advance
> That Princely Order first, our first that conquered *France*;
> The Temple of *Saint George*, wheras his honored Knights,
> Upon his hallowed day, observe their ancient rites. . . . (XV. 314 ff.)

Garter symbolism, already potent under Elizabeth as an instrument of
the reformed religion, is now seen to be elaborately bound up with the
Druidic and Egyptian mysteries. The home of the Garter is on the banks
of the river-son of Isis because the Garter itself, that ancient
'Chivalrous' order, has its origin in a king's chivalry to a woman. Selden
speculates that it might have a 'more ancient Original' than the reign of
Edward III.[27] Drayton implies that its meaning and significance are
traceable to Isis and her fusion with those powerful relatives of her dead
husband, the British Druids.

[iii] *Druids and shepherds in Milton and Lovelace:* Lycidas *and*
Aramantha

In *Poly-Olbion* the Mercurian element disappears into a vague
alchemical Hermeticism which embraces on the one hand the poem's
Egyptian theme and on the other its Druidism. All three are aspects of
the poem's Arthurianism and its attempts to define the nature of the
ancient faith restored by Henry VIII and sustained by his successors. The
dedication to Prince Henry is crucial, though, in directing us to the
element of hope: not now (under James), says Drayton, but under you,
another Henry, and, by virtue of blood as well as title, a true Prince of
Wales and custodian of Welsh traditions.

In many ways Drayton's poem provides a context for the
revolutionary ecclesiastical politics of *Lycidas*, in which 'monody the
author bewails a learned friend, unfortunately drowned in his passage
from Chester on the Irish Seas, 1637. And by occasion foretells the ruin
of our corrupted clergy then in their height'. This epigraph, which heads

the 1645 text of the poem, juxtaposes geography and reform to render provocatively explicit what was already explicit in the narrative. King's death off the Welsh coast gave Milton the opportunity to meditate not just on death but on renovation. The rock struck by King's ship becomes the pristine Peter, 'pilot of the Galilean lake' of line 109, the renewed church itself.[28] But that church, which is also shadowed forth in the resurrection of Lycidas 'Through the dear might of him that walked the waves' (l. 173), is a strange mixture of Christian, Druidic and Arthurian. The significant paragraph for this interpretation begins at line 50:

> Where were ye nymphs when the remorseless deep
> Closed o'er the head of your loved Lycidas?
> For neither were ye playing on the steep,
> Where your old bards, the famous Druids, lie,
> Nor on the shaggy top of Mona high,
> Nor yet where Deva spreads her wizard stream:
> Ay me, I fondly dream!

The same paragraph introduces Orpheus, which reminds us that *Lycidas*, like *L'Allegro* and *Il Penseroso*, is overtly Orphic, a poem about the journey to the wisdom that lies beyond darkness. Orpheus was an ancient theologian. So were the Druids, however, and it is their bones that the bones of Edward King have mingled with off the coast of Mona, because the Druids were slaughtered on Mona by the Romans. When Lycidas rises so, presumably, do the Druids and the British liberty they represent. Hence the singing of the poem 'to the oaks and rills' at line 186, which on one level are the mundane version of the New Jerusalem's 'other groves, and other streams' (l. 174) now enjoyed by the dead King, but on another level are Druidic oaks. In regenerating King through the power of song the 'swain' has regenerated his despairing self into a Druidic bard.[29]

This will seem less speculative if we glance at *Mansus* (1639), where Druids are again remarkably in evidence. Indeed, their presence turns this poem, too, into a statement about revolutionary intention as much as a statement about Milton's poetic aspirations in a merely literary sense. For Milton refers here to his muse as nourished 'beneath the frozen Bear' (later specified as the 'seven-starred wagon') and reminds us that this is the same muse that inspired the Druids, who were bards as well as worshippers of Phoebus. That muse, operating through him, will, he hopes, enable him to 'bring back to life in [his] songs the kings of [his] native land and Arthur . . .'.[30]

The Bear is Arthurian. It is 'frozen' in its manifestation as Charles, whose icy reign at the moment inhibits revolutionary action. (An alternative name for the Bear, we recall, was Charles's Wain. *Il Penseroso* is in one sense about the conflict between the false Caroline Bear and the true Hermetic Bear.) The northern island of Britain will be warmed by Phoebus (religious truth) when the true Bear reigns in the heavens, and this true Bear is not just Hermetic but specifically Arthurian. Furthermore, because of Gregory's interpretation of the seven stars of Ursa Major as a symbol of the universal church, it was associated with ecclesiastical reform. Arthur reborn is the agent of reform. His herald is the Druidic bard whose Druidism asserts a religious and a British purity and liberty. Apollo himself, Milton remarks in what is almost a 'proof' of his Druidic proposition, would often sing to his lute 'beneath a dark oak tree'.[31]

If we now return to *Lycidas* we can see that the conjunction of Druids with Deva's 'wizard stream' is more than accidental. King set sail from Chester up the Dee, which thus becomes the poem's presiding river. The Dee 'marks the northern border between Wales and England';[32] so that *Lycidas* appears to be a thematic counterpart, on the matter of religious and moral reform, to *Comus*, with its celebration of the old southern boundary, Severn. Why 'wizard', though? Because, say the commentators, the Dee was attributed with prophetic power. When it inclined towards its Welsh bank it promised victory to Wales over England; when it inclined towards its English bank it promised victory to the English over the Welsh.[33] It is more precisely 'wizard', however, if we understand Milton as alluding to Merlin and Arthur. To do this he need only be following Spenser, who has 'the great Magicien *Merlin*' visiting the young Arthur in a valley 'Under the foot of *Rauran* mossy hore, / From whence the river *Dee* as silver cleene / His tombling billowes rolls with gentle rore' (I. ix. 4).

As I see it, the drowned Lycidas fuses in the poet's mind with the vanished Druids and the dead Arthur to produce a despair that embraces the fallenness of a once-pure British religion as much as the death of King as an individual. Yet despair yields to hope. The swain sings to 'oaks' and anticipates a 'tomorrow'. The Druidic spirit that inspired *Lycidas* and *Mansus* is much closer, I think, to the one we detect in the second edition of *The Doctrine and Discipline of Divorce* (1644) than it is to the hostility that we later find in *The History of Britain*. In 1644 Milton exhorts parliament to introduce divorce legislation by appealing to the precedent of the reforming Druids:

It would not be the first, or second time, since our ancient *Druides*, by whom this Island was the Cathedrall of Philosophy to *France*, left off their pagan rites, that *England* hath had this honour vouchsaft from Heav'n, to give out reformation to the World.[34]

The Druids were pagans but ancient theologians. In the line of Hermes Trismegistus, Orpheus, and the Sibyls, they were nearer to divine truth than the ecclesiastical establishment with its 'Blind mouths' (*Lycidas*, l. 119). Hence Anglican shepherds are to be displaced by the reforming shepherd whose arrival is heralded by the Druidic-bardic shepherd.

Shepherds belong naturally to Christian pastoral, and so it is easy to assume rather than question their presence in *Lycidas*. When it is questioned we come up with the possibility of a Mercurian shepherd in the poem. The swain plays an instrument that is at once strung and a wind instrument: 'He touched the tender stops of various quills' (l. 188).[35] As a lyre his instrument may be Orphic (and Druidic). And yet he is a shepherd, and Mercury is a shepherd god and inventor of the lyre, which he subsequently bestowed upon Phoebus.[36] Maybe Mercury as shepherd–musician presides over *Lycidas*, so that in this elegy we detect the final reversal of the myth of the Mercurian monarch which Milton had explored and refined in *L'Allegro*, *Il Penseroso*, and *Comus*. Milton now turns his eye to the Mercurian shepherd, whose revival of the Golden-Age rusticity of ditties 'Temper'd to the oaten flute' (l. 33) will announce the expulsion of the faithless clerics' 'lean and flashy songs' as they 'Grate on their scrannel pipes of wretched straw' (ll. 123–124). They 'scarce themselves know how to hold / A sheep-hook'; but 'the faithful herdsman' does (ll. 119 ff.). As we saw from Book VI of *The Faerie Queene* the sheep-hook is the pastoral equivalent of the caduceus.[37] Milton's 'swain' himself possesses a sheep-hook caduceus as well as Mercurian lyre, perhaps. To his Mercurian power is added Druidic inspiration. What he is inspired to see is the purification of the church in the shape of a returned Arthur, whose sceptre will release the sheep-hook to its ancient function as the emblem of rightful ecclesiastical authority.

Some eleven years after the first publication of *Lycidas* Lovelace published his miscellany *Lucasta* (1649). The title page draws attention to the inclusion of one particular poem by stating: 'to which is added *Aramantha, a Pastorall*'. *Aramantha* is the longest poem in the collection. It is also the most riddling, not least because it belongs to that seventeenth-century tradition of Egyptian–Druidic–Mercurian works that we have gradually been uncovering.

In the poem Aramantha turns out to be the supposed-dead Lucasta, beloved of the shepherd Alexis whose lament for her death has been overheard by Aramantha—Lucasta in a grove. On a narrative level it is about separation and reunion. Politically it is about the sequestration and purification of England and the restoration of the Golden Age, since we are told that Aramantha has fled, like Astraea, from civil war 'to this yet living Wood' (l. 340) where she has been instructed in the language of birds by the 'heavenly one' (Caelia; l. 343).[38] When we meet her at the beginning of the poem she is also Flora ('Our *Flora* to the meadow hies'; l. 84), to whom the flowers pay tribute as their sovereign and who therefore restores not only the flowers themselves to a new-born spring earth but the specific qualities that those flowers possess (the monarchical because sun-following '*Heliotropian*', for example, and the 'loyall golden *Mary*' (Henrietta Maria)).

Lovelace is precise about the emblematic nature of the grove as a revised paradigm for a monarchical state:

> From hence her various windings roave
> To a well ordered stately grove;
> This is the Pallace of the Wood,
> And Court oth' Royall Oake, where stood
> The whole Nobility. . . . (ll. 147 ff.)

But it is entered only after Aramantha has encountered a sacred heifer, upon whose milk she breakfasts and who, in her quasi-divinity and sacrificial destiny, becomes a double for Aramantha herself:

> But 'tis decreed when ere this dies,
> That she shall fall a Sacrifice
> Unto the Gods, since those that trace
> Her stemme, show 'tis a God-like race. . . . (ll. 103 ff.)

She is related to Io, is white ('more white / Then is the *milkie way* in Night'), and compared to the moon ('And in her beauteous crescent shone, / Bright as the Argent-horned Moone'). Io is Isis, the moon goddess who was also worshipped as a white cow.[39] The political meaning of the poem somehow depends, as in *Poly-Olbion* and *The Faerie Queene*, on a recognition of the ancient strengths of the Egyptian religion.

We are also told something more. This white heifer must be sacrificed by 'the *hallowed knife*' (l. 132), which suggests Druidic ritual as reported by Selden from Pliny:[40]

In such gloomy shadows, as they [the Druids] most usually for contemplation retired their ascending thoughts into, after exact search, finding an Oake, whereon a Mistletoe grew, on the VI. day of the Moone (above all other times) in which, was beginning of their yeare, they religiously and with invocation brought with them to it a ceremoniall banquet, materials for sacrifice, with two white Bulles, filleted on the hornes, all which they plac'd under the Oake. One of them . . . clothed all in white, climbs the tree, and with a golden Knife or Sith cuts the Mistletoe. . . . Then did they sacrifice the Buls, earnestly calling on the *All-healing* Deity [Apollo], to make it prosperous and happy on whom soever they shal bestow it. . . .

The mistletoe may be missing; the bull is a heifer. But the Druidic (as well as Egyptian) meaning of the poem seems clear enough. The 'Royall Oake' is reborn as a Druidic oak through Aramantha who, apparently dead and then restored to life, signifies renewal as Flora, as Isis, and as the Druidic heifer. Confirmation for this reading comes from direct allusions to Druids, an incidental one at line 246, a more significant one at lines 325 ff.:

> LUCASTA to him doth relate
> Her various chance and diffring Fate:
> How chac'd by HYDRAPHIL, and tract,
> The num'rous foe to PHILANACT,
> Who whilst they for the same things fight,
> As BARDS Decrees, and DRUIDS rite,
> For safeguard of their proper joyes,
> And Shepheards freedome, each destroyes
> The glory of this Sicilie. . . .

Both sides cry 'liberty'; both appeal to ancient, Druidic, precedent.[41] Meanwhile pastoral Sicily suffers. The fighting must stop, sacrifice yield now to rebirth. Hearing her tale Alexis finally hangs up his arms and breaks his sword: 'he betook / Himself unto the humble Crook' (ll. 366–367) and, like a bishop, is installed 'in a SEE of flow'rs'. As in *Lycidas*, but in mirror image, we find the Mercurian shepherd, a royalist Anglican one. Against all the odds – against hope – he has found his Flora. This is the swan song of the monarchical *Mercurius Ver* who is metamorphosed into a republican reforming Mercury, again connected with Druids, in Marvell's *Upon Appleton House*, a direct answer, it would seem, to *Aramantha*.[42]

[iv] *Marvell: Hermes and the Druids in* Upon Appleton House

Upon Appleton House: To my Lord Fairfax is the last of the small group of mid-seventeenth-century political poems concerned with Druids and the Mercury theme that I have been able to trace. It is about Fairfax's retirement and Marvell's own decision to retire with Fairfax to become tutor to his daughter Mary. Inevitably obsessed with the horrors of civil war, it can find its model for a renewed England only after consideration and banishment of the vices unleashed in bloodshed. Fairfax's main vice, suggested at stanzas 68–70, was to have been a warrior and to have been implicated in the regicide. He might now have withdrawn to Nun Appleton and be fighting soul-saving battles through the emblematic structures of his house and garden, but there was Biblical precedent in God's refusal to allow David to build the temple for the ark of the covenant 'because thou hast bene a man of warre, and hast shed blood' (I Chronicles 28: 3)[43] for suspecting that he was so tainted by blood-guilt that the future of the new England had to be found elsewhere, in the second generation. God chose David's son Solomon to build the temple and rule Israel because he was destined to be a peacemaker. Marvell attributes a similar peace-bringing (and Mercurian) role to Mary Fairfax, whom the poet encounters at the poem's end.[44]

Mary comes, like a visitation, when images of civil war have finally been purged from the poet's mind. One of the most compelling of these images of civil-war slaughter has concerned the mowers (st. 49 ff.):[45]

> The tawny Mowers enter next;
> Who seem like *Israalites* to be,
> Walking on foot through a green Sea. . . .
>
> With whistling Sithe, and Elbow strong,
> These Massacre the Grass along:
> While one, unknowing, carves the *Rail*,
> Whose yet unfeather'd Quils her fail. . . .
>
> The Mower now commands the Field;
> In whose new Traverse seemeth wrought
> A Camp of Battail newly fought:
> Where, as the Meads with Hay, the Plain
> Lyes quilted ore with Bodies slain. . . .

The comparison with Israelites is followed a few stanzas later (55) by an Egyptian allusion when the field stacked with hay stooks becomes 'like the *Desert Memphis Sand*' dotted with 'Short *Pyramids* of Hay'. The image of Jewish deliverance may yield here to a reminiscence of the *Asclepian* lament on the collapse of the old Egpytian religion:[46]

> To thee, most holy Nile, I cry . . . swollen with torrents of blood, thou wilt
> rise to the level of thy banks, and thy sacred waves will be not only
> stained, but utterly fouled with gore. . . . this land, which once was holy,
> . . . will go beyond all in cruel deeds. The dead will far outnumber the
> living; and the survivors will be known for Egyptians by their tongue
> alone, but in their actions they will seem to be men of another race. . . .
> And so the gods will depart from mankind . . . the fruits of the earth will
> rot; the soil will turn barren . . . all things will be disordered and awry.

It is perhaps only a Hermetic context that makes easy sense of Thestylis's
indignation as she refers to the simile in stanza 49 'And cryes, he call'd us
Israelites' (st. 51) and then perversely tries to make it true. The
implication could be that she wants to be regarded as an Egyptian, but is
unworthy of the honour; so that the mowers are an image of blood-guilty
Civil War England in the form of the fallen Egyptians of the *Asclepian*
lament doing unworthy things. They are mistaken for Israelites because
'in their actions they . . . seem to be men of another race'.[47]

Another Egyptian allusion occurs after the woodland episode. From
the wood, the escape into which has been precipitated by a 'Flood' (st.
61), the poet emerges to adopt the contemplative pose of an angler[48]
which results in the climactic vision of Mary at stanzas 82 ff. The angling
pose and the vision are preceded by a reference to the Nile (st. 79):

> For now the Waves are fal'n and dry'd,
> And now the Meadows fresher dy'd;
> Whose Grass, with moister colour dasht,
> Seems as green Silks but newly washt.
> No *Serpent* new nor *Crocodile*
> Remains behind our little Nile. . . .

The 'swollen' Nile of the lament has receded. In terms of the poem's
imagery, the meadows so recently stained with the blood of civil
slaughter re-emerge greener than they were before the mowers trod
through them as if on 'a green Sea'. This is the ultimate image of rebirth,
based on Ovid's description of the fertile Nile mud impregnated by the
sun's rays in *Metamorphoses*, I. 422 ff. But whereas Ovid's Nile mud
begets the gigantic and evil Python (ll. 438–440), this new world has 'No
Serpent' – be it Python, Pharaoh, or Satan. Neither has it the Nile
crocodile traditionally identified with hypocrisy.[49]

I suspect, too, with Maren-Sofie Røstvig,[50] that the next stanza, 80,
where the river is compared to '*a Chrystal Mirrour*' in which the sun,
seeing himself reflected, pines 'for his shade . . . *Narcissus* like' hints at
another Hermetic image, appearing as it does in a creation context. In

the Hermetic *Pimander*, Pimander himself (Mind) appears in a vision to Hermes telling him of the creation; of how darkness changed to water; of how Light and Word came forth and ordered the water into the world. Eventually Pimander tells how man was conceived: 'Mind the Father of all, he who is Life and Light gave birth to Man, a Being like to Himself'. God delighted in him 'for it was God's own form that God took delight in'. Man learns the nature of the heavenly bodies, then breaks through the last of the planetary spheres in order to view the earth below (or Nature). He loves her, and she, seeing his God-like form, loves him. The Narcissus image – present by implication in God's love of man – reappears:

> And Nature, seeing the beauty of the form of God, smiled with insatiate love of Man, showing the reflection of that most beautiful form in the water, and its shadow on the earth. And he, seeing this form, a form like to his own, in earth and water, loved it, and willed to dwell there.[51]

This Narcissus stanza looks back to the earlier 'creation' stanzas 56–58, which follow the mowing episode and immediately precede the withdrawal to the wood. As the scene, masquelike, changes to reveal 'A new and empty Face of things', the poet looks at the grazing cattle:

> They seem within the polisht Grass
> A Landskip drawn in Looking-Glass.
> And shrunk in the huge Pasture show
> As Spots, so shap'd, on Faces do.
> Such Fleas, ere they approach the Eye,
> In multiplying Glasses lye.
> They feed so wide, so slowly move,
> As *Constellations* do above.

It is a moment of calm in a world of violence and disorder, confirming, like stanza 80, the reflective relationship of earth and heaven. And it, too, emits a faint Hermetic overtone. For this might be the expulsion of the beast in the form of the Jovian bull. If the animals are now on earth, miming the constellations, the implication seems to be that the constellations 'above' have been purified of their bestial qualities; and being purified the way is now open for the subsequent purification of the earth through the influence of the virginal Mary Fairfax, herself stellar not only because she has been 'in *Heaven* try'd' (st. 86) but because she is the daughter of Fairfax and Anne Vere, the 'starry *Vere*' of stanza 91.[52]

In discussing Mary we may begin with J. M. Wallace's fine insight into her Mercurian characteristics: 'A long simile involving the halcyon makes her seem to fly, and the hush which greets her arrival can be paralleled by other accounts of Mercury's descent'.[53] Wallace thinks here of epic interventions of the god. But we are now in a position to see her rather as Marvell's revolutionary inversion of the Mercurian ruler bestowing order and virtue through wisdom. She is Mercury as pacifier and, like Mercury, she has command of tongues:[54]

> *She* counts her Beauty to converse
> In all the Languages as *hers*;
> Nor yet in those *her self* imployes
> But for the *Wisdome*, not the *Noyse*;
> Nor yet that *Wisdome* would affect,
> But as 'tis *Heavens Dialect*. (st. 89)

The halcyon simile of stanzas 84–85 does more than give Mary Mercurial wings, however. It identifies her with, and makes her the new religion's equivalent of, the Virgin Mary (whom emblematic tradition associated with the halcyon),[55] and it confirms her role as restorer to earth of the peace and tranquillity lost through the corruptions of monarchy and the consequent Civil War because of the halcyon's habit of nesting on the sea during the calm of the winter solstice. She is the new halcyon expelling the depraved halcyon of Caroline propaganda which saw Britain as 'the halcyon's nest' inhabited by Henrietta Maria as the queen of peace and beauty 'with fair / And halcyon beams becalm[ing] the air'.[56] She is, moreover, divinely and Mercurially birdlike in a way only postured at by the poet groping earlier for illumination in the darkness of the wood: 'Give me but Wings as they, and I / Steight floting on the Air shall fly' (st. 71).

It is possible to be more precise about Mary's iconographical characteristics. As peace-bringing Mercury she is also a virginal Astraea descending with the disappearance of Iron-Age strife to herald the return of the Golden Age. Her affinities with the Virgin Mary suggest the restoration of the Golden-Age religion. But she is not destined for a perpetually virginal role, since it is her duty and destiny to marry and beget a new race to people and establish the new Britain (st. 93), thus exorcising for ever the ghosts of the corrupt Catholic nuns to whom Nun Appleton once belonged (st. 11–35). And so to his virgin Marvell adds Venerean characteristics to produce a *Venus virgo* on the model of Spenser's Belphoebe and Britomart. Hence, Venus-like, she is lady of the gardens (st. 87–88; 94), though since she is crowned with flowers (st. 88) she is also the spring goddess Chloris–Flora, who was, as we have seen, frequently identified with Venus and intimately connected with Mercury as a spring god. We therefore suspect a pun on Mary's maternal family name, for *Vere* is not only Truth, the poem's contemplative goal, but *ver*, the spring of a reborn world, as well. And so it is her function to bestow 'sweetness' (st. 87) on those meadows which were earlier strewn with bodies (st. 53), since Venus traditionally tempers Mars to produce Harmony.[57] As a Venus, too, she moderates and supersedes the martial disposition of her warrior father.

If we now turn to the woodland episode we can see how Marvell fuses his Hermeticism with Druidism. The poet escapes, like Noah, from the flood released over the meadow in stanza 59 into the 'yet green, yet growing Ark' of the wood (st. 61). It appears dark:

> When first the Eye this Forrest sees
> It seems indeed as *Wood* not *Trees*:
> As if their Neighbourhood so old
> To one great Trunk them all did mold.
> There the huge Bulk takes place, as ment
> To thrust up a *Fifth Element*;
> And stretches still so closely wedg'd
> As if the Night within were hedg'd.
>
> Dark all without it knits; within
> It opens passable and thin;
> And in as loose an order grows,
> As the *Corinthean Porticoes*.
> The arching Boughs unite between
> The Columnes of the Temple green. . . . (st. 63–64)

As the wood darkens it becomes a symbol of the first chaos like Spenser's wood of Error: via Noah the poet has moved backward through Genesis and other creation tales in order to glimpse the primal matter from which the cosmos was formed. Or, in Hermetic terms, he is viewing the primal matter within himself before undergoing moral and spiritual renewal. As Pimander says to Hermes: 'Learn my meaning . . . by looking at what you yourself have in you'.[58] What he then sees, in a recapitulation of the creative act, is darkness lightening again to become a green temple, where green is the colour of creation and hope (we have met it before; but this green of the temple is only on its way to being the 'newly washt' green of stanza 79 which heralds the vision of Mary),[59] and where the temple is the created earth in its guise as God's 'most august temple' (to quote a phrase of Pico's).[60] Moreover, the '*Corinthean Porticoes*' confirm that the wood-temple is a symbolic prefiguring of Mary, hinting that the poet is still preparing for his vision of her but has not yet attained it, for according to Vitruvius the Corinthian order imitated 'the slenderness of a maiden' and commemorated a freeborn Corinthian girl who died when 'just of marriageable age'.[61] '*Corinthean*' establishes Mary's maidenliness (the order was used, for example, for the temples of Vesta at Rome and Tivoli), then, and anticipates her marriage. Appropriately, the Corinthian order was used, too, for temples of Venus and Flora.[62]

The '*Fifth Element*' is traditionally identified with Mind, the 'heaven which intellectually is within us' of Bruno's *Expulsion*. Not Hermetic in itself, it takes on Hermetic resonance from its context of unified and aspiring trees and their connection with the tree-body of stanza 71:

> Thus I, *easie Philosopher*,
> Among the *Birds* and *Trees* confer:
> And little now to make me, wants
> Or of the *Fowles*, or of the *Plants*.
> Give me but Wings as they, and I
> Streight floting on the Air shall fly:
> Or turn me but, and you shall see
> I was but an inverted Tree.

The image derives from Plato and is commonplace, but it seems more than relevant than an inverted tree appears in the first part of the *Asclepius*, in a passage distinguishing between vegetable life, animal life, and man. All creatures which 'possess soul have roots extending downward to them from above. . . . The soul is nourished by . . . the higher elements; the growth of bodies is supplied from . . . the lower elements. Mind, a fifth component part, which comes from the aether, has been bestowed on man alone'. It is through Mind alone that man 'can attain to knowledge of the truth concerning God'.[63]

These tree stanzas, 63–64 and 71, frame stanzas dealing with another tree, the oak that is felled by the woodpecker (68–70). Obviously an emblem of sin and the specific corruptions of the monarchy that led to Charles's execution, its message is that of the necessity for willing self-sacrifice, the voluntary purgation of vice within the self: 'the Oake seems to fall content'. Applied to the poet the oak's message seems to be that he must abandon the too-easy contemplative half-way house of the wood, with all its opportunities for self-display and regression, in order to confront the outside world in which the flood has now subsided. This new outside world, contrary to what the poet appears to believe, is neither frightening nor excessively rigorous. While he dreamed and role-played in the wood the world was purged in preparation for the arrival of perfect

Mary. All he has to do is to go out to meet this girl who, heaven-descended, will, like the oak tree, achieve herself through self-sacrifice:

> Hence *She* with Graces more divine
> Supplies beyond her *Sex* the *Line*;
> And, like a *sprig of Misleto*,
> On the *Fairfacian Oak* does grow;
> Whence, for some universal good,
> The *Priest* shall cut the sacred Bud;
> While her *glad Parents* most rejoice,
> And make their *Destiny* their *Choice*. (st. 93)

It is at this point that the Hermetic resonances fade and are replaced explicitly by the more domestic strains of Druidism. This is Druidic mistletoe, and we may now suspect that the descending oak leaves of stanza 74 which 'embroyder' the poet are Druidic too: 'Under this *antick Cope* I move / Like some great *Prelate of the Grove*'. D. C. Allen and others, however, assume the Druidic symbolism without exploring it.[64]

As we have seen, Druidism goes hand-in-hand with Hermeticism at this period. The poet's identification of himself with Noah suggests that he is recalling the legendary descent of these ancient inhabitants of Britain renowned for their wisdom, their combination of bardic and priestly roles, and for their adherence to the first religion – that of the Golden Age – in its purest form.[65]

Marvell develops those themes that we have traced in *Lycidas* and *Aramantha* to analyse mid-century corruption and vice, both royalist and republican, in terms of the fallen Egypt of the *Asclepian* lament. He anticipates the return of a pure religion in the symbolic Mary Fairfax by offering us the specifically British version of the ancient wisdom and theology in the shape of a Mercurian girl who is the sacrificial gift of a Druidic priest. It is possible that Marvell derived much of his knowledge of the Druids from Selden, in which case we might note that Selden's most elaborate comment on the Druids, appended to Song IX of *Poly-Olbion*, follows shortly after his remark on Snowdon's boast that 'Nere could that Conquerors [William I] sword (which roughly did decide / His right in *England* heere, and prostrated her pride) / Us to subjection stoope, or make us *Britains* beare / Th'unwieldy *Norman* yoke' (ll. 279–282). This could lead to the inference that the poet, in stanza 73, does indeed become the true alternative bardic priest to the Archbishop of York (the '*Prelate* great' of stanza 46), heralding the arrival of Mary and liberation from Norman tyranny. But it is a hint in Dio Chrysostom's *Orations* that gives a final clue to the relationship of the oak-leaf-covered poet with the felled oak tree of stanzas 68–70. For Dio comments that it is the wise Druids who are the true rulers, and not the monarchs:[66]

> Without the Druids, who understand divination and philosophy, the kings may neither do nor consult any thing; so that in reality they are the Druids who reign, while the kings (tho' they sit on golden thrones, dwell in spacious palaces, and feed on costly dishes) are onely their ministers.

The new religion and the new world belong to the bardic priest and his oak. It is to elevate the adviser to ruler (and this is Marvell's answer to Lovelace) that the royal oak was felled. Moreover, the symbolic function of Druids during the Civil War period, and particularly after the regicide, is made clearer if we recall that, according to Strabo and Caesar, Druids were used as judges, deciding not only public and private disputes but also arbitrating in cases of war and murder.[67] It is Druidic wisdom that is required to repair the ravages of war.

The final Druidic image in the poem belongs to Mary. She is the '*sprig of Misleto*' that 'On the *Fairfacian Oak* does grow' whose 'sacred Bud' must soon be cut by 'The *Priest*'. As Pliny noted, 'anything growing on oak-trees they think to have been sent down from heaven, and to be a sign that the particular tree has been chosen by God himself'. Sacrificial mistletoe, like the halcyon, is rare; given in drink it imparts fertility.[68] Here, then, the poem reaches its climax as the new race and religion are assured by a sign of divine intervention. The fertile mistletoe berries cancel out, across the poem, the virginal pearls to which the nun in the house's earlier history had compared herself, Isabel Thwaites (Mary's historical antecedent), and other sisters:

> Where you may ly as chast in Bed,
> As Pearls together billeted.
> All Night embracing Arm in Arm,
> Like Chrystal pure with Cotton warm. (st. 24)

Mistletoe gathered and sacrificed 'on the VI. day of the Moone'[69] aptly transcends the lunar pearls to remind us of Mary's own lunar qualities and hence, ultimately, her affinity – through the poem's Egyptian symbolism – with the moon goddess Isis. Mary appears, after all, when the flood subsides and 'our little *Nile*' has returned to its normal size. Isis 'was the daughter of the floud Inachus'. She holds

> in one hand a Cymball, and in the other an earthen vessell of water, whereupon (as *Servius* sayth) many supposed her to bee the Genius of Ægypt … understanding by the Cymball … that uncouth noise and

farre-heard murmure which Nilus roareth forth, when with her tumbling and furious billowes shee over-washeth the spacious fields of Ægypt: and by the other vessell of water, the many Rivers, Pooles, and Lakes in which that Country excelleth.[70]

Marvell's Egyptian metaphors in *Upon Appleton House* combine with his Druidic allusions to offer yet another and climactic prospect of how 'the *World*' can be 'what once it was'.

Notes

1 Walker, *The Ancient Theology*, pp. 2, 20, 63, 73 ff., 87–88, 94 ff.
2 The most recent reliable review of the material is by A. L. Owen, *The Famous Druids: a Survey of Three Centuries of English Literature on the Druids* (Oxford: Clarendon Press, 1962). Also valuable are E. Davies, *The Mythology and Rites of the British Druids* (London, 1809); T. D. Kendrick, *The Druids: a Study in Keltic History* (London: Methuen, 1927), and Lewis Spence, *The History and Origins of Druidism* (1949; new imprn, London: Aquarian Press, 1971). Main ancient sources include Diodorus Siculus, V. xxviii; Caesar, *Gallic War*, VI. xiii–xiv; and Pliny, *Natural History*, XVI. xcv.
3 Text from Nichols, *Progresses . . . of King James*, I. 564 ff.
4 Ashmole, *Theatrum Chemicum Britannicum*, sigs A2^V–B3^V.
5 Dio Chrysostom, *Orations*, XLIX; see below, n. 66.
6 Quotations from Hebel's edn of the *Works*, vol. IV. On the eagle and Merlin, see Selden's note, pp. 44–45, and Rupert Taylor, *The Political Prophecy in England* (New York: Columbia U.P., 1911), pp. 21 ff. William Lilly's anti-royalist *The Prophecy of the White King* (1644) is based on the eagle prophecy: Harry Rurche, 'Prophecies and Propaganda, 1641–1651', *English Historical Review*, 84 (1969), 757 ff. Drayton's political argument leads him to modify the topography of Camden's *Britannia*: W. H. Moore, 'Sources of Drayton's Conception of *Poly-Olbion*', *SP*, 65 (1968), 787.
7 The poem also alludes to the building of gold statues to James (l. 325) and to his outshining of Arcturus and Orion (ll. 199 ff.), details that would seem to have particular significance in view of what we have gathered of the Hermetic statues in the court masque and the Arcturus–Orion symbolism of *The Faerie Queene*. Text from *The Poetical Works of William Drummond of Hawthornden*, ed. L. E. Kastner, 2 vols (repr. New York: Haskell, 1968), I. 141 ff.
8 Brinkley, *Arthurian Legend in the Seventeenth Century*, pp. 29 ff. and 68 ff. comments on Selden's notes and remarks on his reservations about monarchical absolutism. B. C. Ewell observes the 'focal celebration of the nuptials of Tame and Isis' in 'Drayton's *Poly-Olbion*: England's Body Immortalized', *SP*, 75 (1978), 303. From the retrospective viewpoint of the complete thirty-song *Poly-Olbion* the marriage is central and sovereign, appearing as it does in Song XV.

9   Ed. cit., p. 358.

10 For Isis as daughter of a river god, see below, n. 70. Drayton probably follows Spenser in making the river Isis female: J. B. Oruch, 'Spenser, Camden, and the Poetic Marriages of Rivers', *SP*, 64 (1967), 623. Oruch's article is a useful account of the tradition of Tame–Isis spousal poems, dealing incidentally with William Vallans and John Leland's *Cygnea Cantio*, and concentrating mainly on William Camden and Spenser's proposed *Epithalamion Thamesis*. See also T. P. Roche, Jr, *The Kindly Flame: a Study of the Third and Fourth Books of Spenser's 'Faerie Queene'*, pp. 170 ff.

11 In Geoffrey's *History*, the goddess's revelation to Brutus of the western island 'beyond the setting of the sun' is granted to him after he has sacrificed to Jupiter, Mercury, and Diana. He sacrifices to Jupiter as king of heaven, and to Mercury, presumably, as lord of the western, Hesperian, land. Brutus's westward journey is thus essentially Mercurian (Penguin edn, I. xi, p. 65).

12 P. 16. Bound Saturn appears in a Golden-Age context in Drummond's *Forth Feasting*, ll. 359–360. Selden cites Plutarch, *The Obsolescence of Oracles*, 419–420 as a source (where the binding of Saturn in company with Briareus off the coast of Britain is, significantly, narrated in conjunction with references to British holy men and the death of Pan: for Drayton, perhaps Saturn will awaken when Pan revives), and *The Face on the Moon*, 941–942 (at 941F Saturn's imprisoning cave 'shines like gold': *Moralia*, Loeb edn (London and Cambridge, Mass.: Heinemann and Harvard U.P., 1957), XII. 187, tr. Harold Cherness and W. C. Helmbold). The lunar context of this latter reference is important in view of *Poly-Olbion*'s Isis symbolism.

13 For Japetus–Japhet, see Ross, *Mystagogus Poeticus*, p. 192.

14 Cf. Gerald of Wales, *Speculum Ecclesiae*, II: 'It is called Avalon [perhaps] from the Welsh word "aval", which means apple, because apple-trees and apples are very common there' (tr. Lewis Thorpe in *Journey through Wales*, Penguin edn, p. 286; cf. p. 283).

15 Pp. 233–234. Cf. Geoffrey, *History* (Penguin edn), VI. xi, pp. 156–157. On Drayton's attitude to the Saxons, see, e.g., Brinkley, ch. II and pp. 206–212, and I. Gourvitch, 'The Welsh Element in the *Polyolbion*', *RES*, 4 (1928), 69–77. W. H. Moore, art. cit. (n. 6), pp. 789 ff. emphasises 'Drayton's Anglo-Saxon sympathies', however.

16 On the alchemical meaning of red and white, see ch. I, sec. ii above, and *ibid.*, n. 32. Arthur's coffin is mentioned by Selden, p. 66, following Gerald of Wales, *Speculum Ecclesiae*, II (Penguin *Gerald*, p. 287). For Druid and oak, see Selden's elaborate note to Song IX. 417, p. 192.

17 Pp. 27–28.

18 Selden comments on Llewelyn and Mona on p. 190; and cf. p. 200. He was of course an ancestor of James I (e.g. Brinkley, p. 16). For Mona, the Druids, and the Romans, see Owen, *Famous Druids*, pp. 23–24 citing Tacitus, *Annals*, XIV. xxx (concerning the year 60 A.D.); also W. H. Moore, art. cit. (n. 6), p. 789.

19 Selden describes the rites in detail on pp. 192 ff., following Pliny, *Natural History*, XVI. xcv. See also R. C. Cawley, 'Drayton's Use of Welsh History', *SP*, 22 (1925), 253–254.

20 See ch. I, n. 92 above. For the Druids' religion, of a Golden-Age purity, see Owen, *Famous Druids*, p. 41.

21 Selden's note to Song IX. 417 (p. 197); *Aeneid*, VI. 201 ff. (Penguin transln).

22 Cranbourne Chase has nourished 'many a goodlie Oake' (II. 188); '*Chute*' is renowned for its dryads, 'Nymphs that live & die with Oakes' (II. 217 and marginal note).

23 As Selden, p. 46, notes, Bevis was contemporary with 'the *Norman invasion*'.

24 Geneva gloss on Gen. 18: 1 ('plain of Mamre'): '*Or, oke grove*'. See also Owen, *Famous Druids*, p. 9, citing Theophilus Gale on 'this *Oke Religion* (of the *Druides*)' as deriving 'from the *Okes* of *Mamre*'.

25 See n. 10 above. Although male, however, Camden's Isis nevertheless sits as king in a cave where 'painted is the Moon that ruls the sealike Crystall glasse': *The Marriage of Tame and Isis*, tr. Philemon Holland, Fragment IV, l. 11 (from the *Britannia*). Quoted from *Poems by William Camden*, tr. and ed. G. B. Johnston, *SP*, 72 (1975), Texts and Studies, p. 89. B. C. Ewell, *SP*, 75 (1978), 299 (see n. 8 above) follows Angus Fletcher, *Allegory: the Theory of a Symbolic Mode*, p. 236 n. in seeing the frontispiece engraving of Albion herself, wearing as her robe a map of England and holding sceptre and cornucopia, as the ultimate (as well as initial) statement about the nature of the poem's unity. We may go further: Albion as a goddess is the white goddess Isis with her emblems of imperial power (cf. plates 6 and 7).

26 Selden, p. 42.

27 *Ibid.*, p. 312. On the Garter, see ch. II, nn. 78 and 82. For its importance to Denham in *Cooper's Hill* (1642 etc.), see *The Poetical Works of Sir John Denham*, ed. T. H. Banks, Jr. (New Haven, Conn. and London: Yale U.P., O.U.P., 1928), pp. 69–70, significant enough to be quoted by Ashmole, *The Institution . . . of the Garter*, p. 130. Ashmole is also keen to connect Garter emblems and rituals with those of the ancient Egyptians: e.g., *ibid.*, p. 218 (Garter collar and collars round images of Isis and Osiris) and p. 506 (pre-feast Garter vigil and vigils in temples of Isis). Isis–Osiris allusions in Herrick's *Hesperides* (1648) suggest the later royalist continuity of the tradition: e.g., 'A Song to the Maskers' and 'The Welcome to Sack'.

28 For the circumstances of King's death, see *Variorum Milton*, II(ii). 545. The 'pilot's' identity is disputed (*ibid.*, p. 679), but he is accepted as Peter by the *Variorum* eds. (e.g., pp. 672 ff.). D. S. Berkeley, however, identifies him firmly as Christ: *Inwrought with Figures Dim: a Reading of Milton's 'Lycidas'* (The Hague, Paris: Mouton, 1974), pp. 73 ff.

29 My reading adds a mystical 'political' meaning to the sympathetic accounts in Owen, *Famous Druids*, pp. 52 ff.; *Variorum*, pp. 654 ff.; Berkeley, *op. cit.*, pp. 46–48 and 53.

30 I have used Carey's transln; Longmans' *Milton*, pp. 265–267.

31 This is not, of course, to exclude the presence of the prophetic oak of Dodona as well: Pausanias, *Description of Greece*, I. xvii. 5; VII. xxi. 2–4, etc.

32 Gerald, *Description of Wales*, I. v (Penguin edn, p. 230).

33 Drayton, *Poly-Olbion*, X. 200 ff. (the only interpretation admitted by the *Variorum* eds, pp. 656–657).

34 *Complete Prose Works of John Milton*, ed. D. M. Wolfe *et al.*, II (1959), 231. In *Areopagatica* (also 1644) he went further: according to many, 'ev'n the school of *Pythagoras*, and the *Persian* wisdom took beginning from the old Philosophy of this Iland': *ibid.*, II. 551–552. For Milton's hostility, see *The History of Britain*, II, in Yale *Prose Works*, V (i) (1971), pp. 60–61.

35 The combination of wind and strings refers to the tradition that the soul contained within itself the qualities of lyre (the higher part) and flute (lower): J. B. Friedman, *Orpheus in the Middle Ages* (Cambridge, Mass.: Harvard U.P. 1970), pp. 80 ff. The wind/string ambiguity is noticed by A. D. S. Fowler, ' "To Shepherd's Ear": the Form of Milton's *Lycidas*', in Fowler (ed.), *Silent Poetry: Essays in Numerological Analysis*, p. 176 (*stop* signifies the finger hole of a wind instrument and the action of placing one's finger on a string to raise the pitch).

36 Selden identifies Orphic and Druidic–bardic harp–lyre at p. 121 (note on Song VI. 106), with a marginal note drawing attention to Mercury's creation of Apollo's lyre (on which see ch. I, n. 133 above). Orpheus, son of Apollo, was given his lyre by Mercury: Friedman, *Orpheus*, p. 140 (citing Boccaccio); and cf. Comes, *Mythologiae*, VII. xiv, *De Orpheo*.

37 Ch. I, sec. viii above.

38 She is Astraea at l. 289, 'that Virgin-star a Maid'. Quotations from *The Poems of Richard Lovelace*, ed. C. H. Wilkinson (Oxford: Clarendon Press, 1930).

39 Linche, *Fountaine of Ancient Fiction*, sigs. Hiv ff.; Ross, *Mystagogus Poeticus*, pp. 206 ff.: 'the Cow in respect of her benefit to mankind, was by the Egyptians worshipped for their god: and Io after her death was worshipped by the Egyptians: hence arose the fable of *Io's* being turned into a Cow'; '*Io* [is] *Isis*'.

40 Selden, pp. 193–194 (note to *Poly-Olbion*, Song IX. 417), echoing Pliny, *Natural History*, XVI. xcv.

41 Philanact represents the royalist cause (Wilkinson's note, p. 296), presumably by analogy with Brutus's son Albanact (to whose name the white of the heifer also relates).

42 James Turner notices similarities between *Appleton House* and *Aramantha* in *The Politics of Landscape* (Cambridge, Mass.: Harvard U.P., 1979), pp. 95–96.

43 Cf. I Chron. 22.

44 King James gloss on I Chron. 22: ('his name shall be Solomon'): 'That is, *Peaceable*'.

45 Quotations from *The Poems and Letters of Andrew Marvell*, ed. H. M.

Margoliouth; 3rd edn, rev. P. Legouis and E. E. Duncan-Jones, 2 vols. (Oxford: Clarendon Press, 1971).

46 *Hermetica*, ed. Scott, I. 341 ff.

47 The orthodox viewpoint based on an Old Testament reading (Egyptians bad, Israelites good) is followed by M.-S. Røstvig, *The Happy Man: Studies in The Metamorphoses of a Classical Ideal*, 2 vols., Oslo Studies in English, II, rev. edn (1962), I. 180, 186–187, and J. M. Wallace, *Destiny his Choice: the Loyalism of Andrew Marvell* (Cambridge: C.U.P., 1968), pp. 246–247. Wallace usefully confirms the Egyptian nationality of the mowers by commenting on their tawny colour (st. 49): cf. Milton's metrical version of Psalm 136, ll. 53–54: 'But full soon they did devour / The tawny king with all his power'.

48 Cf. Marcia Vale, *The Gentleman's Recreations* (Cambridge: D. S. Brewer, 1977), pp. 52–57. A courtly equivalent to Marvell's vision here would be the post-tempest emergence of the 'bowre of *Chloris*' accompanied by a rainbow in Jonson's *Chloridia* (1630): *Works*, ed. Herford and Simpson, VII. 756. M. C. Bradbrook was the first to demonstrate just how far a masque ethos pervades Marvell's work in 'Marvell and the Masque', pp. 204–223 of *Tercentenary Essays in Honor of Andrew Marvell*, ed. Kenneth Friedenreich (Hamden, Conn.: Archon Books, 1977).

49 On these see Røstvig, *op. cit.*, I. 187 (the dragon-pharaoh of Ezekiel 29: 3); P. Ansell Robin, *Animal Lore in English Literature* (London: John Murray, 1932), pp. 53–55 (hypocrisy).

50 Røstvig, I. 188 (the Hermetic passage is cited on p. 164).

51 *Hermetica*, ed. Scott, I. 121; Nock and Festugière, I. 11. Fairfax, the poem's dedicatee, was working on a transln of François de Foix's commentary around this time: C. R. Markham, *A Life of the Great Lord Fairfax* (London, 1870), p. 368.

52 *Vere* suggests *truth* (*Verus*). The epithet alludes specifically to the Vere coat of arms, which incorporates a star: E. E. Duncan-Jones in Margoliouth, *Marvell*, I. 292. Cf. Markham, *op. cit.*, p. 397.

53 Wallace, *Destiny his Choice*, p. 251. James Turner, *The Politics of Landscape*, pp. 64 ff., offers a scrupulous and illuminating analysis of this simile; and see his pp. 74 ff. for a perceptive account of Mary, which, however, is at variance with my own by emphasising the 'private' and 'domestic' nature of her destined role.

54 One of the alchemical Mercuries was identified with the halcyon and rebirth: 'The arcanum is the entire virtue of a thing, multiplied a thousandfold. . . . *Mercurius vitae*, the third [and penultimate] arcanum, has a purifying action; like a halcyon, which puts on new feathers after moulting, it can remove the impurities from man . . . and make him grow anew': Paracelsus, *Selected Writings*, ed. Jacobi, p. 222.

55 D. P. Picinello, *Mundus Symbolicus*, 2 vols. (Cologne, 1694), Book IV. iv. 59 ff., esp. 69 (the halcyon as emblem of Mary as mother of the prince of peace) and 70, the halcyon as emblem of Mary's own birth which heralded the end of tempests.

56 Townshend, *Albion's Triumph*, l. 417 (O and S, II. 457); Carew, *Coelum Britannicum*, ll. 1028–1029 (O and S, II. 579). To royalists, halcyon days were to return with the restoration: Gerard Reedy, S.J., 'Mystical Politics: the Imagery of Charles II's Coronation', in P. J. Korshin (ed.), *Studies in Change and Revolution*, p. 29. The history of the idea in the mid-century has now been written by Dolores Palomo, 'The Halcyon Moment of Stillness in Royalist Poetry', *HLQ*, 44 (1981), 205–221, noting in passing (p. 206) the crucial connection of the halcyon (via the Ceyx and Alcyone myth in Ovid, *Metamorphoses*, XI) with conjugal affection and the begetting of offspring.

57 Wind, *Pagan Mysteries*, pp. 86 ff.

58 *Hermetica*, ed. Scott, I. 117; Nock and Festugière, I. 8–9.

59 On green and hope see Cesare Ripa, *Iconologia* (Rome, 1603), pp. 469–470. Røstvig, *Happy Man*, I. 180–181 connects the green with the Hermetic–alchemical *benedicta viriditas*, the creative spirit clothed in nature's colour (see also *ibid.*, p. 167).

60 *Oration: on the Dignity of Man; Opera omnia*, 2 vols. (Basel, 1572), I. 314.

61 Vitruvius, *De architectura*, IV. i. 8–10, tr. M. H. Morgan (New York: Dover, 1960), pp. 104–106.

62 *Ibid.*, p. 105 (Vesta); I. ii. 5 (p. 15), the fertility goddesses. In Davenant's *The Triumphs of the Prince d'Amour* (1636) Venus's temple is 'an eight square of the Corinthian order': *Trois Masques à la Cour de Charles Ier d'Angleterre*, ed. Murray Lefkowitz (Paris: Centre National de la Recherche Scientifique, 1970), p. 132.

63 *Hermetica*, ed. Scott, I. 297; Nock and Festugière, II. 302–303.

64 Allen, *Image and Meaning: Metaphoric Traditions in Renaissance Poetry* (Baltimore, Md: Johns Hopkins U.P., 1960), p. 143.

65 Owen, *Famous Druids*, p. 41 comments on their religion.

66 Dio Chrysostom, *Orations*, XLIX; as quoted in John Toland, *History of the Druids*; new edn, ed. R. Huddleston (Montrose, 1814), p. 200.

67 Strabo, *Geography*, IV. iv. 4; Caesar, *Gallic War*, VI. xiii.

68 Pliny, *Natural History*, XVI. xcv; Loeb edn, IV. 549–551 (on mistletoe); Aristotle, *History of Animals*, V. ix (542 B) (on the rarity of the halcyon).

69 Selden, p. 194.

70 Linche, *Fountaine of Ancient Fiction*, sig. H iv[r] and our plate 7. This is perhaps why Mary appears after the 'flood' and, indeed, out of the flood (via the poet as angler). For lunar pearls, see Agrippa, *Three Books*, I. xxiv, p. 54: among lunary stones are 'Pearls, which are generated in shels of fishes from the droppings of Water ...'.

[V]

'Fear of change': magic and absolutism in 'The Rape of the Lock'

As well as being a magician the Mercurian monarch had always been Mercurian because of his wisdom and his custodianship of the arts. Martianus Capella's Mercury is the embodiment of Jupiter's 'trust, . . . speech, . . . beneficence, and . . . true genius'. He is 'the loyal messenger and spokesman of my mind, the sacred Nous . . . he knows the bond that joins the contrary elements, and I, the father, enforce those bonds through him . . .'. And so he marries Philology, 'extremely learned and his equal in study'.[1] Mercury married to Philology expresses one aspect of the ideal monarch as James had explained it to Prince Henry: 'besides your education, it is necessarie ye delight in reading, & seeking the knowledge of all lawfull thinges . . . knowledge and learning is a light burthen, the waight wherof will never presse your shoulders'.[2]

This in turn helps explain Dryden's *MacFlecknoe*, a poem from one point of view about the death of the Mercurian monarch in its enthroning of a creature 'design'd for thoughtless Majesty', the professional torturer of 'one poor word Ten thousand ways', an anti-Aeneas who has never sought (and so never been granted) the golden bough. In other words the 'Art' that is inherited by King Shadwell at the end of the poem is the opposite of all those arts possessed by the Mercurian king.[3] The same is true of Pope's *Dunciad*, offspring of *MacFlecknoe*, with its portrayal of a realm over which 'a STUART reigns' no more.[4] Dryden warns a Stuart; the *Dunciad*'s dark world has been perpetrated by the Hanoverian shadow which eclipses '*Art* after *Art*' through the power of its surrogate Dulness, the 'cloud-compelling Queen' who presides as a perverted Isis over an infected Troynovant and its rivers.[5] In Book IV even the old magical metaphors still sound, for Walpole is Dulness's 'WIZARD OLD' (l. 517), and earlier, in the

Argument to Book IV, he is '*the* Magus', offering a '*Cup ... which causes a total oblivion of all Obligations, divine, civil, moral, or rational*'. The tradition of the magician adviser has been revived in the office of prime minister. Monarch and officer together have conspired to kill the magician king.

It is a long way from the idealism of *Windsor Forest* to *The Dunciad*. Between the two poems in their various forms Hanover succeeded Stuart and a world passed. The major doctrinal poem to intervene between 1713 and 1728 is the revised *Rape of the Lock* of 1714, in which the *Dunciad* is prepared for with almost scrupulous care by an analysis of the monarch's loss of constitutional power which is, in effect, a statement about the loss of magical power, the corollary of absolutism.[6] In this poem Belinda is a surrogate for Anne, limited by the constitution inherited from William III.[7] The governing image of the five-canto *Rape*, a noon-day sun that declines until, identified with Belinda, it 'sett[s]' at the poem's end, is an emblem of the loss of absolutist dominance.[8] The fleeing of the sylphs announces Belinda's loss of magical stature. These are the assumptions I shall try to support in the following reading of the poem.

[i] *Queen Belinda*

A useful introduction to *The Rape*'s imagery of courtly ceremonial is Carew's *In answer of an Elegiacall Letter upon the death of the King of Sweden from Aurelian Townsend* (in *Poems*, 1640).[9] In it Carew recalls Townshend's shrovetide masque for the queen, *Tempe Restored* (1632):

> ... in their Angel-shapes
> A troope of Deities came downe to guide
> Our steerelesse barkes in passions swelling tide
> By vertues Carde, and brought us from above
> A patterne of their owne celestiall love.
> Nor lay it in darke sullen precepts drown'd
> But with rich fancie, and cleare Action crown'd
> Through a misterious fable (that was drawne
> Like a transparent veyle of purest Lawne
> Before their dazelling beauties) the divine
> *Venus*, did with her heavenly *Cupid* shine. ...
> It fill'd us with amazement to behold
> Love made all spirit, his corporeall mold
> Dissected into Atomes melt away
> To empty ayre, and from the grosse allay

Of mixtures, and compounding Accidents
Refin'd to immateriall Elements.
But when the Queene of Beautie did inspire
The ayre with perfumes, and our hearts with fire,
Breathing from her celestiall Organ sweet
Harmonious notes, our soules fell at her feet,
And did with humble reverend duetie, more
Her rare perfections, then high state adore. (ll. 60 ff.)

It was the queen herself who took the role of Divine Beauty, and it is this courtly background of the Caroline masque that Pope revives in *The Rape*. Belinda is, on one level, a parody Venus Urania, 'Queene of Beautie', claiming worship of her 'high state', accompanied by Ariel as 'her heavenly *Cupid*'. As the *Key to the Lock* has it she is also Anne, and often a mock Anne, a vehicle for reminding one of how the myth of the '*British* QUEEN' could die.[10] Ultimately, then, Belinda is far removed from her prototype in Arabella Fermor. She is, instead, the complex heroine of a poem that, in its enlarged version which was 'finished' by 8 December 1713, belongs very much to the period of Anne's increasing illness and the furore over the question of the succession which included strong Whig suspicion of the queen's Jacobite sympathies.[11] And yet the poem's origin in Arabella Fermor must not be forgotten. Pope was a Catholic. The poem was written to heal the breach between the Fermors and Petres, two important Catholic families and friends of Pope, caused when the high-spirited Robert, seventh Lord Petre, cut off a lock of Arabella's hair. Catholic union is the clue to the poem's larger meaning which embraces adverse criticism of the Whig settlement and, by implication, some kind of support for the Jacobite cause.[12]

Before considering Belinda, we must begin with Anne's one appearance in the 1714 (as in the 1712) version of the poem. This is in canto III, the central, sovereign canto, in a context which affirms her princely power by alluding to the Thames as enclosed by 'Meads for ever crown'd with Flow'rs' and to Hampton Court as 'a Structure of Majestick Frame': 'Here Thou, Great *Anna*! whom three Realms obey, / Dost sometimes Counsel take – and sometimes *Tea*' (III. 7–8). We should perhaps imagine her taking tea and counsel in the drawing room whose ceiling is dominated by Verrio's allegorical apotheosis of Anne as Justice (with raised sword) and, among other things, queen of love (she is attended by the Graces and Mercury).[13] On the ceiling is the ideal. In the room is the maimed reality, a queen compromised by the constitution, forced to consult with those male councillors whose counsel is often worth much less than tea.[14] The results are immediate: heroes and nymphs who spend their time at court talking of 'Who gave the *Ball*, or paid the *Visit* last' (1. 12), and a corrupt legal system:

> Mean while declining from the Noon of Day,
> The Sun obliquely shoots his burning Ray;
> The hungry Judges soon the Sentence sign,
> And Wretches hang that Jury-men may Dine. . . . (ll. 19 ff.)

Pope is echoing a favourite complaint against judges. But as it is stated here it is a direct result of the absolutist sun's decline from its meridian height. Pope alludes on the one hand to a major constitutional point concerning the role of the king in parliament: the absolutist monarch alone made laws in parliament; after the Whig revolution of 1688, law-making belonged to 'king, lords, and commons'. The way was now cleared, as Weston and Greenberg comment, 'for the theory of parliamentary sovereignty'. Pope alludes on the other hand to the monarch's continuing duty to appoint judges, whose inefficiency in executing the law nevertheless reflects sympathetically the sovereign's diminished law-making power. And over all this presides, perhaps, Anne as *Justitia* in Verrio's ceiling allegory.[15]

In other words, the poem's sovereign centre concentrates attention on Anne's peculiar difficulty as a Stuart brought up a Protestant, with no issue of her own, and an inheritor of the constitutional settlement which resulted from the revolution of 1688. Anne's own status was, indeed, ambiguous. Her position grew increasingly difficult towards the end of her reign. Pope sees her, I think, as the ideal monarch for a Catholic such as he was in a Protestant country, and this despite the limitations imposed on her by the Bill of Rights and the Act of Settlement.[16] But those very limitations are a source of deep worry which Pope explores in Anne's double, Belinda, the mock queen who plays a role because she no longer has the central part in the realm; a mock queen, moreover, whose anger and despair resulting from the loss of her lock of hair (or, to make the still historically possible equation, solar corona) are directed at the man responsible, who thus becomes a symbol for William III and the limiting government he bequeathed to Anne. Hence the culminating battle of women against men, belles against beaux, in the final canto. Seen from this point of view, Clarissa's call to common sense and 'good Humour' (V. 30) in the speech added to '*subsequent Editions*' of the poem is a prudent reminder, as much to Pope himself as anyone else, of the benefits of a temperate reaction not just to the inherited constitution but also to the Hanoverian succession which had now taken place.

Anne's magical powers were affirmed in her reign by her revival of the practice of touching for the king's evil, a practice which William had discontinued as a superstitious vestige of the old divine right theory.[17] Within the poem we are reminded of these magical powers first in Ariel's reference to the angel who 'guard[s] with Arms Divine the *British Throne*' (II. 90),[18] and second in that problematic line at the beginning of canto III, 'Here Thou, great *Anna*! whom three Realms obey'. What are the 'three Realms'? Great Britain, France, and Ireland, annotates the Twickenham editor; England (and Wales), Scotland, and Ireland, suggests a more recent commentator.[19] Both answers might serve, but there is a third possibility which I believe provides a more satisfying solution, namely the 'three-fold World, Elementary, Celestiall, and Intellectual [or super-celestial]'[20] traditionally commanded by the magus. It is this that 'the *Rosicrucian* Doctrine of Spirits' guides us to identifying as the ultimate sign of absolute power. Pope's introductory epistle to Arabella Fermor seems to encourage flippancy with regard to these celestial beings – not surprisingly, in view of contemporary rationalist suspicion of the supernatural. But, in the light of the evidence presented in the earlier chapters of this book, it seems that what he is in fact reviving, by allusion to the supernatural machinery of epic, is the idea of the magician monarch. His tone in the letter to Arabella Fermor, as in the poem as a whole, deliberately masks a deeply serious purpose. Anne is the magician queen 'whom three Realms obey' by virtue of her Stuart blood and beliefs. Belinda is her surrogate who fails to control her demons because she thinks of a man, the shadow, it might be, of William III. To compromise even for a moment is to lose your authority as magus and queen.

What Ariel actually detects, of course, is 'An Earthly Lover lurking at [Belinda's] Heart' (III. 144). In other words, her compromise is considerable and Pope's statement, read as political allegory, almost treasonable. Consequently Pope gently shifts the metaphorical weight of his statement onto *Le Comte de Gabalis*, which we are introduced to in the prefatory epistle and invited to consider as a jest: 'For they [the Rosicrucians] say, any Mortals may enjoy the most intimate Familiarities with these gentle Spirits, upon a Condition very easie to all true *Adepts*, an inviolate Preservation of Chastity'. This apparently outmoded and ludicrous doctrine, based on the tradition of the adept's chastity or virginity, provides an aptly comic support for a poem about the battle between the sexes. There is, from the point of view of a male-oriented society, nothing wrong in having a secret 'Earthly Lover'. What is outrageous is the thought of a girl's obsession with her virginity. So the Rosicrucian–magical paraphernalia in effect blinds the reader to the poem's political meanings, since Pope can confidently expect anti-magical bias and appear to conspire with it. Treason is thus masked by laughter.[21]

From the political aspect, however, the insistence on Belinda's virginity simply confirms the extent of Pope's devious indirection. For if chastity or virginity are prerequisites of magical power, and if the absolutist monarch is traditionally a magician, then who is the sovereign most obviously a candidate for the role of magician monarch through her constant elevation of her virginity to symbolic status and her insistence on her divine election to sovereignty? The answer is Elizabeth, whose motto, *Semper eadem*, Anne adopted for her own a few months after her accession in 1702. Despite her anti-Catholicism it is Elizabeth's mantle, through Anne, that lies over this poem and helps define Belinda.[22] Anne is a more tolerant Elizabeth, a Stuart Elizabeth, whose constitutional inheritance prevents her from re-enacting the Elizabethan imperial absolutist dream. The extent of her constitutional limitations are enacted by Belinda, the clues to whose monarchical significance we must now examine.

The sun is the major emblem of absolutist sovereignty. Hence, in the revised edition of the poem, Belinda awakens when the sun is at its midday height to conflate the *lever de la reine* with the familiar image of Christ as the midday *sol iustitiae*.[23] It is noon at I. 15; the two previous lines read: '*Sol* thro' white Curtains shot a tim'rous Ray, / And op'd those Eyes that must eclipse the Day'. The politically naïve reader detects Petrarchan hyperbole here; the alert friend of Pope's might have recalled something like Davenant's shrovetide masque for the queen, *Luminalia* (1638), where the sun hands over the task of lighting the hemisphere to Henrietta Maria, '*the queen of brightness*', because, as Aurora says, should the sun 'appear he were undone, / And eclipsèd though in his pride of noon'.[24] Or he (or she) might have recalled the phenomenon that when the future Charles II was born, 'Heaven took notice of him, and ey'd him with a Star appearing in defiance of the Sun at Noon-day'.[25]

Belinda's solar qualities are equally to the fore at the opening of canto II:

> Not with more Glories, in th' Etherial Plain,
> The Sun first rises o'er the purpled Main,
> Than issuing forth, the Rival of his Beams
> Lanch'd on the Bosom of the silver *Thames*.

'Glory' here signifies solar corona. Belinda's 'glory' is her hair, and specifically the 'two Locks' of line 20. The cutting-off by the baron of one of those locks, appropriately accompanied by a reference to the 'hew[ing] of Triumphal Arches to the Ground' (III. 176),[26] immediately plunges the poem in darkness as sooty-winged Umbriel visits the black and melancholic underworld palace of Queen Spleen, who is thus the result of a solar eclipse (the disappearance of solar absolutism), the poem's ultimate emblem of the diminishing of Stuart monarchy through the 1688 revolution and the securing of the Hanoverian succession. *The Rape of the Lock* is, on one important level, a meditation by a Catholic admirer of a sick Anne on the Miltonic simile:

> . . . as when the sun new risen
> Looks through the horizontal misty air
> Shorn of his beams, or from behind the moon
> In dim eclipse disastrous twilight sheds
> On half the nations, and with fear of change
> Perplexes monarchs. (*Paradise Lost*, I. 594 ff.)

The key to this poem about a young virgin's loss of a lock of hair is Pope's own 'fear of change' in 1713–1714, his obsession with the mutability of the bearer of that proudly talismanic motto *Semper eadem*.

If the monarch is solar a female monarch is also Venerean. *The Faerie Queene* celebrates Elizabeth as Venus as well as virgin; Henrietta Maria was often the queen of love. And so Belinda, too, is Venus. As she sits, at the end of canto I, in front of her mirror, itself an attribute of Venus, 'A heav'nly Image in the Glass appears' (I. 125) to hint beyond an earthly to the celestial Venus, Carew's 'divine Venus' with which we began this section.[27] A few lines later 'Unnumber'd Treasures ope at once, and here / The various Off'rings of the World appear' (I. 129–130), which, read in conjunction with the voyage down the Thames at the beginning of canto II, identifies her as a version of the sea-born (and sea-borne) Venus, the Venus anadyomene, to be interpreted as an emblem of British mercantile power. On the one hand this might be a compliment to Anne; on the other it is a reminder that mercantile power means Whig power. The luxury trade becomes another symbol of the diminishing of the sovereign's status.

Pope completes his Venerean tableau in canto II:

> But now secure the painted Vessel glides,
> The Sun-beams trembling on the floating Tydes,
> While melting Musick steals upon the Sky,
> And soften'd Sounds along the Waters die.
> Smooth flow the Waves, the Zephyrs gently play,
> *Belinda* smil'd, and all the World was gay. (ll. 47 ff.)

Music belongs to Venus, the 'mother of Harmony',[28] and the description as a whole recalls the beneficent spring Venus of the opening of Lucretius's *De rerum natura*.[29] In addition, the 'Zephyrs' here and a few lines later (l. 58) remind us of Venus's identification with Chloris–Flora. In *The Faerie Queene* the female monarch was depicted as a Venus–Flora accompanied by her beloved Zephyrus who was, in turn, frequently identified with Mercury. In the court masque, too, we are familiar with the mythological identification of king with Zephyrus–Mercury and queen with Venus–Flora. When Pope gives us Belinda–Venus complete with attendant zephyrs, then, we are to understand an allusion to this version of the Mercurian monarch.

At a moment like this it might seem that the poem's politics have yielded before the beauty of the verse. However, it is Pope's triumph, like Spenser's before him, to have written verse that was both exquisite and politically inspired. Indeed, the present passage invites a particularly alert political response. Venus and Zephyrus require our attention but so, too, does the clear reminiscence of Shakespeare's and Dryden's Cleopatra on the Cydnus. Venus and Zephyrus suggest the ideal inherited by Anne from traditions of Tudor and Stuart panegyric (we have seen Marvell modify the ideal to republican ends in the person of Mary in *Upon Appleton House*); Cleopatra is a corrupt and limited monarch.[30] For Belinda to be able to parade like Cleopatra is as ominous a warning of something wrong in the realm as the presence of unjust judges.

It is only a short step from consideration of Venus to consideration of Belinda's hair, the teasing subject of the poem which we have already considered as a solar symbol. For from the Venerean point of view it relates to the poem's preoccupation with monarchy and marriage.

With her locks arranged as they are Belinda appears to be dressed in the height of contemporary fashion, as we would expect. But the context in which we encounter Belinda's 'Locks, which graceful hung behind' offers the possibility that Pope is remembering the English custom that brides wore their hair long. After the marriage, the hair was worn up. In Jonson's *Hymenaei*, for example, we find 'a personated *Bride*, . . . her hayre flowing';[31] in chapter II we encountered the Princess Elizabeth at her wedding of 1613 with 'her amber-coloured haire, dependantly hanging playted downe over her shoulders . . .'. This is the convention that is utilised in the 'Rainbow' portrait of Queen Elizabeth, in which orderly 'shining Ringlets' not too dissimilar to Belinda's do indeed conspire 'to deck . . . the smooth Iv'ry Neck' (II. 21–22) so noticeably that the painting is now generally recognised as a bridal portrait depicting Elizabeth as the bride of England or of Christ.[32] The Belinda who teases with her bride-like hair can now be seen not just as a coquette but as a queen acting out the ritual of marriage to her country. The loss of her lock to a mere man who is himself a symbol of the curbing of monarchical power under William prevents, as it were, marriage to the realm. Hovering delicately near the poem's surface we detect Pope's graceful tribute to Anne's own dedication to her realm despite ill-health and the indifference of ministers.

The reading offered here might be supported by the following lines describing the sylphs that attend on Belinda:

> Loose to the Wind their airy Garments flew,
> Thin glitt'ring Textures of the filmy Dew;
> Dipt in the richest Tincture of the Skies,
> Where Light disports in ever-mingling Dies,
> While ev'ry Beam new transient Colours flings,
> Colours that change whene'er they wave their Wings. (II. 63 ff.)

The description reminds us of the Cupids surrounding Cleopatra, and of Spenser's Mercilla accompanied by 'little Angels' (*Faerie Queene*, V. ix. 29), which we related earlier to its Mercurian and magical courtly context. More simply, however, the sylphs catch sunlight like a rainbow – a detail which raises the more complex possibility that Belinda is being visited by a manifestation of Iris, the goddess of the rainbow and celestial messenger-counterpart to Mercury, who bestows monarchical power on Belinda through the 'Azure Wand' of the chief of these rainbow-like sylphs, Ariel (l. 72).[33]

If I am right about Belinda's hair, though, there is the possibility of an iconographical connection with the tradition exemplified in Elizabeth's 'Rainbow' portrait, in which the queen holds a rainbow in her right hand instead of a sceptre as a demonstration of her role as peace-bringer to her country through a religious dedication to its well-being. Indeed, as the divine sun she has actually engendered the rainbow which she is holding; hence the portrait's motto, *Non sine Sole Iris* (no rainbow without the sun). At the beginning of canto II of *The Rape of the Lock* Belinda is compared to the sun; her hair is arranged in such a way as to recall an English seventeenth-century bridal custom which had monarchical sanction; around her are the rainbow-like sylphs. This poem, which even Aden sees as little more than 'a playful and politically blameless excursion into social satire', is vibrant with political meaning and iconographical innuendo.[34]

We last see the lock at the end of canto V:

> A sudden Star, it shot thro' liquid Air,
> And drew behind a radiant *Trail of Hair*.
> Not *Berenice's* Locks first rose so bright,
> The Heav'ns bespangling with dishevel'd Light. (ll. 127 ff.)

Its stellification is modelled on the astral immortality of the Roman emperors and the often Brunian adaptation of that tradition into Spenserian and seventeenth-century monarchical panegyric. Berenice's lock was stellified by Venus, so that, as Pope says, 'This, the blest Lover shall for *Venus* take' (l. 135). But Catullus's imitation of Callimachus's poem on Berenice tells us that this new constellation, *coma Berenices*, was placed among the ancient constellations, 'close by Callisto . . . point[ing] the way before slow Boötes'.[35]

The Great Bear and Boötes have been almost as much a constant in this book as Mercury. They are the constellations of Arthur and of the reform of England in both Spenser and Milton. It seems that *The Rape of the Lock* points in that most nostalgically idealising direction of all, the salvation of Britain through the implied connection of the Stuarts with Arthur. The satirical and jesting overtones that often surround Belinda as a mock queen (to contrast her with Anne, who retains vestiges of her Stuart rights) here disappear. To all intents and purposes Belinda is Anne. Her lock shines immortally as a reminder of the historical Berenice's 'sunny' hair[36] and as a hope for the restoration of the absolutism that the hair in part signifies, a hope made the more telling by the association of *coma Berenices* with Ursa Major and Boötes and the tradition of reform that they represent. The lock of hair in Catullus's poem, after all, wishes to return to its queen: 'Why do the stars keep me here? I would fain be the queen's lock once more' (l. 93). If such a thing could be, Belinda–Anne would rule as the divinely appointed monarch on earth, the restored 'Rainbow' bridal queen. As it is the lock remains in heaven, to be read by the astrologer Partridge and his kind. Partridge is, of course, foolish to interpret this new constellation as presaging 'The Fate of *Louis*' (V. 140). The death of *le roi soleil* was, at least on the symbolic level, the last thing Pope wanted, and the last thing that the poem says he wants.

[ii] *Belinda and Agamemnon*

Before we consider the poem's Rosicrucian symbolism we must pause over its most overtly political passage. These are the lines in which Belinda attacks the baron with a bodkin:

> Now meet thy Fate, incens'd *Belinda* cry'd,
> And drew a deadly *Bodkin* from her Side.
> (The same, his ancient Personage to deck,
> Her great, great Grandsire wore about his Neck
> In three *Seal-Rings*. . . .) (V. 87 ff.)

Pope's own note directs our reading: '*In Imitation of the Progress of* Agamemnon's *Scepter in* Homer, *Il.* 2.' In Pope's translation (1715) the relevant lines are:

> The King of Kings his awful Figure rais'd;
> High in his Hand the Golden Sceptre blaz'd:
> The Golden Sceptre, of Celestial Frame,
> By *Vulcan* form'd, from *Jove* to *Hermes* came. . . . (II. 127 ff.)

And he appends the note: 'In the Passage of the *Sceptre, Homer* has found an artful and poetical manner of acquainting us with the high Descent of *Agamemnon*, and celebrating the hereditary Right of his Family; as well as finely hinted the Original of his Power to be deriv'd from Heaven . . .'.[37]

Belinda attacks the man who cut off her lock, emblem of her monarchical supremacy, with what should be an equally potent emblem of her divinely bestowed right to rule. Her bodkin is in effect a sceptre, a sceptre that has been transmitted through Mercury (if we take the *Iliad* allusion) and has been metamorphosed, in its long history, into a seal of royal authority and sovereign sway over the 'three Realms' of the opening of canto III (the three signet- or '*Seal-Rings*').[38] But the fact obstinately remains that it is now a bodkin and not a sceptre because Belinda–Anne's rights are diminished. Ariel's wand is a reminder earlier in the poem of the magical power the sceptre once conveyed; Umbriel's 'Branch of healing *Spleenwort*' (IV. 56) is its dark antithesis, a parody golden bough and golden sceptre, and therefore, like the bodkin, a testament to muted authority.

The crux of *The Rape of the Lock*, and one clearly implied in the

Rosicrucian symbolism which introduces magic into the discussion about monarchy, is divine right. This is confirmed by Pope's note on Agamemnon's sceptre with its reference to the king's heaven-derived authority. Pope was not politically naïve. Whatever his reservations about the 1688 revolution and its consequences for the reign of Anne, he was not a simple-minded absolutist. He did not like the idea of Hanover. Equally, I suspect, he had reservations about the Old Pretender, particularly if James Francis Edward thought that divine right opened the way for a return to earlier Stuart absolutism. As Pope saw it both alternatives were fraught with potential difficulties. His perplexity at these difficulties is what *The Rape* of 1714 reflects. Part of him yearns for absolutist certainties: Belinda is Anne, the queen of love who is also the sun queen, whose loss of absolutist dominion the poem laments. Part of him realises that Anne's middle-way monarchy, for all its limitations, is best and safest. Before him lies an unknown and potentially frightening future.

This, then, is why at the poem's climax its heroine is associated with Agamemnon. Belinda is a warning to the Old Pretender not to require too much of his divine right. Agamemnon is a king, appointed by heaven and 'the Care of Heav'n' (*Iliad*, I. 278). But Achilles, too, is 'the Care of Heav'n' (*ibid.*), and it is a moot point how far the blame for the quarrel between them is to be apportioned. From Pope's *Iliad* of 1715, however, we can perhaps infer that Pope agreed with Nestor when he reproves Achilles not to 'treat our Prince with Pride; / Let Kings be just, and Sov'reign Pow'r preside' (I. 364–365). Equally, we might infer that he believes with Agamemnon that ' 'Tis mine to threaten, Prince, and thine to fear' and 'That Kings are subject to the Gods alone' (I. 240, 250).[39] And yet Achilles calls him 'Tyrant' (I. 388), an accusation all absolute monarchs are vulnerable to. Anne's successor will inherit a bodkin rather than a sceptre. If that successor should be George it is best it remain a bodkin. If that successor by the remotest of chances should be James Francis Edward it might be hoped that the bodkin could become a sceptre again, in which case the new king must avoid at all costs the accusations of tyranny that had been levelled at the seventeenth-century Stuarts.

[iii] *Ariel and* Le Comte de Gabalis

The presence of Ariel in the poem reminds us of *The Tempest* and of Prospero, the magician ruler who has to learn to drown his book and break his wand in order that he may return to his kingdom. The play does not say that magic and monarchy are incompatible, merely that total preoccupation with 'secret studies' in Agrippan cabbalist magic prohibits the just exercise of kingly power. The true magician monarch holds a sceptre, not a wand. But the sceptre subsumes the powers of the wand.[40]

If Pope had one eye on Shakespeare's *Tempest*, however, he probably had his other eye on Dryden's and Davenant's adaptation of it into *The Tempest, or the Enchanted Island* (1670), where Prospero's magic is a matter of more than passing interest. Indeed, as a recent editor notes, the Restoration version demythologises Prospero and makes him lose his magical power. Whereas Shakespeare's 'Ariel acts entirely as Prospero's agent, the Ariel of Dryden and Davenant is more strictly an independent agent ... it is Ariel and the elemental spirits who work the magic, not their master'. This is what we would expect from our knowledge of Dryden's reservations about monarchical absolutism: magic is a symbol of the monarch's absolutist power; to withhold the magic is a way of registering reservations about the limits of monarchical power.[41] It was with both versions of *The Tempest* before him that Pope began *The Rape of the Lock*, and in view of what we have just seen of the Dryden-Davenant adaptation it becomes immediately significant that Ariel has greater power than Belinda. It is he who sees 'some dread Event impend' by gazing into 'the clear Mirror of [Belinda's] ruling *Star*' (I. 108–109); it is he who leaves her when the 'Earthly Lover' is found 'lurking at her Heart'. It would seem that the demonic machinery is final confirmation that the poem is concerned with monarchy and the concept of the magician king. Anne controls the 'three Realms'. Belinda does not. Her failure in this respect is not so much the result of personal inadequacy as a statement about the post-Hobbesian rationalist attitude to monarchy. Monarchs could once summon angels, Pope appears to be saying: Anne does control 'three Realms'; but we really know that these realms are earthly kingdoms and not the realms once dominated by the magician monarch; let us anyway give the old idea a new airing while Anne still reigns. It is here that *Le Comte de Gabalis* is relevant.

This is a strange work (its title means 'The Cabbalistic Count') which Pope's critics have, by and large, been shy of. And yet here perhaps more than anywhere else the Jacobite heart of the poem lies. For de Villars's 'Diverting History of the Rosicrucian Doctrine of Spirits, viz. Sylphs, Salamanders, Gnomes, and Dæmons ...' gave Pope a ready-made amusing yet potentially serious vocabulary through which to revive the memory of the magical power of monarchs.[42] Moreover, Rosicrucianism was connected from its beginnings with general ideas of reform, a point evident from the sequel to de Villars's work, *La Suite du Comte de Gabalis*, which has as a main figure 'Monsieur le Docteur Jean le Brun' (Giordano Bruno), who appears to the narrator to tell him that he knows from God of his zeal for the reformation of the Christian world and informs him of his own reforming zeal.[43] As a Rosicrucian poem *The Rape* is not necessarily just satirical and nostalgic. It might in the end be visionary and prophetic.

In de Villars's system the sylphs are of primary importance. Hence the sylph Ariel's dominant role in *The Rape*, and hence his name, which defines his elemental quality since, as the cabbalistic count tells the narrator, each of the elemental beings is made of the purest part of the element they inhabit and contains (unlike man) only one element: sylphs are composed of the purest atoms of air.[44] It is the duty of these elemental demons to minister to the pleasure of the magician-adept, and, we are told, the narrator has been chosen by heaven to be the greatest cabbalist of his century in the tradition of Hermes Trismegistus, Paracelsus, Robert Fludd, and others.[45]

Even allowing for ironies in *The Rape of the Lock* and light-heartedness in *Le Comte de Gabalis* certain serious implications for our theme of the magician monarch begin to emerge. Belinda, like de Villars's narrator, is 'elected', as Ariel tells her in her dream at the beginning of canto I. By implication, then, she, too, is in the line of Hermes Trismegistus and his followers, a Hermeticist who is also a monarch (because of the solar and related symbolism surrounding her). Indeed, the relationship between magic and monarchy is actually touched upon in the second discourse of *Le Comte de Gabalis* when the count explains the fundamentals of his occult philosophy to the narrator: he is destined to command nature (including, of course, 'tous les Peuples invisibles, qui habitent les quatre Elemens'), God alone will be his master.[46] At this point the count exclaims, echoing the tradition of Pico's *Oration on the Dignity of Man*: 'ô Grand Dieu! d'avoir couronné l'homme de tant de gloire, & de l'avoir etably Souverain Monarque de tous les Ouvrages de vos mains'.[47] The magician is a king and answerable only to God. To him is allowed that sovereignty over nature that was Adam's before the Fall. The monarchical implications of magic continue with Paracelsus's arrival in the 'kingdom of wisdom' and of his control of the sceptre of that kingdom.[48]

There is a crucial difference between Belinda's role and that of the narrator in *Le Comte de Gabalis*, however, and it is one that we have already touched upon in connection with *The Tempest*: Belinda does not control or instruct Ariel; in de Villars's system the sages control and instruct the sylphs. Indeed, 'the least of our sages is more knowledgeable and powerful than all those little creatures'.[49] It is here, as we have already seen, that Belinda fails as a magician monarch. And yet there might be one moment in canto I, after Ariel's disappearance, when we detect Belinda consciously trying to summon him back to consult him. This is when she sits in front of her mirror and 'A heav'nly Image in the Glass appears' (I. 125). There are several things going on in this densely allusive line: Belinda is, for example, at once Narcissus and Milton's Eve. She is also the monarch inspecting her magic glass, for as the count informs the narrator in *Le Comte de Gabalis*, one consults aerial oracles by means of mirrors. Similarly, if one wishes to attain mastery over the 'empires' of the elemental spirits of earth, water, fire, or air, one must first purify the relevant elements within oneself. Thus, to regain the sovereignty over the sylphs that was lost with the Fall one must concentrate air, by means of concave mirrors, in a glass globe. If the practice of 'the art' is followed, the air within will be purified and will then sympathetically exalt the air within the body, with the result that the inhabitants of the sphere of air will become our 'inferiors'.[50]

And so the poem's Rosicrucian machinery directs us not just to the theory of the magician monarch but also to the old and related dream of repairing by magical arts the effects of the Fall of man. Is this, perhaps, why *The Rape of the Lock* echoes so insistently the fourth and ninth books of *Paradise Lost*?[51] We should, I think, end with a question, because Pope's poem ends with a question to which he could, at the time of its publication, foresee no answer. It was a question involving his faith and his life, and it was framed around the concept of the magician monarch.

Notes

1 *The Marriage of Philology and Mercury*, tr. W. H. Stahl *et al.*, I. 92–93, pp. 31–32.

2 *Basilicon Doron*, ed. Craigie, I. 143–145.

3 Quoted from *The Poems of John Dryden*, ed. James Kinsley, 4 vols. (Oxford: Clarendon Press, 1958), I. 265 ff. For the *Aeneid* allusions (including an echo of the Sibyl of Book VI) see Kinsley's notes, IV. 1913 ff. The lute and reference to Arion at ll. 35 ff. might suggest Mercury, since Tooke's *Pantheon*, for example, had associated Amphion and Arion,

remarking that Amphion 'receiv'd his *Harp* or *Lute* from *Mercury*' (1713 edn, p. 371).

4   *Windsor Forest*, l. 42.

5   Pope quotations from the Twickenham edn, 11 vols. (London and New Haven, Conn.: Methuen and Yale U.P., 1939–1969). *The Dunciad* is in vol. V, ed. James Sutherland (1953). The lines cited are from Book IV. 640 (1742) and I. 79 (B text, p. 275). The poem's river symbolism should probably be related not just to Lord Mayor's Day processions but to the Isis tradition that we have traced in Spenser and Drayton: compare, e.g., IV. 193 with *Windsor Forest*, ll. 329 ff. The identification of Dulness as an anti-Isis is confirmed by Aubrey Williams, *Pope's 'Dunciad': a Study of its Meaning* (London: Methuen, 1955), pp. 26 ff., who sees her as Cybele, the Great Mother, etc. (i.e., on Apuleius's authority, *Golden Ass*, XI. v, Isis), and by T. C. Faulkner and R. L. Blair, 'The Classical and Mythographic Sources of Pope's Dulness', *HLQ*, 43 (1980), 213–246. It is also confirmed, albeit indirectly, by W. H. Marshall's article on IV. 637 ('As Argus' eyes by Hermes' wand opprest'): 'Medea's Strain and Hermes' Wand: Pope's Use of Mythology', *MLN*, 76 (1961), 224–232. An interpretation not offered by Marshall is that the killing of Argus released Io, who subsequently fled to Egypt and became Isis. In other words, *The Dunciad* ends with a vision of the anti-Isis dead and, perhaps, a hope for the true Isis to be restored (cf. Tooke, *Pantheon*, p. 103). Pat Rogers's brilliant '*Windsor-Forest, Britannia* and River Poetry', *SP*, 77 (1980), 283–299, is implicitly suggestive in this direction, too.

6   The *Iliad* and *Odyssey* translations are omitted as being too substantial to consider here and as not being strictly related to the Mercurian magician theme. Suggestions as to their political content have been made by J. M. Aden, *Pope's Once and Future Kings: Satire and Politics in the Early Career* (Knoxville, Tenn.: Univ. of Tennessee Press, 1978), the implications of whose findings are considerable. A. S. Fisher observes that for Pope there was still ' "divinity" in kings': 'Cheerful Noonday, "Gloomy" Twilight: Pope's *Essay on Criticism*', *PQ*, 51 (1972), 832–844. When writing *The Rape* Pope had clearly not decided on a positive attitude to the future George I, and Bolingbroke's *Patriot King* lay even further in the future (cf. Oswyn Murray, 'Divine Right in *The Dunciad* (IV, 175–188)', *N and Q*, 213 (1968), 208–211). For Pope's later objections to absolute monarchy as inhibiting the liberty of the subject, see Malcolm Kelsall, 'Augustus and Pope', *HLQ*, 39 (1975–1976), 117–131. In connection with *Windsor Forest*, however, J. R. Moore was right to detect with Elwin denunciation of the 1688 revolution: '*Windsor Forest* and William III', *MLN*, 66 (1951), 451–454; and cf. E. R. Wasserman on Jacobitism in *Windsor Forest* in *The Subtler Language* (Baltimore, Md.: Johns Hopkins U.P., 1959), ch. IV, esp. pp. 108–109 and 160–161. Pope's Jacobitism has now been firmly established by Howard Erskine-Hill in 'Literature and the Jacobite Cause', *Modern Language Studies*, 9 (1979), 15–28, and 'Alexander Pope: The Political Poet in his Time', *ECS*, 15 (1981–2), 123–48.

7 E.g., the Bill of Rights, 'An Act declaring the Rights and Liberties of the Subject, and Settling the Succession of the Crown' (1689), and the Act of Settlement (1701), 'An Act for the further Limitation of the Crown, and better securing the Rights and Liberties of the Subjects': D. Oswald Dykes, *Source Book of Constitutional History from 1660* (London, New York, Toronto: Longmans, 1930), pp. 105 ff. and 115 ff.

8 Quotations from Twickenham *Poems*, vol. II, ed. Geoffrey Tillotson (1962 edn).

9 Quoted from Dunlap's edn, pp. 74–77.

10 *Windsor Forest*, l. 384. The *Key* (1715 and written by Pope) is reprinted in *The Prose Works of Alexander Pope*, ed. Normal Ault, I (Oxford: Shakespeare Head Press, 1936), pp. 173 ff. The identification of Belinda with Anne is made on pp. 185–186 (where Belinda's 'white Breast' also makes her Albion).

11 For the date, see *The Correspondence of Alexander Pope*, ed. George Sherburn, 5 vols. (Oxford: Clarendon Press, 1956), I. 201 (Pope's letter to Swift, 8 December 1713). Anne had been in slightly better health in the summer to autumn of 1713 (but 'better' must be understood relatively: on 13 September 'she walked for the first time since February'); her final illness did not 'officially' begin until Christmas Eve, 1713: see Edward Gregg, *Queen Anne* (London, Boston and Henley: Routledge and Kegan Paul, 1980), pp. 374–375. For suspicions of Anne's Jacobitism, see *ibid.*, pp. 363 ff.; *Dictionary of National Biography*, I. 467 ff. (s.v. *Anne*); David Green, *Queene Anne* (London: Collins, 1970), p. 268.

12 On the Fermors and Petres, see Tillotson's edn, Appendix A (pp. 371 ff.). As Tillotson notes (p. 87), Pope may not have known Arabella Fermor and did not know Lord Petre. The invitation to write *The Rape* came from his great Catholic and Jacobite friend John Caryll. Interestingly, the first (1712) version of the poem seems to have been composed at the time Pope wrote his epitaph on John, Lord Caryll, who had been with James II and Mary in exile at St Germains: 'Just to his prince, and to his country true' (*Correspondence*, I. 133–134; Tillotson's edn, pp. 83–84). Pope's letter to Caryll of 9 January 1714 (*Corr.* I. 207) states of the dedication to the revised *Rape*, 'the best advice in the kingdom, of the men of sense has been made use of in it, even to the Treasurer's' (i.e. Robert Harley, Earl of Oxford and Mortimer); and Oxford, together with Bolingbroke, was at this time negotiating with James, the Old Pretender, about the possibility of his conversion to Anglicanism and the repealing of the Act of Settlement: Gregg, *Queen Anne*, pp. 375–376; Green, *Queen Anne*, pp. 298 ff. The possibility of Jacobitism in *The Rape* is discussed by Howard Erskine-Hill in the articles cited in n. 6 above.

13 Green, *ibid.*, p. 188 and plate facing p. 137.

14 For Anne's jealousy of her prerogative to appoint, which often meant that she failed to consult ministers, see Gregg, *Queen Anne*, p. 135.

15 For the absolutist sun, see Ernst Kantorowicz, 'Oriens Augusti-Lever du Roi', *Dumbarton Oaks Papers*, 17 (1963), 117–177. For the king-in-parliament, see C. C. Weston and J. R. Greenberg, *Subjects and*

Sovereigns: the Grand Controversy over Legal Sovereignty in Stuart England (Cambridge: C.U.P., 1981), p. 259 and *passim*; for the complaint against judges, see Twickenham *Rape*, p. 170; and for the sovereign's continuing right to appoint judges, see Gregg, p. 144, who also observes 'In her judicial role the queen acted as the final court of appeal . . . [she] was obliged to hold regular consultations with her judges about individual cases' (*ibid.*).

16 Cf. Aden, *Pope's Once and Future Kings,* pp. 32 and 43.

17 Gregg, pp. 147–148 (noting the pro-Jacobite suspicions that attended it); Green, pp. 104–105; and Marc Bloch, *The Royal Touch: Sacred Monarchy and Scrofula in England and France,* tr. J. E. Anderson, *passim,* but esp. pp. 211–223 (the practice was continued by the Old Pretender).

18 Tillotson in his edn, p. 165 n., cites Dryden's *Discourse concerning the Original and Progress of Satire* on the commonness of the 'doctrine' of the guardian angels of kingdoms, a doctrine accepted by Protestants as much as Catholics: *Essays*, ed. W. P. Ker, II (Oxford: Clarendon Press, 1926), 34 ff. They become of magical significance in *The Rape* only in conjunction with the Rosicrucian spirits.

19 Twickenham edn, p. 169; John McVeagh, 'Pope and the three Realms of Queen Anne', *N and Q*, 224 (1979), 23–24, noting that the allusion is to Waller's *On St. James's Park* (1661) and thus associates Anne with Charles II.

20 Agrippa, *Three Books*, I. i, p. 1.

21 The allusive function of *Le Comte de Gabalis* in the poem is discussed below, sec. iii. Its political status is potentially remarkable: A. E. Waite observes, commenting on a long-recognised problem, that de Villars's *Comte* is 'little more than an unacknowledged translation of "The Key to the Cabinet of the Chevalier Borri" . . .': *Lives of Alchemystical Philosophers based on Materials collected in 1815 and Supplemented by recent Researches . . .* (London, 1888), p. 208. Giuseppe Francesco Borro (1627–1695) believed in universal reform based on the abolition of all anti-Catholic religions but embracing certain 'heresies'. Having been declared a heretic, he eventually took refuge in Denmark where he became court alchemist, complete with familiar demon, to Frederick III, who had recently (10 September 1660) been proclaimed absolute hereditary monarch. Borro remained in Denmark for a while under Frederick's absolutist successor Christian V, brother of the Prince George of Denmark who married Anne (Waite, pp. 208–210). There is thus a perhaps crucial Danish connection between *Gabalis*, magic, absolutism, and the last of the ruling Stuarts. Waite is, however, wrong on one point: Borro translated part of his *Key* from *Le Comte de Gabalis* (1670) and not *vice versa*. This does not, of course, affect the Danish connection. Borro's *Key* (*La Chiave del gabinetto del cavagliere Giuseppe Francesco Borri . . .*) was published in 1681 along with Borro's *Instruzioni politiche date al Re di Danimarca*. On Borro and Frederick, see J. H. Birch, *Denmark in History* (London: John Murray, 1938), p. 246, and Lynn Thorndike, *A History of Magic*

and Experimental Science, vols VII and VIII (New York: Columbia U.P., 1958), 383–385. For a full account of Borro, see *Dizionario Biografico degli Italiani*, XIII (Rome, 1971), *s.v.*, and esp. p. 12. For the English reaction to Danish absolutism, see Ethel Seaton, *Literary Relations of England and Scandinavia in the Seventeenth Century* (Oxford: Clarendon Press, 1935), pp. 109–110. Ariel's abandoning of Belinda because of the 'Earthly Lover' is even more politically pointed if we admit, with G. A. Boire, an allusion to Dryden's *Annus Mirabilis*, ll. 893 ff. ('Our Guardian Angel saw them where he sate / Above the Palace of our slumbering King, / He sigh'd, abandoning his charge to Fate . . .'): 'A Note on Pope's Ariel', *N and Q*, 222 (1977), 232. A crucial point is that magical and alchemical allusiveness was common in Jacobite propaganda, as in the anonymous *The Golden Age* of 1702 (*Poems on Affairs of State: Augustan Satirical Verse, 1660–1714*; vol. IV, 1697–1704, ed. F. H. Ellis (New Haven, Conn. and London: Yale U.P., 1970), 451–465), and that there was a tradition, maybe only in part satirical, which saw the Jacobites as embodying the remnants of ancient Egyptian wisdom and the purity of the 'Primitive Church': an early example is Josephus Abudacnus, *The True History of the Jacobites, of Ægypt, Lybia, Nubia, &c.* (London, 1692), *passim*. On p. 3 it is noted that the Jacobites-Copts 'were converted to the Faith by St. *Mark*, then Bishop of *Alexandria*'.

22 On Richard Blackmore's *Eliza* (on Anne as Elizabeth), see Brinkley, *Arthurian Legend*, p. 184. For Elizabeth and Anne, see Gregg, pp. 123, 152, and 165, and Green, pp. 109–112. Green, p. 112 reproduces the announcement of December 1702: 'It was her Majesty's pleasure that whenever there was occasion to embroider, depict, engrave, carve, or paint her Majesty's arms, these words SEMPER EADEM should be used for a motto, it being the same that had been used by her predecessor Queen Elizabeth of glorious memory'. The *Rape*'s Elizabethan symbolism is an extreme, absolutist, form of Augustan nostalgia for Elizabeth, on which see Isaac Kramnick, *Bolingbroke and his Circle: the Politics of Nostalgia in the Age of Walpole* (Cambridge, Mass. and London: Harvard U.P. and O.U.P., 1968), pp. 6, 25, 77, 134, 178 and 230–3, and Vincent Carretta, 'Anne and Elizabeth: the Poet as Historian in *Windsor Forest*', *SEL*, 21 (1981), 425–37. When the succession crisis has passed, Pope will abandon his flirtation with absolutism, though not his Jacobitism.

23 Belinda-as-sun has been analysed by R. P. Parkin, 'Mythopoeic Activity in *The Rape of the Lock*', *ELH*, 21 (1954), 30–38, and T. E. Maresca, *Epic to Novel* (Columbus, Ohio: Ohio State U.P., 1974), pp. 83 ff. For Christ as the *sol iustitiae*, see Erwin Panofsky, *Meaning in the Visual Arts* (Garden City, N.Y.: Doubleday, 1955), pp. 261 ff.

24 Ll. 284–285, O and S, II. 708–709.

25 Aurelian Cook, *Titus Britannicus* (London, 1685), sig. A8^r, cit. Gerard Reedy, S.J., 'Mystical Politics: the Imagery of Charles II's Coronation', p. 28.

26 Perhaps, though not necessarily, triumphal arches erected for coronations: Defoe, for example, still remembers James I's coronation

arches in *A Tour through England and Wales* (1724–1726): Everyman edn, introd. G. D. H. Cole, 2 vols. (London and New York: Dent and Dutton, 1928), I. 352.

27 For the mirror and Venus, see Meg Twycross, *The Medieval Anadyomene: a Study in Chaucer's Mythography* (Oxford: Basil Blackwell, 1972), pp. 82 ff. The identification of Belinda with Venus is made at greater length in my 'The Mythology of Love: Venerean (and related) Iconography in Pope, Fielding, Cleland, and Sterne', in P.-G. Boucé (ed.), *Sexuality in Eighteenth-Century Britain* (Manchester: M.U.P., 1982).

28 Martianus Capella, *Marriage of Philology and Mercury*, tr. Stahl *et al.*, VII. 737, p. 281.

29 'KIND *Venus*, Glory of the best Abodes, / Parent of *Rome*, and joy of Men and Gods; / Delight of all, comfort of Sea and Earth; / To whose kind Powers all Creatures owe their Birth. / At thy approach, Great *Goddess*, streight remove / What e're are rough, and Enemies to Love. . . . / The well pleas'd Heaven assumes a brighter Ray / At thy approach, and makes a double Day', etc.: *Titus Lucretius Carus, His Six Books, of Epicurean Philosophy*, tr. Thomas Creech, 4th edn (London, 1699), I. 1 ff.

30 Cf. Isabel Rivers, *The Poetry of Conservatism 1600–1745: a Study of Poets and Public Affairs from Jonson to Pope* (Cambridge: Rivers Press, 1973), p. 119, and pp. 151 ff. on Dryden's Epistle Dedicatory to *All for Love* (1678), with its praise of Charles II's government as bearing 'all the Marks of Kingly Sovereignty without the danger of a Tyranny' and its observation that 'no Christian Monarchy is so absolute, but 'tis circumscrib'd with Laws'. For Cleopatra on the Cydnus, see *Anthony and Cleopatra*, II. ii. 190 ff., and *All for Love*, Act III (1678), p. 35. For comments on the despotism of Shakespeare's Cleopatra, cf. P. L. Rose, 'The Politics of *Antony and Cleopatra*', *Shakespeare Quarterly*, 20 (1969), 382.

31 *Jonson*, ed. Herford and Simpson, VII. 211, and cf. the note on this, *ibid.*, X. 470, observing that this is an English, not a Roman, custom.

32 Roy Strong, *Portraits of Queen Elizabeth I*, pp. 84–86 and plate 17; René Graziani, 'The "Rainbow Portrait" of Queen Elizabeth I and its Religious Symbolism', *JWCI*, 35 (1972), 247–259. Graziani, pp. 258–259, comments on bridal hair with specific reference to Princess Elizabeth's wedding. E. R. Wasserman's point about the ancient custom of dedicating a lock of hair to a goddess of virginity which one left behind in one's childhood bed on one's marriage day is relevant here ('The Limits of Allusion in *The Rape of the Lock*', *JEGP*, 65 (1966), 428–429), as, too, is Isis's cutting-off of a lock of her hair to lament the death of her sun-husband Osiris (Plutarch, *De Iside et Osiride*, 356D). The bridal and ecclesiastical themes have a direct relationship with Anne through her choice of Isaiah 49: 23 as the text for her coronation sermon: 'And kings shall be thy nursing fathers, and their queens thy nursing mothers' (Gregg, p. 130). This was a key text in the debate over the monarch's paternalistic function and is, e.g., quoted at the end of Abudacnus's *True History of the Jacobites*, p. 32.

33 Cf. 'the painted Bow' of II. 84. Iris and a rainbow accompany Henrietta Maria as Chloris in *Chloridia* (1630): *Jonson*, ed. Herford and Simpson, VII. 756 ff.; and see ch. II, sec. iii above. Pope is presumably aware of the tradition that angels could assume a body of air which reflected 'divers kindes of colours': John Salkeld, *A Treatise of Angels* (1613), cit. Robert Ellrodt, 'Angels and the Poetic Imagination from Donne to Traherne' in John Carey (ed.), *English Renaissance Studies Presented to Dame Helen Gardner in Honour of her Seventieth Birthday* (Oxford: Clarendon Press, 1980), p. 167. The vari-coloured sylphs also symbolise the imagination – that power through which magicians (as well as poets) operate: T. R. Edwards, Jr, 'The Colors of Fancy: an Image Cluster in Pope', *MLN*, 73 (1958), 485–489.

34 Aden, *Pope's Once and Future Kings*, p. 121. For her first address to Parliament on 11 March 1702 Anne 'wore a robe of red velvet lined with ermine . . ., around her neck a heavy gold chain with the badge of St George hanging on her bosom. Upon Anne's head was the red velvet cap surmounted by the crown of England. . . . It was said that she had used a portrait of Queen Elizabeth as a model': Winston Churchill, *Marlborough: his Life and Times* (London: Harrap, 1947 repr., 2 vols.), I. 499. This is not the 'Rainbow' portrait, more likely one of the 'Garter' portraits (Strong, *Portraits*, p. 62), but it does confirm the real presence of Elizabethan iconography in the reign of Anne. For *The Rape* itself it is confirmed by the poem's Spenserian echoes, particularly of the marriage poems *Epithalamion* and *Prothalamion*. The echoes of *Prothalamion* are significant in view of that poem's political meanings (especially strong in the last two stanzas) and its connection with the Petre family: Twickenham *Rape*, ed. Tillotson, p. 376, and A. W. Hoffman, 'Spenser and *The Rape of the Lock*', *PQ*, 49 (1970), 530–546. Compare, too, Kathleen Williams's sensitive comments on *Prothalamion* and *Windsor Forest* in 'The Moralized Song: Some Renaissance Themes in Pope', *ELH*, 41 (1974), 578–601.

35 Catullus, LXVI, ll. 66–67, tr. F. W. Cornish in Loeb *Catullus, Tibullus, and Pervigilium Veneris* (London and Cambridge, Mass.: Heinemann and Harvard U.P., 1968). At line 56 the lock is placed in Venus's bosom. We should perhaps link the possible allusion to Boötes and Callisto here with *Windsor Forest*, line 390 ('Where clearer Flames glow round the frozen Pole'), since the Bears are circumpolar constellations. The apocalyptic overtones of this passage, which focusses on the Thames, have been associated by Pat Rogers with Garter symbolism: '*Windsor-Forest*, *Britannia* and River Poetry', pp. 296–297. Under a Stuart the true Bear is restored through the reinvigoration of the Garter, and 'moist *Arcturus*' (*Windsor Forest*, l. 119) redeemed for posterity. For earlier examples of Callisto–Bear symbolism, see ch. III above, on *Il Penseroso*.

36 Catullus, LXVI, ll. 61–62. The verb is *fulgor*, the rich political implications of which for Milton are explored by Stevie Davies, 'Triumph and Anti-triumph: Milton's Satan and the Roman Emperors in *Paradise Lost*', *Etudes Anglaises*, 34 (1981), 398. Berenice is significant to *The*

Rape because she was a murdered queen: William Smith, *Dictionary of Greek and Roman Biography and Mythology*, I (London, 1864). 483. *The Rape*'s echoes of the *Aeneid* (e.g. Belinda on the Thames suggests Aeneas on the Tiber in Book VII) confirm its preoccupation with the Stuart-British myth.

37 Twickenham text, *Poems*, vol. VII (1967), ed. Maynard Mack. The Homeric sceptre passage had been recalled earlier by Swift in his anti-Godolphin satire, 'The Virtues of Sid Hamet the Magician's Rod' (1710), which also alludes to Moses's serpent-rod and the caduceus.

38 Barnivelt equates bodkin with 'the *British Scepter*, so rever'd in the Hand of our late August Princess' (*A Key, ed. cit.*, p. 195). The bodkin is inherited from Belinda's mother (V. 95); in an earlier manifestation it was 'three *Seal-Rings*'. If we take the passage allegorically in relation to Anne, the mother is Anne Hyde and the 'Seal-Rings' might allude to the lord chancellor's Great Seal, held under Charles I by Anne Hyde's father. Gregg comments on the lord chancellor's role: he was 'the monarch's chief minister. ... The queen's maternal grandfather, the first Earl of Clarendon, had been the last lord chancellor to serve in fact as principal minister. After the Restoration, the Treasury had increasingly become more important. This pre-eminence naturally grew after 1688. ... The closer connection between the Treasury and the monarch disappeared under Queen Anne' (*Queen Anne*, pp. 138–139). Anne returns to earlier Stuart practice; Pope condones this in the allegory of the bodkin. Barnivelt, however, simply equates the three rings with 'the three Kingdoms' (*A Key*, p. 196).

39 John Dennis regarded this last line as yet another instance of Pope's pernicious Jacobitism: Aden, p. 153 (and cf. p. 30).

40 The Agrippan–cabbalistic aspects of the play have been well noted by Frank Kermode in his New Arden edn of *The Tempest* (London: Methuen, 1961 edn), pp. xlvii ff. Compare Yates, *Shakespeare's Last Plays*, pp. 94 ff.

41 *The Works of John Dryden: Plays*, X (Berkeley, Los Angeles, London: Univ. of California Press, 1970), ed. M. E. Novak and G. R. Guffey, 341. For Dryden's concern over absolutist monarchy becoming tyranny, see n. 30 above, and A. T. Barbeau, *The Intellectual Design of John Dryden's Heroic Plays* (New Haven and London: Yale U.P., 1970), p. 46. It is worth noting that Ariel was the angel of monarchical Leo and was 'the Lion of God': Agrippa, *Three Books*, III. xxviii, pp. 435–436.

42 I quote here from the title page to the London, 1714 transln. This transln was a reissue of the Ayres-Lovell transln of 1680 (Twickenham *Rape*, appendix B, pp. 378 ff.). The most elaborate account of the 'faery'/sylph background to *The Rape* (which, however, avoids interpretation), is Pat Rogers's 'Faery Lore and *The Rape of the Lock*', *RES*, n.s. 25 (1974), 25–38. Rogers's observation that *The Rape*, I. 91 ff. echoes a magical-Druidic passage in William Diaper's *Dryades* (1712), 318 ff. is – in view of the overall argument of the present book – particularly significant. For Jacobitism and magic see n. 21 above. As a 'faery' poem it continues the

tradition of political 'faery' poetry that we have glanced at in connection with Milton's *L'Allegro* and *Il Penseroso* and that also includes Herrick's *Oberon* poems.

43 Quotations from *Le Comte de Gabalis, ou Entretiens sur les Sciences Secretes* (Amsterdam, 1715), bound with *La Suite du Comte de Gabalis, ou Nouveaux Entretiens sur les Sciences Secretes, touchant la Nouvelle Philosophie* (Amsterdam, 1715). Separately paginated. Present reference to *La Suite*, p. 9. This is the first edn of *La Suite*, which is not by de Villars and which it is highly unlikely that Pope could have seen when he was writing *The Rape*, though manuscript circulation is always a possibility.

44 *Comte*, pp. 26–27.

45 *Ibid.*, pp. 32–33. Cf. 1714 English transln, *The Count de Gabalis*, p. 6: 'Adore, my Son, adore the thrice-good and thrice-great God of the Sages'.

46 *Comte*, p. 19.

47 *Ibid.*

48 *Ibid.*, p. 36 (Adam) and p. 47 (Paracelsus).

49 *Ibid.*, p. 14.

50 *Ibid.*, pp. 37–38; cf. p. 54 on 'les Oracles Aëriens dans des miroirs'.

51 E.g., B. K. Lewalski, 'On looking into Pope's Milton', *Etudes Anglaises*, 27 (1974), 481–500.

Select bibliography

Abudacnus, Josephus. *The True History of the Jacobites, of Ægypt, Lybia, Nubia, &c.* London, 1692.

Aden, J. M. *Pope's Once and Future Kings: Satire and Politics in the Early Career.* Knoxville, Tennessee: University of Tennessee Press, 1978.

Agrippa, Henry Cornelius. *Three Books of Occult Philosophy*, tr. J. F. London, 1651.

Alan of Lille. *The 'Anticlaudian' of Alain de Lille*, tr. W. H. Cornog. Philadelphia, Pa., 1935.

Allen, D. C. *Image and Meaning: Metaphoric Traditions in Renaissance Poetry.* Baltimore, Md: Johns Hopkins U.P., 1960.

—. *The Harmonious Vision: Studies in Milton's Poetry.* Baltimore, Md. and London: Johns Hopkins U.P., 1970.

Allen, R. H. *Star Names: their Lore and Meaning.* New York: Dover Publications, 1963.

Andrewes, Abraham. *The Hunting of the Green Lyon.* See Ashmole, Elias, *Theatrum.*

Anglo, Sydney. *Spectacle, Pageantry, and Early Tudor Policy.* Oxford: Clarendon Press, 1969.

Aptekar, Jane. *Icons of Justice: Iconography and Thematic Imagery in Book V of 'The Faerie Queene'.* New York and London: Columbia U.P., 1969.

Ashmole, Elias. *Theatrum Chemicum Britannicum.* London, 1652.

—. *The Institution, Laws and Ceremonies of the most noble Order of the Garter.* London, 1672.

Backhouse, William. *The Magistery.* See Ashmole, Elias, *Theatrum.*

Barbeau, A. T. *The Intellectual Design of John Dryden's Heroic Plays.*

New Haven, Conn. and London: Yale U.P., 1970.

Batman, Stephen. *The Golden Booke of the Leaden Goddes*. London, 1577.

Bennett, J. W. 'Spenser's Venus and the Goddess Nature in the *Cantos of Mutabilitie*'. *PMLA*, 30 (1933).

—. 'Britain among the Fortunate Isles'. *SP*, 53 (1956).

Bergeron, D. M. *English Civic Pageantry 1558–1642*. London: Edward Arnold, 1971.

Bible. Geneva transln. London, 1599 (?)

—. Douai transln. *The Holie Bible Faithfully Translated into English*. Facsimile, 2 vols. Ilkley, Yorks. and London: Scolar Press, 1975.

Birch, J. H. *Denmark in History*. London: John Murray, 1938.

Bloch, Marc. *The Royal Touch: Sacred Monarchy and Scrofula in England and France*, tr. J. E. Anderson. London and Montreal: Routledge and Kegan Paul, McGill-Queen's U.P., 1973.

Bongo, Pietro. *Numerorum mysteria*. Bergamo, 1599.

Bradbrook, M. C. 'Marvell and the Masque'. In Kenneth Friedenreich (ed.), *Tercentenary Essays in Honor of Andrew Marvell*. Hamden, Conn.: Archon Books, 1977.

Brinkley, R. F. *Arthurian Legend in the Seventeenth Century*. Johns Hopkins Monographs in Literary History, 3. Reprint, London: Frank Cass, 1967.

Brooks-Davies, Douglas. *Spenser's 'Faerie Queene': a Critical Commentary on Books I and II*. Manchester and Totowa, N.J.: Manchester U.P. and Rowman and Littlefield, 1977.

Bruno, Giordano. *The Expulsion of the Triumphant Beast*, tr. and ed. A. D. Imerti. New Brunswick, N.J.: Rutgers U.P., 1964.

—. *The Heroic Frenzies*, tr. P. E. Memmo, Jr. University of North Carolina Studies in the Romance Languages and Literatures, 50. Chapel Hill, N.C.: University of North Carolina Press, 1964.

Butler, E. M. *The Myth of the Magus*. Cambridge: Cambridge U.P., 1948.

Camden, William. *Remains Concerning Britain*. London, 1870.

—. *Poems by William Camden*, tr. and ed. G. B. Johnston. *SP*, 72 (1975).

Campion, Thomas. *Works*, ed. Percival Vivian. Oxford: Clarendon Press, 1909.

Carew, Thomas. *The Poems of Thomas Carew with his Masque 'Coelum Britannicum'*, ed. Rhodes Dunlap. Oxford: Clarendon Press, 1949.

Cartari, Vincenzo. *Le Imagini de i Dei gli Antichi*. Venice, 1571.

Catullus. *Poems*. In *Catullus, Tibullus, Pervigilium Veneris*, tr. F. W. Cornish, J. P. Postgate, J. W. Mackail. Loeb. London and Cambridge, Mass.: Heinemann and Harvard U.P., 1968.

Cawley, R. C. 'Drayton's Use of Welsh History'. *SP*, 22 (1925).

Charnock, Thomas. *Ænigma ad Alchimiam*. See Ashmole, Elias, *Theatrum*.

Christopher, G. B. 'The Virginity of Faith: *Comus* as a Reformation Conceit'. *ELH*, 43 (1976).

Churchill, Winston. *Marlborough: his Life and Times*. Reprint, 2 vols. London: Harrap, 1947.

Comes, Natalis. *Mythologiae, sive Explicationum Fabularum Libri Decem*. Venice, 1567. Facsimile, ed. Stephen Orgel. New York and London: Garland Publishing, 1976.

Comte de Gabalis. See under Villars.

Corpus Hermeticum. Ed. and tr. A. D. Nock and A.-J. Festugière. 4 vols. Paris: Société d'Edition 'Les Belles Lettres', 1945–1954.

Council, Norman. 'Ben Jonson, Inigo Jones, and the Transformation of Tudor Chivalry', *ELH*, 47 (1980).

Creigh, Geoffrey. 'Samuel Daniel's "The Vision of the Twelve Goddesses" '. *Essays and Studies*, n.s. 24 (1971).

Daniel Samuel. *The Vision of the Twelve Goddesses*, ed. Joan Rees. In T. J. B. Spencer and Stanley Wells (eds.), *A Book of Masques in Honour of Allardyce Nicoll*. Cambridge: Cambridge U.P., 1970.

Davidson, Clifford. 'The Idol of Isis Church'. *SP*, 66 (1969).

Davies, Sir John. *The Poems of Sir John Davies*, ed. Robert Krueger and Ruby Nemser. Oxford: Clarendon Press, 1975.

Davies, Stevie. 'John Milton on Liberty'. *Memoirs and Proceedings of the Manchester Literary and Philosophical Society*, 117 (1974–1975).

—. 'Triumph and Anti-triumph: Milton's Satan and the Roman Emperors in *Paradise Lost*'. *Etudes Anglaises*, 34 (1981).

Dee, John. A Translation of John Dee's *Monas Hieroglyphica* (Antwerp, 1564), with an Introduction and Annotations by C. H. Josten. *Ambix*, 12 (1964).

Demaray, J. G. *Milton and the Masque Tradition*. Cambridge, Mass.: Harvard U.P., 1968.

Dempsey, Charles. '*Mercurius Ver*: the Sources of Botticelli's *Primavera*'. *JWCI*, 31 (1968).

Denham, Sir John. *The Poetical Works of Sir John Denham*, ed. T. H. Banks, Jr. New Haven and London: Yale U.P., Oxford U.P., 1928.

Drayton, Michael. *The Works*, ed. J. W. Hebel. 5 vols. Oxford:

Shakespeare Head, 1961.

Drummond, William. *The Poetical Works of William Drummond of Hawthornden*, ed. L. E. Kastner. 2 vols. Reprint. New York: Haskell, 1968.

Dryden, John. *The Poems of John Dryden*, ed. James Kinsley. 4 vols. Oxford: Clarendon Press, 1958.

Duncan, E. H. 'The Alchemy in Jonson's *Mercury Vindicated*'. *SP*, 39 (1942).

Dunseath, T. K. *Spenser's Allegory of Justice in Book Five of 'The Faerie Queene'*. Princeton, N.J.: Princeton U.P., 1968.

Dykes, D. Oswald. *Source Book of Constitutional History from 1660*. London, New York, Toronto: Longmans, Green and Co., 1930.

Eisler, Robert. *The Royal Art of Astrology*. London: Herbert Joseph, 1946.

Ellrodt, Robert, 'Angels and the Poetic Imagination'. In John Carey (ed.), *English Renaissance Studies Presented to Dame Helen Gardner in Honour of her Seventieth Birthday*. Oxford: Clarendon Press, 1980.

Embry, T. J. 'Sensuality and Chastity in *L'Allegro* and *Il Penseroso*'. *JEGP*, 77 (1978).

Enkvist, N. E. 'The Functions of Magic in Milton's *Comus*'. *Neuphilologische Mitteilungen*, 54 (1953).

Erasmus. *The Praise of Folly*, tr. John Wilson. Ann Arbor, Mich.: University of Michigan Press, 1961.

Ewell, B. C. 'Drayton's *Poly-Olbion*: England's Body Immortalized'. *SP*, 75 (1978).

Festugière, A.-J. *La Révélation d'Hermes Trismégiste*. 4 vols. Paris: Gabalda, 1944–1954.

—. *Hermétisme et Mystique Païenne*. Paris: Aubier-Montaigne, 1967. See also *Corpus Hermeticum*.

Ficino, Marsilio. *Marsilii Ficini Florentini . . . Opera*. 2 vols. Basel, 1576.

Fletcher, Angus. *Allegory: the Theory of a Symbolic Mode*. Ithaca, N.Y.: Cornell U.P., 1964.

—. *The Prophetic Moment: an Essay on Spenser*. Chicago, Ill. and London: University of Chicago Press, 1971.

—. *The Transcendental Masque: an Essay on Milton's 'Comus'*. Ithaca, N.Y. and London: Cornell U.P., 1971.

Fowler, A. D. S. *Spenser and the Numbers of Time*. London: Routledge and Kegan Paul, 1964.

—. *Triumphal Forms: Structural Patterns in Elizabethan Poetry.* Cambridge: Cambridge U.P., 1970.

French, P. J. *John Dee: the World of an Elizabethan Magus.* London: Routledge and Kegan Paul, 1972.

Friedman, J. B. *Orpheus in the Middle Ages.* Cambridge, Mass.: Harvard U.P., 1970.

Geoffrey of Monmouth. *The History of the Kings of Britain*, tr. Lewis Thorpe. Harmondsworth, Middx: Penguin Books, 1973.

Gerald of Wales. *The Journey through Wales* with *The Description of Wales*, tr. Lewis Thorpe. Harmondsworth, Middx: Penguin Books, 1978.

Gesta Grayorum. Gesta Grayorum 1688, ed. W. W. Greg. Oxford: Malone Society Reprints, 1914.

Giamatti, A. Bartlett. 'Proteus Unbound: Some Versions of the Sea God in the Renaissance'. In Peter Demetz, Thomas Greene and Lowry Nelson, Jr. (eds), *The Disciplines of Criticism: Essays in Literary Theory, Interpretation, and History*. New Haven, Conn. and London: Yale U.P., 1968.

Gourvitch, I. 'The Welsh Element in the *Polyolbion*'. *RES*, 4 (1928).

Graziani, René. 'The "Rainbow Portrait" of Queen Elizabeth I and its Religious Symbolism'. *JWCI*, 35 (1972).

Green, David. *Queen Anne*. London: Collins, 1970.

Greenberg, J. R. *See under* Weston, C. C.

Greene, Thomas. *The Descent from Heaven: a Study in Epic Continuity.* New Haven, Conn. and London: Yale U.P., 1963.

Greg, W. W. See *Gesta Grayorum*.

Gregg, Edward. *Queen Anne*. London, Boston and Henley: Routledge and Kegan Paul, 1980.

Guthrie, W. K. C. *Orpheus and Greek Religion*. London: Methuen, 1952.

Heinemann, Margot. *Puritanism and Theatre: Thomas Middleton and Opposition Drama under the Early Stuarts.* Cambridge: Cambridge U.P., 1980.

Heninger, S. K. Jr. *The Cosmographical Glass: Renaissance Diagrams of the Universe.* San Marino, Calif.: Huntington Library, 1977.

Hermes Trismegistus. See *Hermetica* and *Corpus Hermeticum*.

Hermetica, tr. Walter Scott. 4 vols. Oxford: Clarendon Press, 1924–1936.

Hill, Christopher. *Milton and the English Revolution.* London and Boston: Faber, 1979.

Hobbes, Thomas. *Leviathan,* ed. and introd. C. B. Macpherson. Harmondsworth, Middx.: Penguin Books, 1968.

Hoffman, A. W. 'Spenser and *The Rape of the Lock*'. *PQ*, 49 (1970).

Holmyard, E. J. *Alchemy*. Harmondsworth, Middx.: Penguin Books, 1968.

Hughes, M. Y. (general editor). *A Variorum Commentary on the Poems of John Milton*. 6 vols. London: Routledge and Kegan Paul, 1970–.

Iamblichus. *Iamblichus on the Mysteries of the Egyptians, Chaldeans, and Assyrians,* tr. Thomas Taylor. London, 1821.

Iredale, R. O. 'Giants and Tyrants in Book Five of *The Faerie Queene*'. *RES*, n.s. 17 (1966).

James I and VI, King. *The Basilicon Doron of King James VI*, ed. James Craigie. 2 vols. Edinburgh and London: Scottish Text Society, 1944.

Javitch, Daniel. *Poetry and Courtliness in Renaissance England*. Princeton, N.J.: Princeton U.P., 1978.

Jayne, Sears. 'The Subject of Milton's Ludlow *Maske*'. *PMLA*, 74 (1959).

Jonson, Ben. *The Works of Ben Jonson*, ed. C. H. Herford and P. and E. M. Simpson. 11 vols. Oxford: Clarendon Press, 1925–1952.

Jung, C. G. *Psychology and Alchemy*, tr. R. F. C. Hull. Bollingen Series, 20. New York: Pantheon Books, 1953.

—. *Alchemical Studies*, tr. R. F. C. Hull. Bollingen Series, 20. Princeton, N.J.: Princeton U.P., 1967.

Kantorowicz, E. H. *The King's Two Bodies: a Study in Mediaeval Political Theology*. Princeton, N.J.: Princeton U.P., 1957.

—. 'Oriens Augusti-Lever du Roi'. *Dumbarton Oaks Papers*, 17 (1963).

Kelsall, Malcolm. 'Augustus and Pope'. *HLQ*, 39 (1975–1976).

Kermode, Frank. *Shakespeare, Spenser, Donne: Renaissance Essays*. London: Routledge and Kegan Paul, 1971.

Kipling, Gordon. *The Triumph of Honour: Burgundian Origins of the Elizabethan Renaissance*. The Hague: Leiden U.P., 1977.

Klibansky, Raymond, Panofsky, Erwin, and Saxl, Fritz. *Saturn and Melancholy: Studies in the History of Natural Philosophy, Religion, and Art*. London: Nelson, 1964.

Knight, W. Nicholas. 'The Narrative Unity of Book V of *The Faerie Queene*: "That Part of Justice which is Equity" '. *RES*, n.s. 21 (1970).

Levinson, R. B. 'Spenser and Bruno'. *PMLA*, 43 (1928).

Linche, Richard. *The Fountaine of Ancient Fiction*. London, 1599.

Lindley, David. 'Campion's *Lord Hay's Masque* and Anglo-Scottish Union'. *HLQ*, 43 (1979–1980).

Lovelace, Richard. *The Poems of Richard Lovelace*, ed. C. H. Wilkinson. Oxford: Clarendon Press, 1930.

Lucretius. *Titus Lucretius Carus, His Six Books, of Epicurean Philosophy*, tr. Thomas Creech. London, 1699.

Macrobius. *The Saturnalia*, tr. P. V. Davies. New York and London: Columbia U.P., 1969.

Martianus Capella. *The Marriage of Philology and Mercury*, tr. W. H. Stahl and Richard Johnson with E. L. Burge. Vol. 2 of *Martianus Capella and the Liberal Arts*. 2 vols. Records of Civilization: Sources and Studies, 84. New York: Columbia U.P., 1977.

Marvell, Andrew. *The Poems and Letters of Andrew Marvell*, ed. H. M. Margoliouth. 3rd edn, rev. P. Legouis and E. E. Duncan-Jones. 2 vols. Oxford: Clarendon Press, 1971.

McVeagh, John. 'Pope and the three Realms of Queen Anne'. *N and Q*, 224 (1979).

Merriman, J. D. *The Flower of Kings: a Study of the Arthurian Legend in England between 1485 and 1835*. Lawrence, Manhattan, Wichita: University of Kansas Press, 1973.

Milton, John. *Complete Prose Works of John Milton*, ed. D. M. Wolfe *et al.* 8 vols. New Haven, Conn. and London: Yale U.P., Oxford U.P., 1953–1982.

—. *'A Maske': the Earlier Versions*, ed. S. E. Sprott. Toronto and Buffalo: University of Toronto Press, 1973.

—. *The Poems of John Milton*, ed. John Carey and A. D. S. Fowler. Longmans' Annotated English Poets. London and Harlow: Longmans, 1968. See also Hughes, M. Y.

Moore, J. R. '*Windsor Forest* and William III'. *MLN*, 66 (1951).

Moore, W. H. 'Sources of Drayton's Conception of *Poly-Olbion*'. *SP*, 65 (1968).

Nicholl, Charles. *The Chemical Theatre*. London, Boston and Henley: Routledge and Kegan Paul, 1980.

Nichols, John. *The Progresses and Public Processions of Queen Elizabeth*. 3 vols. New edn. London, 1823.

—. *The Progresses, Processions, and Magnificent Festivities, of King James the First*. 4 vols. London, 1828.

Nicolson, M. H. 'The Spirit World of Milton and More'. *SP*, 22 (1925).

Nock, A. D. See *Corpus Hermeticum*.

Nohrnberg, J. C. *The Analogy of 'The Faerie Queene'*. Princeton, N.J.: Princeton U.P., 1976.

Norton, Thomas. *The Ordinall of Alchimy*. See Ashmole, Elias,

Theatrum.

Orgel, Stephen. *The Jonsonian Masque.* Cambridge, Mass.: Harvard U.P., 1965.

—. *The Illusion of Power: Political Theater in the Renaissance.* London and Los Angeles: University of California Press, 1975.

—, and Roy Strong. *Inigo Jones: the Theatre of the Stuart Court.* 2 vols. London, Berkeley and Los Angeles: Sotheby Parke Bernet and University of California Press, 1973.

Oruch, J. B. 'Spenser, Camden, and the Poetic Marriages of Rivers'. *SP*, 64 (1967).

Ovid. *Fasti*, tr. J. G. Frazer. Loeb. London and Cambridge, Mass.: Heinemann and Harvard U.P., 1951.

Owen, A. L. *The Famous Druids: a Survey of Three Centuries of English Literature on the Druids.* Oxford: Clarendon Press, 1962.

Palme, Per. *Triumph of Peace: a Study of the Whitehall Banqueting House.* London: Thames and Hudson, 1957.

Palomo, Dolores. 'The Halcyon Moment of Stillness in Royalist Poetry'. *HLQ*, 44 (1981).

Panofsky, Erwin. *Meaning in the Visual Arts.* Garden City, N.Y.: Doubleday, 1955.

Paracelsus. *Selected Writings*, ed. J. Jacobi, tr. N. Guterman. Bollingen Series, 28. New York: Pantheon Books, 1951.

Parker, W. R. *Milton: a Biography.* 2 vols. Oxford: Clarendon Press, 1968.

Parkin, R. P. 'Mythopoeic Activity in *The Rape of the Lock*'. *ELH*, 21 (1954).

Parry, Graham. *The Golden Age Restor'd: the Culture of the Stuart Court.* Manchester: Manchester U.P., 1981.

Peacham, Henry. *Minerva Britanna.* London, 1612.

Pellegrini, A. M. 'Bruno, Sidney, and Spenser'. *SP*, 40 (1943).

Philostratus. *Imagines*, tr. Arthur Fairbanks. Loeb. London and New York: Heinemann and Putnam's, 1931.

Pico della Mirandola. *Opera omnia.* Facsimile of Basel, 1572 edn. Ed. Eugenio Garin. 2 vols. Turin, 1971.

Pliny. *Natural History.* Loeb. Vol. 4, tr. H. Rackham. London and Cambridge, Mass.: Heinemann and Harvard U.P., 1945.

Plotinus. *The Enneads*, tr. Stephen MacKenna. 4th edn, rev. B. S. Page. London: Faber, 1969.

Plutarch. *De Facie quae in orbe lunae apparet*, tr. Harold Cherniss and W. C. Helmbold. Loeb *Moralia*, vol. 12. London and Cambridge,

Mass.: Heinemann and Harvard U.P., 1957.

—. *De Iside et Osiride*, tr. F. C. Babbitt. Loeb *Moralia*, vol. 5. London and Cambridge, Mass.: Heinemann and Harvard U.P., 1936.

Pope, Alexander. *The Correspondence of Alexander Pope*, ed. George Sherburn. 5 vols. Oxford: Clarendon Press, 1956.

—. *The Poems of Alexander Pope*, ed. John Butt *et al.* Twickenham edn. 11 vols. London and New Haven, Conn.: Methuen and Yale U.P., 1939–1969.

—. *The Prose Works of Alexander Pope*, ed. Norman Ault. Vol. 1. Oxford: Shakespeare Head Press, 1936.

Raggio, Olga. 'The Myth of Prometheus: its Survival and Metamorphoses up to the Eighteenth Century'. *JWCI*, 21 (1958).

Rattansi, P. M. 'Paracelsus and the Puritan Revolution'. *Ambix*, 11 (1963).

Reedy, Gerard, S. J. 'Mystical Politics: the Imagery of Charles II's Coronation'. In Paul Korshin (ed.), *Studies in Change and Revolution: Aspects of Intellectual History 1640–1800*. Menston, Yorks.: Scolar Press, 1972.

Ripa, Cesare. *Iconologia*. Rome, 1603.

Ripley, Sir George. *The Compound of Alchymie*. See Ashmole, Elias, *Theatrum*.

Rivers, Isabel. *The Poetry of Conservatism 1600–1745: a Study of Poets and Public Affairs from Jonson to Pope*. Cambridge: Rivers Press, 1973.

Roche, T. P., Jr. *The Kindly Flame: a Study of the Third and Fourth Books of Spenser's 'Faerie Queene'*. Princeton, N.J.: Princeton U.P., 1964.

Rogers, Pat. 'Faery Lore and *The Rape of the Lock*'. *RES*, n.s. 25 (1974).

—. '*Windsor-Forest, Britannia* and River Poetry'. *SP*, 77 (1980).

Ross, Alexander. *Mystagogus Poeticus, or the Muses Interpreter*. London, 1648.

Røstvig, M.-S. *The Happy Man: Studies in the Metamorphoses of a Classical Ideal*. Oslo Studies in English, 2. Revised edn. 2 vols. 1962.

Rurche, Harry. 'Prophecies and Propaganda 1641–1651'. *English Historical Review*, 84 (1969).

Scott, Walter. See *Hermetica*.

Scoufos, A.-L. 'The Mysteries in Milton's *Masque*'. *Milton Studies*, 6 (1974).

Screech, M. A. *Rabelais*. London: Duckworth, 1979.

Seaton, Ethel. *Literary Relations of England and Scandinavia in the Seventeenth Century*. Oxford: Clarendon Press, 1935.

Servius. *Servii Grammatici qui feruntur in Vergilii Carmina Commentarii*, ed. G. Thilo and H. Hagen. 3 vols. Leipzig, 1878–1887.

Seznec, Jean. *The Survival of the Pagan Gods*, tr. Barbara F. Sessions. New York: Harper and Brothers, 1961.

Shumaker, Wayne. *The Occult Sciences in the Renaissance: a Study in Intellectual Patterns*. Berkeley and Los Angeles, Calif. and London: University of California Press, 1972.

Simpson, Percy. 'The Castle of the Rosy Cross: Ben Jonson and Theophilus Schweighardt'. *MLR*, 41 (1946).

Spenser, Edmund. *The Faerie Queene*, ed. A. C. Hamilton. Longman Annotated English Poets. London and New York: Longman, 1977.

—. *The Works of Edmund Spenser: a Variorum Edition*, ed. Edwin Greenlaw *et al*. 10 vols. Baltimore, Md.: Johns Hopkins U.P., 1932–1957.

Steadman, J. M. 'Milton's *Haemony*: Etymology and Allegory'. *PMLA*, 77 (1962).

—. *Nature into Myth: Medieval and Renaissance Moral Symbols*. Pittsburgh, Pa.: Duquesne U.P., 1979.

Strong, Roy. *Portraits of Queen Elizabeth I*. Oxford: Clarendon Press, 1963.

—. 'Inigo Jones and the Revival of Chivalry'. *Apollo*, 88 (1967).

—. *Van Dyck: Charles I on Horseback*. London: Allen Lane, 1972. See also Orgel, Stephen.

Svendsen, Kester. *Milton and Science*. Reprint. New York: Greenwood Press, 1969.

Taylor, Rupert. *The Political Prophecy in England*. New York: Columbia U.P., 1911.

Tervarent, Guy de. *Attributs et Symboles dans L'Art Profane 1450–1600*. Travaux d'Humanisme et Renaissance, 29. Geneva: Droz, 1958.

Thomas, Keith. *Religion and the Decline of Magic*. Harmondsworth, Middx: Penguin Books, 1978.

Thorndike, Lynn. *A History of Magic and Experimental Science*. 8 vols. New York: Columbia U.P., 1923–1958.

Toland, John. *History of the Druids*. New edn, ed. R. Huddleston. Montrose, 1814.

Tonkin, Humphrey. *Spenser's Courteous Pastoral: Book Six of 'The Faerie Queene'*. Oxford: Clarendon Press, 1972.

Tooke, Andrew. *The Pantheon, representing the Fabulous Histories of the Heathen Gods. . . .* London, 1713.

Turner, James. *The Politics of Landscape.* Cambridge, Mass.: Harvard U.P., 1979.

Tuve, Rosemond. *Allegorical Imagery: Some Mediaeval Books and their Posterity.* Princeton, N.J.: Princeton U.P., 1966.

—. *Images and Themes in Five Poems by Milton.* Cambridge, Mass.: Harvard U.P., 1967.

Twycross, Meg. *The Medieval Anadyomene: a Study in Chaucer's Mythography.* Oxford: Basil Blackwell, 1972.

Vale, Marcia. *The Gentleman's Recreations.* Cambridge: D. S. Brewer, 1977.

Valeriano, Pierio. *Hieroglyphica, seu de Sacris Ægyptiorum aliarumque Gentium Literis Commentarii.* Lyons, 1602.

Villars, Montfaucon de. *Comte de Gabalis, ou Entretiens sur les Sciences Secretes.* Amsterdam, 1715; *La Suite du Comte de Gabalis.* Amsterdam, 1715.

—. *The Count de Gabalis: Being a Diverting History of the Rosicrucian Doctrine of Spirits.* London, 1714.

Virgil. *The Aeneid*, tr. W. F. Jackson Knight. Harmondsworth, Middx.: Penguin Books, 1974. See also Servius.

Vitruvius. *The Ten Books on Architecture*, tr. M. H. Morgan. New York: Dover Publications, 1960.

Waddington, Raymond. 'The Iconography of Silence and Chapman's Hercules'. *JWCI*, 33 (1970).

Waite, A. E. *Lives of Alchemystical Philosophers based on Materials collected in 1815 and supplemented by recent Researches.* London, 1888.

Walker, D. P. 'Orpheus the Theologian and Renaissance Platonists'. *JWCI*, 16 (1953).

—. *Spiritual and Demonic Magic from Ficino to Campanella.* London: The Warburg Institute, 1958.

—. *The Ancient Theology: Studies in Christian Platonism from the Fifteenth to the Eighteenth Century.* London: Duckworth, 1972.

Wallace, J. M. *Destiny his Choice: the Loyalism of Andrew Marvell.* Cambridge: Cambridge U.P., 1968.

Wasserman, E. R. *The Subtler Language.* Baltimore, Md.: Johns Hopkins U.P., 1959.

—. 'The Limits of Allusion in *The Rape of the Lock'. JEGP*, 65 (1966).

Waters, D. Douglas. *Duessa as Theological Satire.* Columbia, Missouri.:

University of Missouri Press, 1970.

West, R. H. *Milton and the Angels*. Athens, Ga.: University of Georgia Press, 1955.

Weston, C. C. and J. R. Greenberg. *Subjects and Sovereigns: the Grand Controversy over Legal Sovereignty in Stuart England*. Cambridge: Cambridge U.P., 1981.

Williams, Kathleen. 'The Moralized Song: Some Renaissance Themes in Pope'. *ELH*, 41 (1974).

Wind, Edgar. *Pagan Mysteries in the Renaissance*. Rev. edn. Harmondsworth, Middx: Penguin Books, 1967.

Wordsworth, Christopher (ed.). *The Manner of the Coronation of King Charles the First of England at Westminster, 2 February, 1626*. Henry Bradshaw Society, 2 (1892).

Yates, Frances A. 'The Emblematic Conceit in Giordano Bruno's *De Gli Eroici Furori* and in the Elizabethan Sonnet Sequences'. *JWCI*, 6 (1943).

—. *Theatre of the World*. London: Routledge and Kegan Paul, 1969.

—. *Astraea: the Imperial Theme in the Sixteenth Century*. London and Boston: Routledge and Kegan Paul, 1975.

—. *The Rosicrucian Enlightenment*. Reprint. St Albans, Herts: Granada Publishing, 1975.

—. *Shakespeare's Last Plays: a New Approach*. London: Routledge and Kegan Paul, 1975.

—. *Giordano Bruno and the Hermetic Tradition*. London and Chicago: Routledge and Kegan Paul, Univ. of Chicago Press, 1978.

—. *The Occult Philosophy in the Elizabethan Age*. London, Boston and Henley: Routledge and Kegan Paul, 1979.

Index